T0355818

Sunk Cost

SUNK

Who's to Blame for the Nation's Broken Student Loan System and How to Fix It

COST

Jillian Berman

The University of Chicago Press
Chicago and London

The University of Chicago Press, Chicago 60637
The University of Chicago Press, Ltd., London
© 2025 by Jillian Berman
All rights reserved. No part of this book may be used or reproduced
in any manner whatsoever without written permission, except in
the case of brief quotations in critical articles and reviews. For more
information, contact the University of Chicago Press, 1427 E. 60th St.,
Chicago, IL 60637.
Published 2025
Printed in the United States of America

34 33 32 31 30 29 28 27 26 25   1 2 3 4 5

ISBN-13: 978-0-226-82115-3 (cloth)
ISBN-13: 978-0-226-83895-3 (e-book)
DOI: https://doi.org/10.7208/chicago/9780226838953.001.0001

Library of Congress Cataloging-in-Publication Data

Names: Berman, Jillian, author.
Title: Sunk cost : who's to blame for the nation's broken student
    loan system and how to fix it / Jillian Berman.
Description: Chicago ; London : The University of Chicago Press, 2025. |
    Includes bibliographical references and index.
Identifiers: LCCN 2024034380 | ISBN 9780226821153 (cloth) |
    ISBN 9780226838953 (ebook)
Subjects: LCSH: Student loans—United States. | Student loans—
    Government policy—United States. | College graduates—United
    States—Finance, Personal.
Classification: LCC LB2340.2 .B474 2025 | DDC 378.3/620973—dc23
    /eng/20240821
LC record available at https://lccn.loc.gov/2024034380

♾ This paper meets the requirements of ANSI/NISO Z39.48-1992
(Permanence of Paper).

For Judah, may you grow up in a better world.

Contents

Introduction

How Did We Get Here?

When then president Lyndon B. Johnson signed the Higher Education Act into law on a November day in 1965, he described the legislation as the key that would unlock "the most important door that will ever open—the door to education." Johnson went on to tell the rows of spectators seated on the floor and packed into the rafters of the gymnasium at Southwest Texas State College why he chose to stage the signing ceremony at his alma mater: "Here, the seeds were planted from which grew my firm conviction that for the individual, education is the path to achievement and fulfillment; for the Nation, it is a path to a society that is not only free but civilized."[1]

The Higher Education Act, which established America's first broad student loan program, was based on those convictions—that access to higher education would improve both the lives of the individuals who received it and the nation at large—and that therefore the government should eliminate money being a barrier to attending college.

Nearly sixty years later, the student loan program is a far cry from that vision. The roughly $1.7 trillion that Americans hold in student debt, as of this writing, has become an obstacle to some of the traditional engines of the American economy, like homeownership.[2] In many cases, the investment that borrowers made in their education isn't paying off as promised; of those who carried outstanding student loans in 2009, about 25% had larger balances by 2019.[3] Put another way, a large share of student loan borrowers are never going to repay their debt.[4]

If you want more evidence of the challenges student loans pose, just take a brief look at my inbox. As a reporter who began covering student debt for *MarketWatch* in 2015, I receive emails regularly from borrowers describing the havoc student loans have wreaked on their financial lives. "We went to college so that we could get jobs, start families, and buy homes . . . basically the American dream. And now, the one thing that was supposed to lead to the American Dream is a complete nightmare," MaNesha Stiff wrote to me in June 2021.

In a follow-up phone call, Stiff told me she was "scared shitless" for when student loan payments resumed after what was then a more-than-yearlong pause related to the COVID-19 pandemic. She'd just exited a trial payment period to stave off foreclosure on her Chicago-area home, and she was worried her student loan bill would jeopardize her ability to stay current on her mortgage.

Stiff graduated from high school in 1999, about a decade before policymakers, educators, students, and families started to truly grapple with the risk of student loans both to individual borrowers and to the economy. She was set to be the first in her family to go to college, and throughout high school, she never believed she would actually be able to attend. "I just didn't think I was smart enough, and I didn't think that we could afford it," she said. Stiff took a standardized entrance exam, the ACT, on the last day she could and sent the score in as part of her application.

Despite an entire industry of rankings, guidebooks, and media coverage centered on the idea that students and families approach the college application process with copious research to determine the right fit, the reality is that many students pick a college in a way that's similar to how Stiff chose hers.

Most students tend to stay close to home; on average, students enroll in college roughly within one hundred miles of where they grew up, and that distance is likely skewed by the minority of students who travel long distances.[5] About 63% of freshmen who filled out the Free Application for Federal Student Aid, or FAFSA, sent their financial aid information to only one school during the 2022–2023 application cycle.[6]

When Stiff applied to college she was part of that majority. "We really didn't know anything about the process," Stiff said of her and her family's mindset at the time. She visited one school, North Park University, a private college in Chicago about thirty-five miles from her home, liked it, and decided to apply—only there. "It was close enough to home for me to go home when I wanted to and far enough to say that I went away to college," Stiff remembered. Once she got in, she wasn't going to pass up the chance to leave Hammond, Indiana, a manufacturing town in decline, where there was little economic opportunity, with or without a degree, regardless of the financial commitment required.

"My mom is a nurse's aide, my dad is a steelworker," she said, and her tuition was more than $15,000 a year, plus living expenses. Her family wondered where and how they would get that money, Stiff remembers. "When we got the papers, I signed, I signed, I signed, and signed again," she said, referring to the student loan documents.

After college, Stiff worked briefly for TRIO, the federal program that works with low-income and first-generation college students to get them on a path to college, the same program that Stiff herself had been a part of when she was in high school. Soon she began working for her alma mater, first as an orientation coordinator and then as an adviser. Although she was employed, Stiff struggled to make regular student loan payments on her salary. Eventually, Stiff reasoned, she needed to go to graduate school to move up the career ladder in her field, higher education administration. She got a master's degree for free at the college where she worked, but she ultimately signed up for more student loans to get a doctorate in education. But when the college where she worked started layoffs, the degree wasn't enough to protect her. Stiff found herself cobbling together work at Goodwill and other part-time jobs to make ends meet.

During that period, thanks to a government program that allows borrowers to repay their debt as a percentage of income, Stiff's monthly student loan payment was zero dollars, a "blessing in disguise," Stiff called it. She found full-time work in January 2020, but by the time we first spoke, she was bracing for the increase in student loan payments that would come with a higher salary. Stiff worried they'd eat into her ability to afford other bills, like her mortgage and car note. "I'm so afraid," she said.

———

How did we get from the ideals of President Johnson's Higher Education Act to MaNesha Stiff's dread about steep student loan debt? After several years of reporting and writing on the student debt crisis, I have learned the answer to that question. Like thousands of other Americans, MaNesha Stiff is part of a system, one in which promises that higher education will transform students' circumstances are ultimately dampened by the reality of stagnant wages and high tuition costs; one in which employers increasingly demand advanced degrees for even entry-level positions; one in which the cost of housing, childcare, and health care are often out of workers' reach, exacerbating student loan woes; one in which seemingly generous repayment terms can trap borrowers in debt for years; and one in which a gulf between the resources that wealthy (often white) students and poorer students bring to attending and paying for college has allowed the system to reinforce already-existing inequalities instead of ameliorating them.

When I first started covering student loans, I didn't think of the debt in the way Stiff experienced, largely because I was one of those students coming to the process of applying to and paying for college with a variety of resources at my disposal. An only child with a lawyer mom and hospital executive turned real estate agent dad, I was fortunate enough to avoid student loans thanks to a combination of the wealth my family brought to the process and a deal from Congress that allowed students who grew up in Washington, DC, like me, to pay in-state tuition at any public college in the country (up to a cap of $10,000 per year).[7]

During the college application process, few at my high school—counselors, students, parents—talked about the possibility of debt. It was still a few years before our country began to realize the alarming consequences of it, but there was also a sense at my private Jewish high school that with good grades, careful planning, and research, you could avoid student loans or at least greatly minimize the amount you borrowed. And indeed, my high school peers and I were part of a demographic that some colleges would lure with so-called merit aid at the expense of need-based scholarships. Instead of fully subsidizing a student who could pay nothing, these colleges reasoned they would convince families that could afford to pay the bulk of tuition to enroll by subsidizing the price a little bit.[8]

In my own case, my parents and I talked some about the finances of college, but it was more about making a smart financial decision than avoiding debt. My parents figured, Why pay more to attend private schools when many of the public colleges where my family would get a deep discount were just as good?

Once I got to college, I was funneled into a situation of well-documented economic segregation between and on college campuses. I attended the University of Michigan, the type of selective, name-brand school that is often the focus of the media but that actually educates a relatively small portion of the nation's college-going population—and an even smaller share of its low-income students.[9]

I had friends with student loans, but they typically viewed the debt not as a necessity of attending college but as a consequence of a choice they'd made to go to Michigan over other, cheaper options available to them. In addition, by attending Michigan, my friends were at a college with the kind of outcomes that would likely shield them from the harshest consequences of student loans—an opportunity not typically available to Americans who attended less-resourced high schools.

Even with all those advantages, college didn't deliver to us exactly what we and our parents had been sold. We graduated into a recession, and despite our degrees, we took whatever internships and waitressing gigs we could find and moved back in with our parents if we could.

———

I share my experience not because it's unique but because it's typical of one of the most powerful constituencies in American politics—upper-middle-class (often suburban) enclaves that are home to legions of vocal voters, the Capitol Hill and think-tank staffers who write and influence policy, and the financial industry workers who shape the way the country thinks about money and the economy.

It's likely why borrowers similar to the people I knew became the face of the student debt crisis, at least for a while. A typical story from that period: a 2012 article in the *New York Times Magazine* profiling the class of 2011 from Drew University, a small private college in New Jersey "in the middle of the collegiate pack," as the *Times* put it, as they struggled to pay off student loans with unpaid internships and jobs at the Wawa.[10]

When students who attended four-year public and private non-profit colleges—the kind most families and popular culture viewed as leading to a decent job and financial life—started struggling in bulk, the media, politicians, and others couldn't help but take notice. And they started to craft fixes to the student debt problem directed toward this population.

The personal finance literature (including some of my own writing) offered tips to help students find a college that was a financial fit, in addition to a social and academic one. Questions like "Should they choose the most affordable school? Or should they pick the one with more prestige, even if it's a financial stretch, even if it means going deep into debt?" posed by the *New York Times* in 2008 reinforced the notion that student debt was the result of choices made by families who had them.[11] The solutions policymakers proposed assumed that, eventually, these borrowers would be able to repay their loans; they just needed a temporary reprieve while they muddled through an unusually terrible job market.

It wasn't until I started looking for student debt stories that I realized the student loan borrower whom powerful politicians had in their minds when talking about student debt was actually relatively rare. About 14% of those earning $20,000 or less have some student debt, and nearly 20% of those earning between $20,001 and $50,000 have loans. Roughly 25% of those with a two-year college or vocational degree also hold student debt.[12] Not only that, these borrowers' experience in managing their student loans was not a major factor in what's come to be known by many as the student debt crisis.

Instead, the people I encountered didn't have an option not to borrow or to borrow less; like Stiff's, their choice was to take on debt or forgo what educators, policymakers, and their parents had told them was the only ticket to a better financial life. Often they were parents or older working adults themselves trying to find a foothold in the economy in between work and taking care of their kids.

Some of the students I've spoken with attended the cheapest or what they thought was the only option available to them—the local community college or the nearby four-year public or, in some cases, private school. But unlike the two hundred or so schools that are the regular fixation of the media, these colleges didn't have the resources and connections to ensure that their graduates entered jobs that would pay them enough to be able to repay their debt.

I also met borrowers lured into debt by admissions recruiters, paid by the number of students they enrolled, who guaranteed them a job after graduating. These recruiters were hired by companies whose mission was largely not educational but maximizing shareholder value. Only after the students had taken on their loans did they realize the promises were empty.

I've spoken to countless strivers convinced by the glut of bachelor's degrees and employer job listings that a graduate degree is the best way they can secure a decent job, only to find that the pay still doesn't match their credentials—or their debt.

I've heard from borrowers diligently working to repay their loans only to get sidetracked from benefits guaranteed to them under the law by government-hired student loan companies that gave them poor advice. I've talked with borrowers who, even with these obstacles, were able to access the benefits only to learn that they weren't enough to alleviate the financial strain the debt posed.

It's these borrowers you'll meet in this book, because the data indicates that they're the story of the student debt crisis. You'll hear from a borrower who left school without completing her degree. She's one of the roughly four in ten student loan borrowers who leave college with only the debt to show for it. This group accounts for a relatively small share of total outstanding student loan dollars— about 8% by one estimate—which makes sense, given that they've typically gone through less schooling.[13] But they disproportionately face some of the harshest consequences of the student debt system because they are more likely to default—roughly 41% of these borrowers default on their debt, compared with 18% of borrowers overall.[14] Crucially, students who attend for-profit colleges and, to a lesser extent, community colleges are most at risk of dropping out.[15]

You'll hear from multiple borrowers over the age of sixty. Despite that the student loan borrower in popular imagination is a twenty- or thirtysomething with a four-year degree, about 20% of student debt is held by borrowers over fifty. Borrowers between the ages of sixty and sixty-nine have seen their balances grow most quickly over the past several years.[16]

You'll meet borrowers lured into taking on debt for graduate degrees by the idea that the credentials would help them make more money than an undergraduate degree alone. In the next few years, the Department of Education predicts that the federal student loan program will disburse more money for graduate school than for undergraduates for the first time.[17] Despite the expansion in graduate student debt, the earnings premium for graduate degrees hasn't changed since the early 2000s—indicating the return on investment in a graduate degree may have fallen.[18]

You'll hear from so-called nontraditional college students, or those who came to school after a period of working or those for whom college isn't their only or primary responsibility. Although the red-brick dorms and student services at many colleges are built to cater to students who come to school from their parents' homes at the age of eighteen, 37% of college students are twenty-five or older.[19] A large share of students work, many of them full-time.[20]

Despite this reality, which I encounter on a daily basis, this wrong and pernicious idea persists: student loan debt is largely the result of a choice that will ultimately benefit the borrower. And this mistaken notion has major implications for the debate over whether and how we decide to fix the problem. President Joe Biden expressed this incorrect view when he told the *New York Times* columnist David Brooks in May 2021: "The idea that you go to Penn and you're paying a total of 70,000 bucks a year and the public should pay for that? I don't agree."[21]

Biden ultimately came around to the notion that student debt disproportionately affects people who aren't necessarily part of the college-going population in the popular imagination. In announcing his plan to cancel $10,000 in student debt for many borrowers and $20,000 for those borrowers who were low-income when they were in college, Biden argued that the move was "targeted" at "families who need it the most—working and middle-class people hit especially hard during the pandemic."[22] Still, his plan faced both legal and political challenges, in part because of the prominent perception that borrowers who had a choice decided to take on more than necessary in student loans.

This perception has meant that even when aspiring teachers, nurses, court reporters, and others did what our nation expected and told them to do—invest in themselves in hopes of a decent financial life—the government wasn't there for them when it didn't work out. And in many cases, their neighbors, colleagues, and fellow citizens agree that's how it should be. I know because I hear from them too. Mixed in with the messages from borrowers lamenting their loan payments are emails decrying those who chose to attend college when they could have gone straight to work instead, or those who didn't have the financial discipline to pay their debt off quickly. "I don't believe it's fair to the people who paid for their college degrees without government help," reads a November 2020 email typical of these readers.

Borrowers' anguish and others' criticism stem from the same source: a lack of discussion about the system underlying what's come to be known as the student debt crisis. Instead of interrogating the choices policymakers and business leaders have made for sixty years about the design of our college finance system—and getting to the hard work of fixing them—we've blamed the choices of individuals.

Indeed, my reader's comment about unfairness exactly matches the way policymakers have framed the debate over the government's role in financing college for decades: as a zero-sum battle between taxpayers and college goers. But the reality is that you would be hard pressed to find a family who did not get some financial help from the government. Even families who paid out of pocket for a college education likely received some governmental assistance, whether through tax advantages that largely benefit upper-income house-holds or because they attended college several years or even decades ago, when the government subsidized more of it.

So how should we be thinking about it? Politicians often say that households with no college degree holders shouldn't be forced to fund generous higher education benefits. The fact is that, in many cases, these households have actually had contact with the college system, either through shorter training programs required for many occupations—including welders, electricians, and nursing assistants—or because they started college but never finished and have only the debt to show for their experience.[23]

Others say that these students should have never started college at all, that the problem is the emphasis that we, as a society, place on a four-year degree, pushing students who don't belong there toward college instead of providing other pathways to viable careers. It is true that, for decades, policymakers and educators have prioritized increasing access to higher education without necessarily interrogating what exactly we're providing access to. Since the 1980s, during the same period that more women and nonwhite people have started to attend college, it's become a riskier route to economic mobility.

Still, given this messaging and the reality that, on average, those with bachelor's degrees earn much more—by some estimates, $1 million more—over their lifetimes, it's hard to blame so many Americans for trying.[24] It's even harder to blame them for dropping out when the time and money they invested in school doesn't pay off in the ways they had hoped or that our nation promised.

The problem is a perennial one: it takes money to make money, even as far as education is concerned. The ability to harness the power of higher education to improve or maintain a decent financial life is tied closely to the financial resources students bring to it.[25] That data suggests that when politicians and others say that college isn't for everyone, those they're likely shuttling toward another path will end up there simply because they don't have the resources to risk trying college out—not because they're not well suited to it.

This debate today illustrates one of the many ways our country has struggled for decades with the tension between the vision articulated by President Johnson and others—that broad access to higher education could be transformative both for individuals and for the economy—and the financial burden it requires from individuals and their families. So often Americans respond to the vision and instead are confronted with the reality.

The journey from unlocking the door to education to one of the largest consumer finance challenges of our time winds through many familiar stops in American economic history: a well-intentioned goal hijacked by collusion between bad actors, policymakers, and lobbyists; greed on the part of institutions comfortable with the way they benefit from the status quo; incremental changes whose impacts wouldn't be felt for years; declining worker power and the vast gulf in outcomes between rich and poor, Black and white. It's also about how we view investment in higher education and how that's changed from a public to a private good as the demographics of who attends college have changed.

There's evidence that nonprofit and public colleges, which technically don't have a profit motive, have had a role to play in driving up the nation's student loan balance. In some cases, these schools have spent money to attract students and climb college rankings lists, seemingly without regard to how their actions might affect college costs.[26] In other cases, they've used financial aid to lure relatively well-off students at the expense of low-income ones.[27]

Still, to focus too closely on these schools' behavior repeats a mistake that those crafting the student loan narrative in the media and elsewhere have been making for years: it zeroes in on the places where students take their loan dollars in the search for the source of the student debt crisis instead of on the design of the system itself. Of course, colleges have taken steps over the past several decades that have pushed up the debt balances of both individual students and the nation overall. But there are two other factors that have made the debt a crisis and a major public policy problem.

The first is that a federal student loan is onerous to repay. Despite the lofty rhetoric surrounding the education that a student loan is used to pay for, it is at its core a financial product that in many ways has fewer protections than other types of consumer debt. If borrowers could reliably get accurate information from their student loan servicers about the programs the government offers to help them stay current on their loans, if those programs actually provided an insurance policy, if the consequences of defaulting on a student loan weren't so harsh, and if a borrower could discharge the debt in bankruptcy, it would matter a lot less that colleges can convince students to finance overpriced degrees with debt.

The other factor that's turned student debt into a crisis is that there's no public option for college—meaning that for some students, no matter where they go, they will have to borrow. If the nation offered a clear path to a free or debt-free college education, then it would matter much less that schools across the country are more expensive than they need to be for various reasons.

The lack of both regulation and protection surrounding student loans and the dearth of a public option can be traced to decisions made by policymakers at the state and federal levels, who were often influenced by companies that stand to benefit from an increase in student debt. Although there are steps the government and schools can and should take to keep colleges from charging too much, if student debt is still difficult to repay in challenging economic circumstances and students have no choice but to take it on to earn a degree, the student debt problem will still exist.

Ultimately, what makes our college finance system so problematic is that students are asked to assume a financial risk if they want a decent foothold in the economy. Making student loans less onerous to repay and providing a true public option would make taking a stab at higher education much less risky.

———

When it comes to making decisions, we often find ourselves victims of the sunk-cost fallacy, or the idea that we should continue to throw money, time, and energy at something even when it's not working because we've thrown so much money, time, and energy at it already. Our nation's approach to financing higher education fits this bill. Roughly sixty years ago, policymakers decided that the best way to pay for college would be to have the government subsidize some of it but for students and families to take on much of the risk. This was based on the idea that a college degree provides an individual benefit.

We now understand that many of the assumptions underpinning the student debt system turned out not to be true—most crucially that, broadly, borrowers' earnings would be high enough and their debt low enough to make their student loans manageable. In addition, we've seen the ways bad actors can take advantage of sometimes well-intentioned policies. And yet we keep building on and tweaking this system that we've thrown time, money, and energy into, assuming it can be fixed, instead of trying to wipe the slate clean.

This book describes the origins of the student debt system, the ways policymakers have tried to tinker with it, and the harms students and borrowers still face despite those efforts. The first few chapters lay out the history, politics, and impact of some of the federal policies that are the foundation of the student loan system, including the GI Bill, the Higher Education Act, and the Federal Pell Grant Program. Chapter 4 highlights the role that state policymakers have played in keeping college costs high for students. Chapter 5 explores how employers and schools have pushed students toward earning more credentials, driving up debt. Chapters 6 and 7 outline how federal student loans have become so onerous to repay. Chapter 8 takes readers inside the movement to radically transform the student loan system.

This book is both for borrowers and for those with the political power to change borrowers' lives. I have seen the impact of our most consequential student loan policies and heard the stories of the people who are trying to better their situations against all the system's odds. My hope is that this book will show how borrowers' individual student loan bills are a product of their own circumstances *and* of a broader system and will provide some possible steps about how to do it all better. At the very least, those without a student loan bill will know to question the narratives in the news or in political speeches that equate a lack of student debt with a high level of personal responsibility. Instead, they'll recognize that the blame for the student debt crisis rests with a nation that insists on a college degree for economic stability but refuses to fund it—and with the actors who capitalize on that gap for their own gain.

1. The GI Bill

America's First Try at Subsidizing College Students

On a Tuesday in early September 2001, Murray Hastie and his fellow students sat wondering whether their teacher was coming. They mused aloud about how long they would have to wait—Fifteen minutes? Twenty?—before they could assume class had been canceled and continue on with their day.

Although it was the start of Hastie's first year at Fulton Montgomery Community College, it wasn't his first try at college. Hastie grew up in Gloversville, an upstate New York town that, as the name suggests, was renowned in the mid-nineteenth century for its thriving glove-making industry.[1] By the time Hastie came of age, it was "a pretty small, quiet town" near the lake, where Hastie and his friends would usually spend the weekends "doing something crazy." After graduating from high school in 2000, Hastie followed some of those friends to the State University of New York at Plattsburgh. As the year went on, Hastie realized his first attempt at college "just wasn't working out." "It was quite the party school," he said, by way of explanation. So he returned home, opting for more affordable and less socially tempting community college courses.

On that Tuesday morning, Hastie was in class working toward a biological sciences degree. Intrigued by the human body and the way it functions, Hastie had a goal of eventually working for the Centers for Disease Control and Prevention. He kept a list of diseases and health problems he wanted to get rid of. One of the many sources of inspiration for his future career was an eight-year-old girl with rheumatoid arthritis. An encounter with the girl and her mom (who was a friend of Hastie's parents) at the local grocery store when he was in high school left Hastie feeling bereft. Although the girl wasn't crying, Hastie could tell by her slow and tortured movements that she was in pain. "It just made me mad," Hastie said. "I wanted to find out how that happens."

About twenty minutes into the class, students started receiving emails indicating that a plane had hit the World Trade Center's twin towers. Hastie imagined a small prop plane flown by an inexperienced pilot accidentally running into the tall buildings. Then a voice came over the loudspeaker announcing that classes were canceled for the day. Hastie walked to his car, sat in the parking lot, and turned on the radio to listen to the news.

As he drove home, information trickled into his car, allowing Hastie to start to piece together what had happened while he and his classmates were wondering about their professor's whereabouts. When Hastie arrived home, he turned on the television and watched the footage of the twin towers erupting in flames. He saw President George W. Bush's face twist in shock as he learned of the news during a visit to an elementary school. "That was when I realized it was something really big," Hastie said.

A few hours later, Hastie began researching local blood donation centers, looking for a way to help. But by the time he'd begun investigating, they were already overwhelmed. When Hastie realized he couldn't give blood immediately, he started thinking, "What more could I do?"

Hastie wasn't clicking with any of his professors or classmates at school. "I wasn't in the right mindset to go to college and sit at a desk for the rest of my life," he said. And the morning's events had shifted his goals. So he resolved to join the military.

Hastie announced his intention to his parents, and his mother, in particular, was wary of his choice. She'd had a brother who fought in Vietnam, returned home changed, and ultimately died by suicide. Although both his parents were still hesitant to endorse a decision to join the military at a time when it was clear the country was about to go to war, they were happy he'd made a commitment and would follow through with it.

Shortly after the conversation, Hastie walked into the local military recruitment office he'd passed by so many times before. He opened the first door he saw on the left, effectively choosing to enlist in the Marine Corps.

"How can I help you?" the recruiter asked. Hastie responded, "I want to go to war."

The recruiter showed him a video featuring recruits having their heads shaved, swimming laps with their uniforms on, and learning to shoot a gun. By the end of the video, Hastie was asking, "Where do I sign up?"

A few months later, Hastie arrived at the Marine Corps Recruit Depot in Parris Island, South Carolina. A banner declaring We Make Marines hung over the entrance. Growing up, he'd been a pretty good kid, rarely subject to discipline. So to be suddenly punished, often for other people's behavior, took adjusting. The first week or two, he and his fellow recruits would march out of step with one another and struggle to respond in unison to their leaders' commands. But several weeks in, it was as if each member of the group were a clone of the same person.

He spent the summer, fall, and winter of 2002 with his unit in Camp Pendleton, California, while the Bush administration made its case for going to war with Iraq. By the time Hastie arrived in Kuwait in March 2003, he and his unit were simply waiting for Bush to declare war so they could head north into Iraq.

Hastie found fighting Saddam Hussein's army in the desert to be relatively straightforward. Both sides wore uniforms and knew each other. "That was actually quite easy, much easier than I thought it would be," Hastie said. But when he returned to Iraq for his second deployment in 2004, the situation had changed. US forces toppled Hussein and the trappings of his rule, but a violent insurgency had sprouted up in its place. Hastie found himself battling lurking, less obvious enemies—explosive devices hidden on roadsides and snipers targeting Hastie and his fellow soldiers from above.

By the fall of 2005, Hastie had spent so much of his four-year military contract participating in combat that he'd accrued enough benefit time to finish up his service from home. Hastie had dreamed of and waited for the chance to return, but once he arrived back home, it didn't feel like what he expected. He missed his fellow soldiers and the constant activity. Still, he was excited for what lay ahead, figuring that if he could survive two combat deployments in Iraq, he could survive anything.

Hastie knew he wanted to continue his education, and thanks to his military experience, he had more funds to do so. He began searching for schools where he could use his GI Bill benefits, the funds the government provides to veterans to attend college following their service. One website in particular seemed promising: GIBill.com. "I thought it was a government website that shows you what schools will accept the benefits that you earned from the government," he said.

That internet search started a process that would mire Hastie in student debt for years. That a veteran with access to GI Bill education benefits could wind up with student loans that were challenging for him to repay is thanks to a decades-old alliance between policymakers and colleges that earn money for their owners or shareholders.

These schools had access to government education benefits even before the start of the federal student loan program, and their skill at tapping those resources has had implications for the growth of student debt almost since the start of the loan program.

The GI Bill Takes Shape

In a 1943 message to Congress, President Roosevelt outlined the basic rationale for providing returning soldiers, like Hastie, with an education benefit. "Every day that the war continues, interrupts the schooling and training of more men and women and deprives them of the education and skills which they would otherwise acquire for use in later life," he wrote. "Not only the individual welfare of our troops but the welfare of the Nation itself requires that we reverse this trend just as quickly as possible after the war."[2]

The notion that providing an education for veterans would offer both an individual and a societal benefit is one that advocates for veterans and schools emphasized throughout the negotiation process for what would become the GI Bill. That dual purpose also underlies much of the tension surrounding our higher education finance system today—is it to benefit individuals or society?

As stakeholders began debating and drafting what would become the GI Bill, a divide emerged over how the education benefits should be administered. On one side were those representing the veterans who would receive the education, and on the other were those representing the higher education institutions who would provide it. Although in some ways, this wrangling could be understood as a wonky squabble between various sets of insiders, it ultimately became about who had the power to control a program that would later dispense billions in government money each year to support the education of students who were veterans.

In December 1943, a parade of representatives from higher education associations argued before the Senate's Education and Labor Committee that the Office of Education—the precursor to today's Department of Education—not the Veterans Administration, should be responsible for overseeing the veterans' education programs. Guy Snavely, the executive director of the Association of American Colleges, a lobbying group, told the committee, "All things being equal, we think that the agency set up to operate the provisions of this bill should be the United States Office of Education." Representatives from the Land Grant College Association and the National Association of State Universities wrote in expressing similar sentiments.[3]

George Zook, the president of the American Council on Education, the most powerful college lobby, brought to the committee a similar message from the educators he represented. Zook was a creature of the education policy establishment; by the time he testified before Congress that day, he'd run the Office of Education and served as president of the University of Akron.[4] The Office of Education, he told Congress, should oversee the veterans' education benefits "for the simple reason that this is an educational program which is to be carried out through regular educational channels, and the institutions and school systems are accustomed to dealing with the United States Office of Education."[5]

For the educators, maintaining autonomy over their programs was crucial, given the history dating to the country's founding that limited the federal government's role in education. Although the feds would be providing the schools with the money to educate veterans, college representatives were wary of any indication that the government could be involved in the curriculum. The question of the size of the federal government's role in the initiative, and which agency would be responsible for carrying out the government's duties, was not a small one. The agency under which the bill was housed would have the authority to determine the schools where veterans were eligible to use their benefits, funds that could be a boon for some institutions.

Placing control of the entire GI Bill under the auspices of the Veterans Administration was a project the veterans' lobby had been working toward for years. Chief among the architects of that effort was Warren Atherton, the national commander of the American Legion from 1943 to 1944. A World War I veteran, Atherton vigorously fought anything he viewed as undermining what the American Legion argued that soldiers and veterans were entitled to. As his term went on, Atherton used his public appearances and other lobbying activities to portray veterans as a class distinct from other Americans, even those working as part of the war effort. In December 1943, Atherton recounted a visit to a war plant in Newport News, Virginia, to the *Christian Science Monitor*. Of the experience, Atherton said, "It made me sad to see so many young faces." Some of those plants "are offering refuge from uniforms."[6]

Distinguishing returning soldiers from civilians was a key component of the American Legion's strategy to create a sweeping program of benefits exclusively for veterans. He tapped Harry Colmery to draft a bill to propose to Congress.[7] A former American Legion national commander and Pittsburgh-educated lawyer, Colmery's square face, thick neck, and close-cropped hair harked back to his baseball-playing days at Oberlin College.[8] Colmery sensed in advance that the education provisions would face some objections. For one, although previous proposals had included clauses limiting education benefits to soldiers whose schooling had been interrupted by war, this version did not—thus widening the pool of eligible veterans to include those who might not have qualified for college or hadn't been interested in a degree before the war. To those concerned about the cost of offering the benefit to such a wide swath of veterans, Colmery's testimony to Congress offered an argument that echoed Roosevelt's interest in providing an individual and national benefit, as well as Atherton's rhetoric that veterans' specific experience entitled them to distinct rights: "If we spend two hundred to three hundred billion to teach our men and women to kill, why quibble over a billion or so to help them have the opportunity to earn economic independence, and to enjoy the fruits of freedom, and civil and religious liberty—the things for which they fight," Colmery said.[9]

In Colmery's version of the GI Bill, the education benefits, like the other provisions, would remain the purview of the Veterans Administration. Colmery briefly worried that allowing the VA to administer the education benefits provisions could provide opportunities for exploitation. But he ultimately quelled his doubts, writing in response to his own concerns in the margins of a GI Bill draft: "Personally, I think not. Many educators disagree."[10]

As the historian Kathleen Frydl chronicles in her book *The GI Bill*, the American Legion worked to ensure that the veterans' educational benefits would be under the auspices of the Veterans Administration by identifying an ally in Congressman John Rankin, a Democrat of Mississippi. They also lobbied for veterans legislation to be considered only in the House Committee on World War Legislation, which he chaired. That strategy would have consequences for the shape of the bill and who it benefited.[11]

Rankin's approach to policymaking was tinged by his racism—he frequently opposed antilynching laws and offered public support to Nazis charged with war crimes at Nuremberg.[12] He aimed to structure what would become the GI Bill in a way that would preserve racial hierarchy in the South in particular, Frydl told me in an interview.[13] He initially held up the bill over concerns that a provision providing unemployment compensation would benefit Black veterans as well as white ones.[14] This approach created a GI Bill that theoretically offered benefits to all veterans but in practice actually bolstered a middle-class society that was "almost exclusively for whites," Ian Katznelson writes in *When Affirmative Action Was White*.[15] Katznelson provides a useful frame for thinking about the GI Bill—as part of a history of midcentury government welfare programs that, by design, disproportionately benefited white Americans.

That was true of the bill's education provisions. Ultimately, the American Legion helped broker a solution that preserved its interest in having veterans' benefits housed within the Veterans Administration and assuaged Rankin's concerns that the unemployment compensation could upset the racial hierarchy in place in the South: the entitlement would be funded by the federal government through the VA but administered by states, giving local officials some sway in who received the funds.[16]

Lawmakers adopted that model for other provisions, including the education benefit. In that effort, they received some encouragement from private, commercial schools whose leaders worried that if the Office of Education oversaw the bill's education provisions, the agency would deny the participation of many of them, as commercial schools.[17] Even for those schools that did make it past the Office of Education's standards, a bill under the purview of the Veterans Administration would likely provide more access to funds. The VA fully reimbursed schools for the cost of education, while the Office of Education required states to meet part of the cost, an approach that put poor states at risk of being able to fund fewer schools.[18] In light of these concerns, private, commercial colleges wrote to Rankin and other lawmakers, encouraging them to keep oversight of the education benefits under the VA.[19]

Rankin was sympathetic to that view, concerned that allowing the Office of Education to oversee the education provisions of the GI Bill would represent an inappropriate incursion of federal power into education.[20] In the end, policymakers opted for a federal-state hybrid similar to the one they had designed for unemployment benefits. Each state department of education would submit a list of approved institutions, but if veterans wanted to attend a school not on the list, the federal VA administrator had the authority to place it on the list.[21]

The result of this approach allowing the federal government and states to share power in administering the bill was a package of benefits that didn't explicitly distinguish different types of veterans but effectively locked Black veterans out of many of its provisions. In addition, it left taxpayers and veterans—particularly Black veterans in the South—vulnerable to being preyed upon by schools.

The state offices of education, suddenly charged with overseeing schools' participation in the GI Bill program, were new to that kind of responsibility and to interacting with for-profit businesses interested in offering training.[22] That dynamic in part allowed for a proliferation of programs looking to take advantage of the influx of funds that came along with veteran students.

A 1948 report in the *New York Times* headlined "Care Urged on GI's in Picking Schools" describes the challenges some veterans faced as they tried to use the education paid for by the government to reassimilate into civilian society: "One veteran complained that he had completed a course for radio repairman, and upon applying for a job, found that he could only be employed as a helper. Another ex-serviceman finished a refrigeration course in the upper third of his class and discovered that employers considered the course almost worthless."[23]

A 1950 report compiled by Carl Gray, then the administrator of Veterans Affairs, provided more detail: "When the Federal Government was authorized to pay for the education and training expense of thousands of veterans of World War II, the education and training of veterans grew into a billion-dollar business."[24]

Gray documented how executives with no previous experience in education "discovered the lucrative business of training veterans."[25] Roughly 140 trade and vocational schools owned or partly owned by just twenty-four people sprung up between the signing of the GI Bill on June 22, 1944, and the release of the 1950 report. Proprietary school operators had set up dummy corporations to stretch the government funds as far as possible, Veterans Administration employees had left the government to work in the proprietary school industry, and schools were engaging in a "pernicious variety of solicitation and advertising."[26]

One veteran whose testimony appeared in the report recounted responding to an advertisement in his local newspaper for a training course. He discussed the course with the school's representative. "I told him that I had previously been in training under the GI Bill," his testimony reads. The veteran went on, "He assured me that it did not make any difference as long as I had not used all of my entitlement."

He signed up for the course and made a $25 deposit (about $335 in 2024 dollars), then took an aptitude test required to enroll in the class, which he didn't pass. "Therefore I had to give up the training as well as lose the $25 deposit," he said.[27]

When state education departments threatened schools with revoking their access to GI Bill funds, the schools would organize students to protest the decision. In a December 1949 letter, the governor of Ohio described to VA officials the approach of a school that the state's education department had cited for poorly serving its students. "The records of the Department of Education show that out of 15 graduates who applied for positions only two were found to be qualified and those two because of previous experience," the letter reads. The school threatened to close and brought hundreds of students to meet with the state's director of education in response to officials' concerns.[28]

Gray pointed to the 1945 amendments that liberalized the GI Bill, including one that allowed correspondence schools to be included in the program, as a major reason that "individuals whose primary interest is a quick and large return on invested capital" had entered the education sector. In addition, he cited the oversight structure as another reason the behavior proliferated. The state education departments didn't have the resources to keep up with alleged violations, and the VA didn't have much authority to step in.[29]

A 1951 report from the General Accounting Office echoed Gray's findings. By the early 1950s, the report found that two out of three for-profit schools approved by the government to educate veterans had existed only since the passage of the GI Bill.[30] "Many of these schools were organized for the specific purpose of attracting veterans to their courses of study," W. L. Ellis, the chief of investigations at the General Accounting Office, wrote. "And it is doubtful whether they could have existed had they been required to depend upon what the general public was willing to pay for the courses offered."[31]

While veterans of all types found themselves caught up in these scams, Black veterans were more likely to be preyed upon in the

South than their white counterparts were, the historian Frydl notes. In addition, sham school operators opened schools alongside the railroad tracks going north, Frydl told me, which many Black veterans took to get out of the South.[32] Although Black veterans were interested in vocational training, they were often barred from the legitimate programs available.[33] Meanwhile, as waiting lists for legitimate vocational training opportunities grew, shady operators began popping up in the South, looking for ways to lure Black veterans and the GI Bill dollars that came with them. In one particularly egregious example cited by Frydl, a school claimed to be "training" Black veterans in floor sweeping and supplementing those workers' wages with GI Bill funds.[34]

At the same time, the GI Bill was effectively helping to prop up a system of segregated higher education. In the South, to avoid an influx of Black student veterans who might integrate predominantly white colleges, states would pay for a Black veteran to travel to a school out of state or to a historically Black college or university.[35] But decades of state government policies that drastically underfunded colleges educating Black students as compared to those educating their white counterparts meant that these schools struggled to absorb the influx of veterans.[36] They turned away an estimated twenty thousand students during the roughly ten years following the passage of the GI Bill.[37]

Although the law that created the GI Bill and its education provisions didn't technically discriminate against Black veterans, the way it was implemented meant that many Black GIs struggled to find a school where they could use it. By sending money to schools that discriminated against Black students and by allowing states to dictate how the money was spent, the structure of the GI Bill helped to fuel the segregated higher education system that was already in place and that still exists to this day.

The bill propped up that system in another, subtler way as well— by opening the government spigot of higher education funds for the first time to commercial colleges. As Frydl notes, in the years following the passage of the GI Bill, Black veterans in the South were often victims of the ensuing scams of the time. But in the decades since, for-profit colleges have enrolled a disproportionate share of students of color.[38] To their proponents, that's a sign they're serving an underserved population. To their detractors, it's an indicator that they're preying on students who may struggle to access other types of higher education because of the segregation embedded in K–12 and college and university systems.

The differences in the way white students and students of color, particularly Black students, experience college is one of the many contributing factors to the gulf in student debt between Black, white, and Hispanic borrowers. Students of color are more likely to attend for-profit colleges with high costs and poor outcomes, which can make the student loans they borrowed in order to attend difficult to repay.[39] They're also more likely to attend traditional colleges with fewer resources, like historically Black colleges and universities, community colleges, and regional public universities. These schools tend to struggle more than their whiter and wealthier counterparts to provide the right courses at the right time for students to graduate quickly and other resources that get students through school and into a decent-paying job—making it more difficult for students to repay their loans once they leave.[40]

In many ways, the World War II–era GI Bill looks very different from the predominant ways the US finances higher education today. For one, it was limited to veterans, and in addition, it was a grant, not a loan. But as the government's first foray into funding individual students to attend college, the decisions that policymakers made about its structure—in particular, allowing veterans to spend benefits at commercial colleges and using the program to perpetuate the segregated higher education system—still reverberate today.

For veterans themselves, the college education provided by the GI Bill had the potential to be transformative—and in many cases it was. But policymakers' decisions and the behavior of unscrupulous schools and companies in the decades following the establishment of the GI Bill meant that the line between a life-changing opportunity and a life-ruining one was dangerously thin.

The GI Bill's Potential and Peril

Murray Hastie sat at the computer in his parents' house, scanning the list of schools that would accept the benefits he'd earned fighting in Iraq. He typed his interests—still biology and other science courses that could lead him to a career fighting disease—and his personal information into the website GIBill.com. Later that day, Hastie received a phone call from a representative at DeVry University, who said he was in the area and wanted to visit Hastie to talk about the school. The idea that the representative happened to be nearby struck Hastie as strange.

"Nobody is just in the area of Gloversville, New York," he said. "Even if you're in Albany or Saratoga, you're an hour away." Still, Hastie didn't have any reason to be skeptical of the representatives' efforts to help him enroll in school. "I had just come from a place where, if you don't trust the person that's to your left and to your right, you're probably going to die."

The man from DeVry came over the next day. The two talked about Hastie's interests and how he'd pay for school. Hastie wondered about the mismatch between the level of his GI Bill funding and the school's tuition. He didn't understand why he couldn't sign up for the major he was interested in. But every time Hastie asked a question, the representative swatted it away, implying either that Hastie didn't need to worry about the things concerning him or that he was asking a stupid question.

As the conversation wore on, Hastie stopped asking questions. "I didn't want to seem like an idiot or like I didn't know what I was doing." The representative filled out Hastie's personal information on a form, and Hastie signed it, assuming the paper would be used to hold his spot in the courses he was interested in. About two months later, he received a phone call from DeVry letting him know that his classes were going to start soon.

Although Hastie was dumbfounded to learn that he'd actually enrolled at the school, he greeted the phone call with excitement and relief. "I was still waffling on where to go to school and what I was studying," Hastie said. The call indicated that "the decision was already made."

———

A few years later and roughly four hundred miles away, Jennifer Esparza was considering giving college a try while on active duty in the military. As a high school student in Los Angeles, college had felt out of reach for Esparza. She'd never put much effort into school, and her grades showed it. Esparza thought signing up for the military would be a good way to distance herself from any expectations of how she would perform in college. It was October 2001, and 9/11 had just happened, so enlisting seemed like a natural way to get away from that pressure.

By 2009, Esparza had reenlisted twice; had traveled to Iraq, Kuwait, Paris, Okinawa, and mainland Japan; and was working as an administrative chief at the Pentagon. She started thinking about taking some college courses. A friend of hers was studying for a bachelor's degree online through Ashford University. Esparza mulled the idea of attending a local community college in person, but it was difficult to fit those classes in with her schedule—she felt constant pressure to work harder and longer hours to gain respect from her peers and supervisors. Meanwhile, Esparza watched her friend zoom through classes at Ashford. "Why am I looking at anything else then?" she thought.

Ashford was a subsidiary of Bridgepoint Education, a company founded in 2003 with backing from private equity.[41] Two years after its launch, Bridgepoint purchased a nonprofit college in Iowa that enrolled fewer than five hundred students. It used the school almost as a shell for building out a large online program.[42] By the fall of 2009, Bridgepoint enrolled nearly fifty-five thousand students.[43] That growth was fueled in part by aggressive recruiting tactics, according to a Senate investigation, including calling students at least eight times in the first seven days after the school received a lead and telling students who expressed reservations about the cost of the education that they were doing the right thing and would make their parents and role models proud.[44]

At the time, Esparza didn't know anything about Ashford's ties to Wall Street or its approach to luring students; she reached out to Ashford to find out about signing up for classes and was contacted by one of the school's military recruiters. His entreaties to her seemed to go beyond simply wanting information to sign her up for school. He asked Esparza to send him pictures of her with her dog, and he friended her on Facebook. The recruiter kept reassuring Esparza that she was making the right choice and encouraged her to bring any doubts about her decision to him so that he could talk her out of them. Although the behavior made her uncomfortable, Esparza tried to shrug it off.

Because of their age gap, Esparza thought of her older brother, who was eleven years her senior, almost as another father figure. But he was living on the opposite coast at the time, they weren't talking much about the process of enrolling at Ashford, and she didn't want to include him in it. "I thought I was doing the right thing," she said. Once she enrolled, Esparza's brother started gently probing her decision to attend Ashford. When they spoke, he would ask her if she had considered taking some classes in person at a nearby community college.

Eventually, Esparza also started to question the education she was receiving at Ashford. The breaking point came when she realized she could have a couple of drinks at Margarita Wednesdays with her friends, walk home a little bit tipsy, and still be capable of completing her Ashford homework assignments and earning an A. "For me that was embarrassing," she said.

An Attempt to Clamp Down Opens the Doors

The concern over the scam schools that had proliferated following the World War II version of the GI Bill did inspire policymakers to make some tweaks as they approached drafting the Korean War version to clamp down on such operators.

Worried by the evidence presented in Gray's 1950 report and in the media, President Harry Truman instructed Congress to find a way to curb the schools' offenses, telling lawmakers, "In a good many instances veterans have received training for jobs for which they are not suited or for occupations in which they will be unable to find jobs when they finish their training."[45]

Congress convened a committee, led by the Texas congressman Olin Teague, to investigate the education and training provisions under the GI Bill. Teague was known for his tenacity. He earned his nickname, "Tiger," as a high school football player, as he was known for leaving it all on the field. Teague, who'd been awarded a Purple Heart, a Silver Star, and other accolades, was first approached to run for Congress from a hospital bed, and he initially declined.[46]

With thorough research, Teague uncovered voluminous evidence of the ways business owners were taking advantage of veterans' education benefits. In Pennsylvania, for example, all the schools offering carpentry, cabinetmaking, and other trades were made up only of veterans and had existed only since the GI Bill.[47]

Accordingly, Teague offered some proposals that would curb that abuse in the version of the GI Bill for veterans of the Korean War. For example, Teague suggested that Congress require schools to enroll a minimum of 25% nonveterans in order to receive GI Bill funds.[48] Perhaps most crucially, he suggested that instead of the government paying schools directly, the feds provide a stipend to the student to be used in paying tuition. That would encourage students to use their benefit at cheaper schools and would also incentivize schools to keep tuition low.[49]

But Bernard Ehrlich, who lobbied on behalf of the proprietary school industry for decades, indicated the circumstances under which these tweaks to the Korean War version of the bill came about differently. Ehrlich, a World War II veteran himself, began his career in the for-profit college sector in 1949, when he volunteered to help Teague with his investigation into the GI Bill. Ehrlich, twenty years old and at the time a recent law school graduate, was too young to sit for the bar exam but eager to keep busy even if he wasn't drawing a salary. Ehrlich's assignment from the congressman's office was to research for-profit colleges, and even enroll in some, and then report his findings back to the committee.[50]

Through his study of individual schools, Ehrlich decided that certain trade schools that he believed were offering veterans a quality education weren't recognized by the Veterans Administration at the time. This meant they couldn't participate in the GI Bill, even if they were worthy of accessing those federal funds.[51]

Once he came to that realization, Ehrlich dedicated himself to finding a way to get those schools included. A few years later, Ehrlich, by then an attorney, was in a position to ensure that the schools could access the GI Bill funds. "So many people who served in the war were people who had no background and were not college material," Ehrlich recalled in a 2020 interview with me.[52] "My role was to try to help write the bill and to make sure that the bill included all types of schools and made sure that only schools who measured up were part of the program."

Ehrlich's approach to ensuring that only legitimate schools participated in the program was to develop a system of accreditation. He spoke to prominent educators to come up with standards that schools would need to comply with in order to continue to access GI Bill funds.[53] The second GI Bill, which was signed into law in 1952, allowed funds to go to schools as long as they were accredited by governing bodies recognized by the Office of Education.[54]

So, accrediting organizations made up of representatives of member schools would determine whether those schools were eligible for federal education benefits. Essentially, as long as an accrediting organization was approved by the Office of Education, the schools would be policing themselves, and veterans could easily take their funding to an accredited school of their choosing.

Ehrlich testified at the 1952 Senate subcommittee hearing, but not as part of Teague's team. Instead, he represented the National Federation of Private Schools. Ehrlich told the committee he supported Teague's proposal to change to a scholarship system, granting the funds to students instead of schools. When Teague, who also testified at the hearing, questioned whether allowing certain schools to take part in the program could put veterans and taxpayers at risk, Ehrlich responded, "We are not here to protect the schools that came into this business for the purpose of securing all GI enrollments."[55]

"I was sort of proud of the fact that the door was opened to people going for programs that were not just colleges," Ehrlich remembered later.[56]

Ultimately, the Korean War GI Bill ended up with some provisions meant to curb abuses: vocational and trade schools were required to prove that they didn't solely rely on veterans for enrollment—although the cap on veteran enrollment wound up at the VA-endorsed 85% instead of Teague's suggestion of 75%; veterans received one stipend that covered tuition and living expenses, ideally encouraging them to shop around for a quality school that would stretch their funds the furthest; and institutions that voluntarily submitted to accreditation were favored.[57]

But that still left room for schools to take advantage of taxpayers and veterans through the program. For one, supervision of schools remained with individual state departments of education.[58] In addition, by empowering accrediting organizations as part of the oversight process, the Korean War–era GI Bill left a legacy whose implications students and taxpayers are still feeling today. For schools to receive access to federal student aid funds, they still need to have approval from accrediting agencies, essentially private membership organizations that monitor members. Often inherent in this system is a conflict of interest—colleges pay to be members of a group that evaluates them, and if a college fails the evaluation, the organization no longer receives the fee that college was paying.

More than sixty years later, this conflict of interest was still playing out in dramatic fashion. Corinthian Colleges, a for-profit chain that collapsed in 2015 amid accusations it lured students with inflated job placement and graduation rates into enrolling and taking on debt, maintained its accreditation right up until the day the school closed.[59]

The GI Bill's Impact on College Campuses

Of course sham schools and scandal weren't the only or even primary legacies of the education benefits of the GI Bill. An estimated 8.1 million veterans used the bill to attend college in the bill's first few years of existence.[60] Their presence—and the funds that came with them—Frydl argues, swelled the ranks of college campuses and in many ways transformed the "college experience" into what we know today. In the first several years following the passage of the GI Bill, colleges grew their facilities and faculty, and they started using the teaching format of a large lecture broken into discussion sessions led by a teaching assistant—a technique adopted from the military.[61] In addition, colleges, pressured by veterans who were enrolled as training for a job, started to become more explicit about the role of college in preparing students for work, launching the job placement and counseling centers that today's families often expect to see on a campus tour.

Despite the racism embedded in the design of the GI Bill, male students of all types were able to experience transformative benefits from it. Thanks to the GI Bill, Catholics, Jews, and other students who had historically struggled to access graduate school were able to go, diversifying the ranks of many professions.[62] Although many historically Black colleges and universities struggled to accommodate the influx of returning GIs with limited resources, for some schools and their students, the bill was transformational. For example, Howard University used the influx of funds to expand its engineering and law programs, with the latter ultimately becoming a locus of civil rights legal activism.[63]

———

After a few post–happy hour homework sessions, Jennifer Esparza knew she wanted something closer to the quintessential GI Bill experience—attending in-person classes following her service commitment—than what she was experiencing at Ashford. She sent a series of emails to the school until finally she was able to unenroll. Then, she sat tight for a couple of years, finishing up her military contract while she waited to go back to school. During that period, Esparza was often tempted to return to a program like Ashford; her colleagues at the Pentagon were touting their bachelor's degrees, which she still didn't have. Esparza tried to keep focused on her ultimate goal: earning a bachelor's degree that would give her fodder to discuss more than just the credential—she hoped to be able to share what she actually learned instead of just the fact of the degree itself.

"I wanted the college education in the most traditional sense I could possibly get, even though I was thirty years old when I was going to undergrad," she said.

When Esparza was studying at Ashford, she used tuition assistance benefits to fund her education. Part of the reason Esparza turned to that source of funds—which are available to pay for college only to those still in the military—was that she was on active duty. But in addition, because she'd always hoped she'd eventually be able to have an on-campus experience at a more traditional college, Esparza avoided tapping her GI Bill benefits for anything that wasn't that, including Ashford.

As she approached the end of her military career and prepared for what to do next, Esparza decided to lean on her brother's expertise to help her navigate the college application process. He talked about college in a way she wasn't hearing from her peers in the military—as an opportunity to grow both intellectually and personally by studying topics she was interested in, not just as a ticket to move up the career ladder. Together, they decided to target the University of Oregon. That way, once Esparza enrolled she could have access to a reliable support system while in school.

Although Esparza could lean on her brother, who had experience applying to college, she still came up against obstacles faced by many college applicants who aren't eighteen years old and living in their parents' house. For-profit colleges often take advantage of the way these hurdles can throw off a so-called nontraditional student, critics say. The colleges may offer flexibility in the form of application requirements, multiple deadlines and dates throughout a term to enroll, and class schedules outside of standard work hours.

For Esparza, a relatively basic question presented a source of confusion. Would she be enrolling as a freshman? Or as a transfer student, given her experience in the military? In addition, Esparza had never completed one of the standard requirements for entering a four-year public college: taking a college entrance exam. Because she went straight to the military out of high school, Esparza hadn't sat for the SAT or ACT. The application also provided an opportunity for Esparza to address any gaps. In an essay, she used her military background to explain why she didn't meet the school's math requirements.

A month or so after applying, Esparza received a big envelope in the mail with a duck, the University of Oregon's mascot, and "Congratulations" written on it. For Esparza, the acceptance provided reassurance that she was headed in the right direction. Over the course of her twenties, she'd struggled to leave the military, reenlisting twice after her initial contract was up because of the opportunities—to travel the world, for example—and financial stability it provided her. Now, with the chance to attend college in hand, Esparza felt confident about her choice.

Once Esparza arrived on campus, the high-stress environment of her life in the military allowed her to take a more relaxed approach to college than some of her peers who were more than a decade her junior. She knew that if she treated the classes and coursework as her full-time job, she still wouldn't be as busy as she'd been on active duty. Still, Esparza wasn't immune to the jitters that accompany arriving on campus for the first time as a student—she wore her shirt backward for much of her first day.

Almost immediately, Esparza was introduced to the kind of mind- and personality-expanding experience that her brother promised would be available at college. On the first day of Spanish class, the professor asked all the students to write something in Spanish and turn it in. Esparza came from a Spanish-speaking family, with parents who were fluent and grandparents who spoke it exclusively, but she had never been in touch with that part of her background. When she was growing up in the 1980s and 1990s, the prevailing wisdom among immigrant parents like hers was to provide their children with the best chance to assimilate by making sure they knew English.

Still, when Esparza turned in her write-up, it was evident to the instructor that her proficiency was beyond what would be covered in the class. She pulled Esparza aside and encouraged her to enroll in a Spanish heritage class, where other students who came from Spanish-speaking families but weren't necessarily confident in their language skills could improve and also discuss broader issues too.

In addition to exploring her own background, Esparza also started to probe through her coursework some of the experiences she had in the military. Although she'd been deployed to countries where most people practice Islam, Esparza hadn't learned much about the history, culture, and people of the religion. She signed up for an introductory course on Islam and started taking Arabic.

In the years leading up to when Esparza enrolled at Ashford and Hastie started at DeVry, for-profit colleges had become increasingly skilled at, and increasingly interested in, targeting veterans. The original impetus for their push came from a law that was actually aimed at cracking down on for-profit college abuses.

As part of the 1992 reauthorization of the Higher Education Act, Representative Maxine Waters, a Democrat of California, introduced a bill that would require for-profit colleges to receive at least 15% of their funding from sources other than federal student aid. The rule applied the same logic that Teague and the VA had advanced when including a similar provision as part of the changes made to the GI Bill for veterans of the Korean War. Waters had watched as many of her low-income Los Angeles constituents were lured into taking on loans to attend for-profit colleges with promises of a better life, only to find themselves in debt and unable to find a job.[64] She figured that if the schools provided a decent education, at least some students would be willing to spend their own money on them.[65]

Waters's interest in curbing for-profit colleges predated her time in Congress. As a member of the California State Assembly, representing an area of Los Angeles that included, as Waters put it, "a number of housing projects," a lot of her work was focused on ways to help members of her district deal with poverty. "It brought me in contact with a lot of young people who were just hanging out, people were looking for jobs, looking for any kind of resources to support their families," Waters said during an interview for *Fail State*, a documentary about the rise of for-profit colleges. "I learned a lot about how they were being approached by these recruiters." For example, recruiters would come into housing projects and tell residents they could train to become dental assistants and even show them the uniforms they would wear once they graduated. Instead, the students often found classrooms with no teachers or computer training courses with no computers.[66]

"There were a tremendous number of people who were coming into Maxine Waters's office and were coming into legal aid," with stories of misery after enrolling in these schools only to find that they didn't lead to promised jobs, Elena Ackel, an attorney at the Legal Aid Foundation of Los Angeles, who worked with Waters on these issues for years, told me.[67] When Waters got to Congress, she wanted to find a way to deal nationally with what she saw in California, so she looked to the 85/15 idea, which is the notion of limiting the share of a for-profit college's revenue that could come from federal student aid.[68]

Even after Waters's measure was signed into law, lobbyists for the for-profit college industry pushed lawmakers to delay and weaken the provisions. They warned that the rule would hurt a majority of their schools and push others out of business. That, they argued, could put a post–high school education out of reach of the low-income and often minority students they served.[69] That notion—and perhaps the nearly $2 million the schools' trade associations spent on lobbying and advertising in 1992—was enough to convince at least some lawmakers that a delay was warranted.[70] A bipartisan group of eighty-two members of the House of Representatives signed on to a letter that supported delaying implementation of the law until mid-1995.[71]

Once the rule went into effect, enforcement was initially lax, with the Department of Education relying on schools to self-report the share of their funds that came from federal student aid. Not surprisingly, just four out of about two thousand schools admitted that they were over the 85% threshold required to stay in compliance.[72] Just a few years later, Congress relaxed the provision, allowing for-profit colleges to derive up to 90% of their revenue from federal financial aid funds.[73]

Throughout the drafting, tweaking, and implementing of the 85/15-turned-90/10 rule, policymakers continued to leave open a loophole that would allow for-profit colleges to stay in compliance but remain funded almost entirely by the government. The 85% or 90% cap applied only to federal financial aid funds—essentially the Pell Grants and student loans available to the general student population—but military-connected government education benefits, including tuition assistance and the GI Bill, didn't count toward the limit.

"We should have put that in to begin with," Ackel told me years later of a provision that would have banned schools from counting military-related benefits toward the 10%. Both Waters and Ackel wanted to prevent the veterans benefits from counting toward the 10%, but there was so much opposition from lobbyists and the lawmakers they worked with that they couldn't push the bill through with that provision, she said: "We didn't, everything was done very fast and the opportunity opened up. We underestimated the zeal with which the schools went after active duty military and veterans."[74]

When veterans suddenly got access to more education funding through the post-9/11 GI Bill passed by Congress in 2008, they became an attractive target to for-profit colleges looking to stay afloat and stay in compliance with the law. Or as Holly Petraeus, then an official at the Consumer Financial Protection Bureau overseeing servicemember affairs, put it in 2011, "This gives for-profit colleges an incentive to see service members as nothing more than dollar signs in uniform."[75]

Recruiting veterans and their education benefits became key to the schools' survival, so they developed several strategies to lure them. At one for-profit college chain, leadership wrote in internal documents that they viewed growing the military student population as a 90/10 compliance tactic and suggested starting a location of the school next to a military base.[76] The president of one of the schools in that company's portfolio urged staff in a 2009 email to "never give up especially when dealing with important issues such as 90/10" and described the VA funding as a "terrific opportunity."[77]

A *Frontline* documentary highlighted a particularly egregious example of for-profit colleges' drive to lure veterans: a recruiter trolling the wounded-warrior barracks of a military base and signing up students with brain injuries so severe they couldn't remember the courses they took.[78] Schools also devoted resources to creating lead-generating websites that were styled to look like government- or military-backed sources of information, like the GIBill.com site Hastie had found. Instead, they were simply portals for recruiters focused on the military to collect the contact information of aspiring student veterans.

Periodically, lawmakers would try to make veterans less attractive targets for for-profit colleges, but they were often thwarted by their own colleagues. In 2014, Representatives Susan Davis and Mark Takano, both California Democrats, attempted to close the so-called 90/10 loophole, but Representative John Kline, a Republican of Minnesota and then chair of the House Committee on Education and the Workforce, killed the provision within fifteen minutes of the lawmakers introducing it. At the time, the parent company of the University of Phoenix had donated more to Kline's coffers than to any other member of Congress.[79] Between 2010 and when Takano and Davis introduced their proposal, lawmakers had tried to modify the 90/10 rule at least five times, failing every time.

The funds that for-profit colleges received from veterans eventually proved so lucrative that they essentially capitalized the schools when other sources of funding dried up. As the enrollment surge that had bolstered for-profit colleges in the immediate aftermath of the Great Recession began to wane, putting the schools' financial future at risk, they continued to recruit veterans whose GI Bill funds helped to keep the schools afloat.[80] In the two years leading up to fiscal year 2013–2014, for-profit colleges' revenue from enrolling servicemembers grew from $727 million to over $1 billion.[81] That year nearly two hundred for-profit colleges were receiving more than 90% of their revenue from government sources, including military education benefits.[82]

An Unexpected College Experience

As Murray Hastie got closer to starting classes at DeVry, he began to get an inkling that the experience might be different from what he'd expected. Hastie had hoped to attend a DeVry campus in New York, but a representative from the school told him there were no options in the state where he could also live on campus. That was key to Hastie; he didn't have a car, and he wanted to immerse himself completely in school. So he enrolled at a campus in North Brunswick, New Jersey, where he'd been assured that he'd be able to live on campus.

When Hastie arrived, he discovered that the on-campus accommodation he'd been promised was actually an apartment complex two miles from the school. He'd need a bus pass to attend class. What's more, Hastie, a twenty-two-year-old, would be sharing the two-bedroom apartment with three other students. He met two of his roommates, who had traveled to DeVry from Long Island and North Carolina, shortly after he arrived. The three of them bonded over the mutual sense of shock they shared at the difference between where they thought they'd be living and their actual apartment.

Although Hastie felt he'd been misled, he resolved to move forward and keep progressing toward his degree. Complaining about his situation wasn't going to help. Like so many students who sensed something wasn't quite right with their school, he was hesitant to leave after sinking time, energy, and money into enrolling. Still, he realized relatively quickly that continuing his studies would be a challenge. He thought he'd enrolled in a program that would teach him how to work in a lab; instead, he was taking medical coding classes. Never particularly technology savvy, Hastie struggled. Every time he attended a class that wasn't English, math, or public speaking, he felt as if he were going to fail.

Hastie was also experiencing extreme fluctuations in his emotions, which affected his ability to focus in class and study. One semester he'd earn straight As and the next he'd barely attend class. But at meetings with a dean or his advisers, no one brought it up. Meanwhile, Hastie was receiving letters at his parents' house from the student loan company Sallie Mae. When his mom asked him about the letters during the Christmas break of his second year in school, Hastie told her what he'd heard from financial aid officials at DeVry: that the school needed to take loans out on his behalf so he could enroll in his courses, but once his GI Bill funds arrived, they'd pay the loans.

"That doesn't sound right," Hastie's mom told him. "Trust me," he said, and continued to take courses at the school.

One summer day in his third year of college, a group of Hastie's childhood friends came to visit him at DeVry and took him to a Yankees game. When he told them of his experience at the school and his emotional peaks and valleys, the group became worried and brought him back to his parents' home. "They took it upon themselves to kidnap me," Hastie said.

His parents were also concerned and urged Hastie to visit a Veterans Administration office. A few months later, after a battery of tests, doctors diagnosed Hastie with post-traumatic stress disorder and prescribed therapy and other remedies. Hastie also decided to meet with a school placement representative at the VA to determine how to finish his schooling. That representative told Hastie that the credits from the courses he took and passed likely wouldn't transfer to another school. He had earned enough credits from DeVry for an associate's degree, but the VA representative told him that community colleges likely wouldn't accept most of them.

At the time, Hastie thought he was the only one who'd been duped. But in reality, he was the victim of a system designed to lure him and his GI Bill funds. The proprietary business and correspondence schools that had lobbied in the 1940s to be included in the GI Bill were ancestors to DeVry, a modern-day for-profit college listed on the New York Stock Exchange.

During the years Hastie attended DeVry, its enrollment soared from 63,000 to more than 128,000—essentially doubling—according to findings from a Senate investigation published in 2012.[83] To achieve such staggering enrollment growth, DeVry representatives were encouraged to use recruitment tactics like the "tie down," in which they would urge prospective students to say yes as many times as possible so by the time the final question of whether to enroll came up, it would seem ridiculous to say no.

The school also employed tactics specifically to lure veterans. The website where Hastie had first looked into using his education benefits, GIBill.com, was actually run by QuinStreet Inc., a firm DeVry paid to provide its recruiters with military leads.[84] In 2010, the year after Hastie left, GI Bill funds accounted for just over 3%, or $53 million, of DeVry's revenue.[85] But by bringing in veterans, schools like DeVry captured more than just their GI Bill benefit—they also enrolled a student who would help keep them in compliance with the 90/10 rule. In addition, even if the school's tuition were higher than what a veteran's GI Bill would cover, student loans could provide for-profit colleges with the rest. And so between 2009 and 2011, DeVry earned on average $10,214 in revenue per veteran, according to the Senate report, while public schools collected $4,642.[86] In more recent years, DeVry has faced actions from the Federal Trade Commission and the Department of Education over what the agencies have described as its misleading advertising campaigns between 2008 and 2015. The school has said it disagrees with the Department of Education's conclusions.

"While I was in therapy, it really hit me how much I had invested in that school and how much that school is ultimately going to take from my life," Hastie said. Ultimately he owed $90,000 in debt from his time at the school.

In a statement emailed to me, DeVry said that while the university is "grateful" for Hastie's service to our nation and "respect[s] his right to speak out," the school harbors "serious misgivings about his public statements." Because of student privacy laws, DeVry couldn't comment on the specifics of his case, but the university said, "We can confirm, however, the narrative he provides is neither accurate nor complete."

"DeVry University has always been committed to serving learners seeking a ladder of opportunity to a better life, particularly those who have tried and failed in other educational settings or are otherwise unable to thrive within the traditional higher education system," the statement reads. "We are intensely focused on student success and our mission of preparing learners to succeed in careers shaped by continuous technological change."

Although Jennifer Esparza escaped Hastie's fate, she did it narrowly—and she knew it—thanks in large part to support from her brother. It wasn't until she arrived at the University of Oregon with the help of that support unavailable to many veterans and other students who don't fit the mold of the college freshman in popular imagination—an eighteen-year-old high school graduate leaving their parents' house for the first time—that Esparza began to understand what she would have given up had she stayed at Ashford.

When Esparza first started thinking about college, she'd initially been intimidated by the idea of attending a four-year public or private school. She never sat for the SAT and hadn't taken some college prerequisites. What's more, the pull toward a different type of college was strong. "That's a bigger ask of veterans," Esparza said of the idea of attending a more traditional college, "to trust you and walk away from the fast degree and take time to sit in the classroom."

She'd watched others fall prey—including her mother and sister—to the temptation of earning a credential quickly and their own insecurities about their ability to succeed at a more traditional college. For-profit colleges often would fuel those emotions by billing themselves as accommodating the schedules and needs of veterans and other students with responsibilities outside the classroom: "In some cases they do offer these more flexible schedules for people that want a degree but feel like they can't do it because they work full-time or they feel like they're providing for other people in their family—or they're just nervous about a college experience in general," Esparza said. The stoking of that insecurity by the recruiter and the experience of watching her fellow servicemembers plow through to their degrees was a large part of why Esparza ended up starting her college journey at Ashford.

But once at Oregon, Esparza realized that it wasn't uncommon for four-year public and nonprofit schools to have resources available to students like her. It's just that they didn't advertise them or even make them easy to find. When Esparza started at Oregon, she received no special introduction to the school that would help her locate what she needed. Instead, she was pushed into the regular freshman orientation surrounded by students more than a decade her junior in a giant auditorium where session leaders encouraged students to interact with one another. "I did not honestly know how I fit in," she said. Luckily, Esparza had someone else with which to navigate an experience largely geared toward teenagers who had just left high school. Esparza's mom, who was in her fifties, started as an undergraduate at Oregon around the same time that Esparza arrived on campus. She recommended that Esparza inquire about the school's disability services offerings, which had helped her navigate returning to school as an older student.

During the first week of classes, Esparza decided to take her mom's advice and walked into the disability services office. At the time, Esparza was just starting to understand her disabilities, including panic disorder and depression, which had been recently diagnosed. Through the office she was able to receive extra time taking tests, and she started checking in weekly with a counselor who advised her on strategies to bring her stress level down. If Esparza started to feel anxious, she'd take out her headphones and walk slowly between classes, just as the counselor advised.

Those meetings and strategies instilled a confidence in Esparza that made approaching her courses less intimidating than she'd envisioned they would be as a high school student or when she weighed her college options while on active duty. Esparza thrived academically, making the dean's list multiple semesters in a row. "Part of this was I was so supported by my brother," who offered her a stable home while in school, she said. That, she knew, made her time in college different from what many other veterans and older students experience.

Still, initially, Esparza couldn't shake the notion that she should be progressing toward her degree and a job quickly. "A lot of veterans, it's very easy to get caught up in this idea of 'I need to be thinking of my next career now,'" she said. Once again, it was her brother who guided her toward approaching her education as an experience of personal and intellectual growth. He advised her to assess the courses she was taking, figure out what she was good at and what she enjoyed, and use that information to decide on a major. "That's a piece of advice that I really hold dear," she said.

Despite the support Esparza received from her brother, her mother, and disability services, it wasn't enough to protect her from moments in which she was unsure of her place on campus. When she arrived at Oregon, Esparza immediately gravitated toward the campus veteran student group. "I didn't identify as much else than veteran," she said, so the idea of hanging out with those students made sense. "I thought, 'This is awesome. I have people that know my background and will get me.'"

But soon, conversations in the veterans' lounge, a dark room above a rarely used basketball court, turned uncomfortable. There were lewd comments about women marines standing on the steps of the commandant's house, questioning how those women got to work for the highest officer in the Marine Corps. After months of enduring that treatment, Esparza decided it would be healthier for her to step away from the organization, which until that point had been the source of everything from friends to go out with on weekends to a space to sit between classes.

Ultimately, distance from that group and space gave her the opportunity to connect with other types of students and veterans who hadn't been active in student veteran programming but, like her, were focused and passionate about their studies. She sought out other spaces on campus to study, including the student union, where she met the person who would ultimately become her partner—a student veteran who was focused on his studies. She got involved in student groups focused on sexual violence prevention and decided she would do what she could to make the veterans' center a safer one for women, LGBTQ students, and others who previously had been hesitant to use it. Esparza and other student veterans worked with administrators to design a new space that was light and airy and where computers for students to do work—not couches—were the focus. At times, the space was filled completely with women.

Esparza's success academically and on campus made her reconsider a long-forgotten dream of becoming a lawyer. "In high school I told myself I could never go to college because I wasn't smart enough, I didn't have good enough grades," she said. "One day I just realized 'I am not the student I told myself I was in high school.'"

She sat for the law school entrance exam, although because her test date was during finals and she was so focused on getting good grades, Esparza's score wasn't competitive. She decided to send out applications to a few top law schools anyway, reasoning that she probably wouldn't get in and could send off another round the next application cycle. One day in the spring, Esparza walked out into the driveway, picked up the mail, and spotted a regular-sized envelope from Stanford. She opened it and confirmed it was a denial, as she'd expected. Esparza kept going through the mail and saw a letter from Georgetown that looked almost as if it were an invitation or thank-you note. Esparza resigned herself to thinking she would receive two denials in one day, but when she opened the envelope, she saw the word "congratulations." She started crying in the driveway and called her brother immediately to share the news. "In that moment it felt like there was a school willing to give me a chance, based on my background and not just those test scores," she said.

Like so many veterans before her, the GI Bill and the education it paid for altered Esparza's trajectory for the better. But she was constantly reminded of how close she and those GI Bill dollars came to a different fate. Working at a student veterans' advocacy organization, Esparza engaged directly with veterans whose experiences resemble Hastie's more than hers, people who served their country and tried to use the funding provided by the government to improve their educational and financial outcomes but instead were left repaying student loans.

The government's first foray into subsidizing higher education through the GI Bill set the stage for trends that persist in the US college finance system to this day. That includes leaving loopholes open for bad actors to take advantage of and propping up a higher education system that generally offers Black students fewer opportunities. In addition, the GI Bill helped to instill the idea that providing students with a college education could benefit the country—not just the students themselves—and therefore should be subsidized to some degree by the government. The experiences of Esparza and Hastie illustrate the potential and pitfalls of this system.

"Each week—without fail—we receive emails and phone calls from veterans who were cheated out of their benefits and lied to by college recruiters," Esparza told a government rule-making panel in fall 2021. "It's not difficult for me to believe their experiences because I've been there too," she said. "I'm lucky I had a brother who helped me leave Ashford and attend a good school. But most veterans aren't so lucky."

2. The Higher Education Act

When a Plan to Open the Door to Education Gets Complicated

It wasn't until she was a teenager nearly a thousand miles away from home that MaNesha Stiff first became interested in college. Stiff was traveling around Florida with a cohort of students from her local TRIO program, a federal government initiative established in the 1960s to push more low-income students and students who would be the first in their families to go to college toward attending.

The drive, more than fourteen hours from northwestern Indiana, was the farthest Stiff had ever been from home. And in Florida, Stiff saw something she hadn't witnessed before: quads and dining halls filled largely with Black students and the pride that permeates football games and stepping competitions at historically black colleges and universities. At Florida A&M University, a land grant public college in Tallahassee, and at Bethune-Cookman, a private women's college in Daytona Beach, Stiff began to understand that there were "people who looked like me who were in college."

Despite recognizing herself in the mass of students walking through campus, the idea that she would apply to and ultimately attend college still wasn't clicking for Stiff. The excursion to Florida felt less like a nudge toward higher education and more like a field trip. The conversation on the charter bus centered on an outing to Disney World, not on what Stiff and her fellow teenagers thought of the schools or the steps they'd have to take to end up as a student walking through those Florida campuses.

For Stiff, seeing college as an option for herself was going to take a lot more than a few brief encounters with the ivory towers. Stiff lived in Hammond, Indiana, a city where the downtown was once so bustling with shops and offices that one of its department stores was the real-life inspiration for an encounter between the main character Ralphie and Santa in the iconic holiday movie *A Christmas Story*.[1] But by the time Stiff was growing up in Hammond, much of that economic stability was gone. Pullman had stopped manufacturing its famed railroad cars in town, and other steel factories had pulled out too.[2]

With few decent-paying jobs available, Stiff's neighbors were focused on the basics of paying for food and housing, not extras, like filling out college applications. "When you grow up in an area like I grew up in, it's hard to plan for the future because you're living day-to-day," Stiff said.

In her own home, Stiff's parents encouraged her to do whatever she needed to do to achieve her goals; "they knew that I had the heart and I had the drive to get out," she said. But even though leaving Hammond, where just 14% of residents have a bachelor's degree, would likely require attending college, Stiff's parents didn't talk to her much about it.[3] They never went themselves—Stiff's dad was a steelworker, and her mom was a nurse and became one at a time when that training often took place in trade schools—and weren't familiar with the quirks and minutiae of the process.

Because it was barely mentioned around her dinner table or in her neighbors' yards, the idea of attending college felt out of reach. "I just didn't think I was smart enough, and I didn't think that we could afford it," she said. Still, sometimes a campus tour with TRIO or a conversation with a friend at the high school Stiff attended in a whiter and wealthier neighborhood as part of an integration initiative would pique her interest in continuing her education. But the silence on the topic resumed when she got back home. Days and then months passed without Stiff taking any action on the checklist of tasks involved in preparing a college application.

Stiff graduated from high school in 1999. As the summer started to tick by, she listened as her classmates talked about their plans to leave Hammond for college, including one of Stiff's best friends, who was headed to Northwestern University. Amid all that excitement, "My mom was like, 'Are you going?'" Stiff said.

With just a few months left before fall, the two started figuring out what Stiff would have to do to enroll in college the following semester. So when a representative from North Park University, a private Christian liberal arts school on Chicago's North Side with about two thousand students, called to follow up on a postcard the school had sent her, Stiff arranged over the phone to visit.

Her mom and her aunt joined her on the trip. The campus's tree-lined pathways and red-brick buildings—some with white columns adorning their entrances—were enough to convince Stiff she wanted to attend. The school's location helped too; Stiff liked that North Park was still in Chicago proper but tucked away in a quiet residential neighborhood. Even better, North Park was just forty minutes from Hammond on a commuter train.

Stiff had seen enough—thankfully, because there wasn't much time to see more—she decided to apply to North Park and only there.

By the time Stiff came to that decision, there was just one test date left for the ACT college entrance exam that would produce a score in time for her to attend North Park in the fall. On the day of the test, Stiff showed up to a satellite campus of Purdue University with her pencils and ID and stood around with a handful of other students who were waiting to find out whether they'd actually be able to sit for the test. She watched as other students wandered into the testing room assured that they'd have a seat to take the ACT, sometimes for the second or third time. Stiff signed up so late that she was on standby.

"If there wasn't enough room for us to take it, that was it," she said. And if she got to take the test, "whatever my score was, was it."

Stiff remembered being told on the visit that she needed a 16 to get into North Park. "Of course I got a 16," she said. "I was just happy that I got a 16 to get in—a 16 out of what? I don't even know what the highest score was."

Her score did turn out to be enough to get Stiff into North Park. "When I got the opportunity, I said, 'I'm in,'" Stiff remembered.

Just a few weeks later, Stiff and her parents made the roughly thirty-five-mile drive to North Park's campus. When they arrived, a college representative photographed Stiff and her father as they stood by registration tables. When Stiff saw her room—the first she'd be sharing in years after having a bedroom to herself in high school—she was surprised by how small it was; she hadn't seen the hall where she would be living when she visited North Park's campus initially. Her mom helped her set up her dorm room and realized she'd need a refrigerator while Stiff thought about how she would cope with the lack of privacy that comes with walking down a public hallway to and from the shower.

After the twin long sheets were on the bed and the clothes in the dresser, Stiff and her mom "almost made a clean getaway," she said. But as they walked along a hallway connecting Stiff's dorm to the dining hall, the two looked at each other and realized they were both crying. They turned and hugged each other, and when Stiff opened her eyes, still in her mom's arms, she saw the school's football team running by in their blue, white, and gold practice uniforms. The players reassured her mom that they'd take care of Stiff after she left.

A Government Plan to Help Students Pay for College

A family of limited means tearily dropping their child off at college, surrounded by football players, a dining hall, and the other trappings of residential campus life is perhaps one of the images lawmakers had in mind when they began conceiving of the student loan program in the early 1960s. Ultimately, they would create that student loan system through the Higher Education Act. The program would shift over the ensuing decades in response to the needs of participants in the system, including lenders, servicers, politicians, and students—often with unforeseen consequences.

By the early 1960s, the government was already experimenting with providing loans to students. President Dwight D. Eisenhower had signed the National Defense Education Act in September 1958, which was designed to provide low-interest loans to students with financial need to study science, math, foreign languages, and other defense-related topics.[4] The rationale behind the subsidizing of these students was essentially an extension of the rationale behind the GI Bill. Just as lawmakers believed that providing an education to returning veterans would benefit the country, they also thought that unleashing more college graduates with scientific skills would help the nation in its arms race.

Sputnik, the Soviet Union's successful space satellite launch roughly a year before the passage of the National Defense Education Act, had spooked Eisenhower and other lawmakers about whether the United States had the scientists to compete with its Cold War foe. The president and other lawmakers and experts turned to strengthening the nation's education system to mitigate the problem. In a November 1957 address to the American people, Eisenhower fretted that the Soviet Union had more scientists and engineers than the United States. He vowed that the federal government would "do its part," but Eisenhower also called on schools, parents, and students to push to enhance science and math education.

"My scientific advisers place this problem above all other immediate tasks of producing missiles, of developing new techniques in the Armed Services," Eisenhower told the nation.[5]

About a month later, Marion Folsom, Eisenhower's secretary of health, education, and welfare, offered specific proposals for Congress to consider to address Eisenhower's goals. The Eisenhower administration called for, among other provisions, matching grants to states to test students' aptitude earlier and more thoroughly, fellowships for graduate students to help them prepare for college teaching careers, and ten thousand scholarships—but no loans.[6]

The idea behind the scholarships, in part, was "to stimulate high-school students to do their best and to take courses qualifying them for entrance to college," as lawmakers put it in an August 1958 report on National Defense Education Act draft bills. But by the time the act became law, the scholarships had been dropped in favor of loans—the result of a combination of ideological opposition to providing government funding to what lawmakers deemed nonneedy students and political wrangling.

In the back-and-forth between Eisenhower and the two houses of Congress as they drafted and negotiated the proposal, the president urged lawmakers "to make sure no tax dollars are paid to any scholarship winner who does not need those dollars to finance his education."[7] Some members of Congress wanted to go even further, whittling down scholarships and replacing them with loans, because it was "the American way of doing things."[8] Others, like Senator John Sherman Cooper, a Republican of Kentucky, argued that proposals to cut scholarship aid in favor of loans would "bring into the program young people more eager to study seriously," the *New York Times* reported.[9]

By the time the bill got to conference—or the process that aims to reconcile the Senate and House versions of a proposal—one bill had no scholarships and the other had severely limited them, leaving scholarship supporters with little leverage.[10] In the end, the law would provide a loan fund that began at $47.5 million in the first fiscal year and increased over the following four fiscal years.[11]

Although the National Defense Education Act initiative was only a precursor to a widespread national student loan program, the debate over it anticipated many of the themes that would drive America's approach to financing higher education in the decades to come. That tension between the societal and individual benefits that was present during the debate over the GI Bill also influenced the act's design. It was primarily conceived as a way to boost a national policy objective, with the low-interest loans provided to individual students serving as a sort of ancillary benefit.

But even the urgency to cultivate American talent to compete with the Soviet Union wasn't enough to assuage lawmakers' and President Eisenhower's concerns that students who were undeserving in some way—either because they could afford college without government help or they weren't "eager to study seriously," as Senator Cooper put it—might receive government assistance in paying for their education. And so a program designed to push students toward helping the country achieve a policy objective and initially conceived of with a major scholarship component ultimately required students to pay the money back.

Private Sector Finds Its Own Route to Financing Students

At the same time that lawmakers were looking for ways to improve science and math education to better compete with the Soviet Union, the private sector was experimenting with its own student loan program.

During the late 1950s, Massachusetts, Maine, New York, and other states began launching their own quasi-public-sector corporations to loan money to students to pay for college. Lending money in order to finance education presents challenges to funders, including the fact that they're often advancing the money to young people with little or no credit history. It can be difficult to predict whether the student's and the lender's investment will provide a return, and unlike a car or a home, a lender can't repossess an education to cover a debt. These corporations aimed to get rid of some of these concerns for banks by guaranteeing the loans that the institutions made to students.

In Massachusetts, for example, the Massachusetts Higher Education Loan Plan guaranteed 80% of loans made to students by banks, with the guaranty funds donated by charities, businesses, and individuals. Unlike the National Defense Education Act, which offered low-interest-rate loans to students, borrowers who used the Massachusetts programs were paying about .05% more than the prime commercial bank rate. In other words, banks stood to earn market-rate interest from students but were on the hook for only 20% of the debt if the student struggled to repay it.[12]

Despite the guarantee, these loans weren't available to all students. As Dudley Harmon, executive director for the Massachusetts program, told the *Wall Street Journal* at the time, "All we ask is that the boy or girl be in good standing at college and appeal to the local bank as a good loan prospect." He told the paper, "The skill and experience of these loan officers in appraising character and credit risk is one of the real assets of this plan."[13]

It didn't take long for someone to develop a plan to take this model to the national level, and like the government's first foray into student loans, the main objective of that effort wasn't easing the burden of college finances on families. Instead, in this case, it was about proving an ideological point.

In the mid-twentieth century, Richard Cornuelle, a libertarian writer, was looking for a way to show that private organizations—hospitals, colleges, philanthropies, and the like—could perform social service functions that in the New Deal, and then post–World War II, had been taken over by the government. Cornuelle first became interested in these organizations, which he dubbed the "independent sector," while working at the William Volker Fund, a charitable foundation that promoted libertarian and free market ideas. Cornuelle was working on a project locating libertarian-leaning academics whom the organization could boost with funding and other support. As he and his colleagues started to understand how wide the universe of potential academics was, they also realized that the initiative would require more funding.[14]

He began to "look jealously" at the money the foundation was spending on "conventional welfare activities," Cornuelle told an interviewer in 2005. While looking more closely at the charitable organizations receiving the foundation's funds, in part as a way to get some of that funding to use for his own programming, "I began to realize that there was out there an alternative to government action on social problems," like improving health care and education, he told the interviewer. Up until that point, he'd largely ignored the role of such organizations because "it had become so much a part of American life it was invisible," he said. "We just thought that was part of the furniture or something."[15]

Rallying support for the idea that this group of organizations should take a more prominent role in "solving the problems of people that were in real distress" appealed to Cornuelle in part because it fit with the libertarian ideal of limited government. Boosting the so-called independent sector also satisfied his notion of himself as a do-gooder, which Cornuelle had developed as the son of a minister.[16] So he set out to prove that the independent sector "could solve most pending public problems."[17]

The test case Cornuelle and his colleagues settled on? Student loans. They started to analyze the extent of the problem and what they learned was that, as college costs were rising, more low-income students were attending and having trouble paying for school. Although commercial lenders were in the market and would likely expand their footprint, particularly with loans to parents, banks wouldn't readily support low-income students whose parents couldn't borrow more.[18]

"When we'd finished our analysis we were convinced we had found a problem needing solution. The commercial sector couldn't fully solve it with the instruments at hand. The question became: How could the independent sector get this job done?" Cornuelle wrote in his 1965 book, *Reclaiming the American Dream.*[19]

Cornuelle and his colleagues realized that the founders of organizations like the one in Massachusetts and other states had already figured it out. "We decided that if the guarantee method could be put to work promptly all across the country, we could solve the student loan problem," Cornuelle wrote.[20]

They launched a nonprofit called United Student Aid Funds, or USA Funds, that aimed "to make it possible for any deserving college student in the nation to borrow money at a bank in his neighborhood with no collateral other than a promising academic record." Cornuelle wrote that the organization was "determined" to tackle the problem "independently—without any government help," although Cornuelle would ultimately head to Washington to lobby for USA Funds to receive tax exemption as a nonprofit.[21]

Under their version of the state guarantee plans, banks would agree to lend $12.50 for every $1 that USA Funds held in a security fund that was made up of funding from foundations, colleges and universities, and businesses. The colleges would direct the foundation toward students who needed to borrow, and the banks would lend the money to students and collect on it starting four months after a student graduated. They expected students to pay the money back in three to four years at a 6% interest rate—double the 3% rate the federal government was offering through the National Defense Education Act program.[22]

Nonetheless, bankers claimed that they weren't profiting off the students; instead, the 6% would cover the cost of servicing the loans.[23] To convince banks to participate, USA Funds used an argument that would lure financial institutions to work with colleges and their students for decades to come: in addition to the 6% interest rate, they'd have the opportunity to be students' first financial transaction, likely establishing loyalty with the bank and its products for the rest of their life.[24]

By early 1961, the experiment to prove that private institutions should be primarily responsible for dealing with society's ills was making its first student loan—to a student studying chemical engineering at a small college in Indiana.[25] By 1962, the organization had landed its first major grant: $2 million from the William Volker Fund, the nonprofit that had financed its start. Cornuelle was predicting that borrowing for college would soon "be as universal as borrowing for automobiles and housing."[26]

Support Builds for the Government to Subsidize Students

While Cornuelle and his colleagues were using student loans to try to illustrate that the government should be a less prominent supporter of social programs, the idea that the government should be taking a more active role in financing higher education was beginning to take hold among the wonks roaming the halls of think tanks in Washington.

Alice Rivlin came to Washington, DC, in 1957 on a fellowship from the Brookings Institution, one of the capital's most prominent think tanks, to finish her economics dissertation. Rivlin, originally a history major, was inspired in college to study economics—an uncommon path for a woman at the time—in large part because she realized the influence the discipline could have on public policy. "Economics is all about choice, it's about limited resources and how do you best deploy them," Rivlin said decades later, explaining why economists are so revered in Washington.[27]

Just a few years after arriving in DC, Rivlin started to wield that influence, making a case for the government to devote more resources to higher education, which drew notice and coverage from the *New York Times* and the Associated Press. In *The Role of the Federal Government in Financing Higher Education*, Rivlin warned that the sector would face a financial crisis in the 1960s as a result of a growing number of college-aged students and the increasing costs of higher education. "The American people and their legislators are going to be called upon to decide, explicitly or by default, what role the federal government should play in resolving it," Rivlin wrote of this impending crisis.[28]

Thus far, Rivlin wrote in the 1961 book, the most salient fact about the federal government's approach to higher education was "there has never been a clearly defined policy." Instead, legislation affecting colleges and students had been "a by-product of some other well-established federal concern," like agriculture, Rivlin wrote.[29] Now, though, it was time to consider higher education a policy issue all its own, Rivlin argued. Relying solely on private lenders that have a profit motive could lead to underinvestment in higher education, because taking on a market-rate loan could be risky for both the borrower and the lender—neither of whom has much insight into how the investment could perform, Rivlin noted.[30]

That dynamic could provide a role for the government to guarantee loans made by private lenders through a scheme that could "cost the government virtually nothing," Rivlin posited.[31] Whether the federal government sent more of its funding directly to students through scholarships and loans or instead to the institutions themselves would depend on policymakers' goals. If they aimed to reduce a waste of talent, then aid to students made the most sense. But if instead the objective was to boost certain types of education to achieve other national priorities—national defense, for example—then sending the funds to institutions made more sense, Rivlin wrote.[32]

When the government was subsidizing students who had given to their country in the form of military service or who were likely to contribute to the Cold War effort, the case for scholarships or low-interest loans was clearer. Once the discussion of subsidizing college students began to go beyond students who provided a direct benefit to the country, the tension grew between the individual benefit students derived from their education and the impact it would have on the country.

Regardless of the approach, Rivlin, who would go on to have a decades-long career as a federal policymaker, including as the first woman head of the Office of Management and Budget, argued that the government should be putting more funding toward colleges and their students.[33] But the answer to a philosophical question would guide the federal government's approach to this investment—and it's one that still today animates the debate over college affordability and student loans.

As Rivlin put it in 1961, "By far the most important issue to be decided by the institutions and the public is the way in which the burden of support for higher education should be shared between the consumers of education and the tax-paying public."[34]

A Force Sets His Sights on Funding College Students

By the early 1960s, the National Defense Education program, the federal government's first major foray into student loans was experiencing wider-than-expected take-up, nonprofits were working to mitigate risks to banks of lending to students, and the notion that the federal government should play a larger role in financing higher education had received a prominent airing. The environment was ripe for federal policymakers to step in—all it took was a force of personality and power unexpectedly assuming the presidency.

Years before Lyndon Johnson became president, he was advocating for a student loan program as the Democratic leader in the Senate.[35] As president, Johnson set his sights on an ambitious domestic policy agenda of which education was a key plank. Even before Johnson provided Congress with his set of priorities in his first State of the Union address, he hinted at the value he would place on boosting the nation's education system. In December 1963, less than a month after the assassination of John F. Kennedy, Johnson told lawmakers assembled in the Cabinet Room at the White House that the legislation they'd passed to boost higher education facilities signaled the "Nation's determination to give all of our youth the education they deserve."[36] About a week later, Johnson fleshed out his plan in a special message to Congress delivered from the White House. In his remarks, Johnson continued to frame increasing the number of students in higher education as both an individual goal for the students themselves and a national objective.

"Higher education is no longer a luxury, but a necessity," he told the lawmakers, noting that existing federal programs, like the National Defense Education Act loans weren't enough.

Still, in the paradigm presented by Rivlin—send money to institutions to boost a national objective or send money to students to avoid a waste of talent—Johnson's proposals aligned with the latter approach. The choice to subsidize students also implied a belief that they, as individuals, would reap something from the education and so should be on the hook for contributing to the cost in some way. Johnson invoked data indicating that every year, one hundred thousand young people who had the ability to go to college didn't attend because of lack of money. For these students, Johnson proposed a combination of targeted outreach, scholarships, and expanded work-study to bring more of them to college.[37]

For middle-class students whose families could generally afford college but might struggle to pay the expense out of pocket all at once, Johnson proposed that the government create a guaranteed loan program, similar to the model operating in several states and through USA Funds—and to one of the ideas Rivlin pitched in her book. "We should assure greater availability of private credit on reasonable terms and conditions," Johnson said, noting that the government could facilitate this by paying part of students' interest cost to lenders and providing a guarantee for their loans. He called that strategy "a more effective, fairer and far less costly way of providing assistance" than another initiative gaining traction in Congress: tax credits for tuition payments.[38]

Who Should Pay? Students or Taxpayers?

From Johnson's outline, congressional lawmakers began hashing out the details. As they debated and probed witnesses, policymakers started to sketch out the federal government's answer to the question of how best to split the costs of higher education between individual consumers and taxpayers—the question posed by Alice Rivlin in 1961.

The first hint came in the form of testimony from Anthony Celebrezze, the secretary of health, education, and welfare. Celebrezze warned the Special Subcommittee on Education of the House of Representatives that the phenomenon of talented students skipping college as a result of money concerns could wind up costing the nation.[39] But that didn't mean the administration intended to fully subsidize these students' education. Instead, the administration was proposing an approach infused with what Celebrezze called "practical realism."[40] Low-income students would contribute to their tuition.

As lawmakers weighed increasing the federal government's subsidy to college students, they worried the students would take advantage of taxpayers' generosity. At various points during the weeks of hearings, lawmakers discussed a report in the *Wall Street Journal* indicating that colleges were struggling to collect on National Defense Education Act loans.[41] Under the program, the government contributed 90% of the loan funds and colleges, 10%, but colleges were responsible for collecting on the loans. "Perplexed college business offices, which have little experience in bill collecting, attribute much of the problem to their inability to keep track of borrowers once they have graduated," the *Journal* reported.[42]

Some of the lawmakers had different theories. Sam Gibbons, a Florida Democrat, told the committee that, given his experience as a lawyer trying to collect money, he knew "that there are many ways in which people can just wave goodby and walk off and leave one of these loans hanging."[43] "I am afraid that these students really have not been impressed with the seriousness of not repaying this money," he added.[44] Because the government wasn't lending directly to students, the guaranteed program would theoretically cost less, and bankers, not college officials in the financial aid office, would be responsible for tracking students down to repay them. Although the structure of the guaranteed loan program ameliorated some of the challenges that members of Congress observed with the National Defense loans, lawmakers were still skeptical of the idea. And their skepticism was encouraged by those in the private sector already making student loans.

Allen D. Marshall, who by then was president of Cornuelle's organization, USA Funds, warned the House committee that a federally guaranteed student loan program "might have the entirely unintended effect of putting non-Federal loan guarantee plans out of business." Marshall assured lawmakers that USA Funds and organizations like it already had the objective of the government's loan program covered. "United Student Aid Funds is convinced that the rapid and continuing growth of State and private nonprofit loan insurance programs is bringing close the day when all needy and deserving students can borrow from banks at low interest rates whatever marginal money they need to stay in school after exhausting savings, work, grants and scholarships," Marshall said.[45]

But when students could access commercial college loan programs, in some cases they were paying exorbitant interest rates. Reports that some lenders were charging families an annual interest rate of 50% was part of what pushed the Johnson administration to consider a loan program of its own as part of the Higher Education Act. A 1965 *Boston Globe* article offered an early indication of the cozy relationship between colleges and lenders that would continue to exist for decades, noting that some colleges "funnel needy students into the outstretched arms of the loan companies without reading the fine print."[46]

The student loan business had become so profitable for banks that two of the largest participants in the market at the time informed Senator Vance Hartke, an Indiana Democrat who had been concerned about the rates students were paying on commercial loans for years, that they would back a federal guaranteed loan program. Although the government loan program would "drastically reduce" the interest rate the companies would charge for such loans, "they would apparently still turn a nice profit," the *Los Angeles Times* reported. But if instead the government opted to directly fund loans to college students in a similar fashion to the National Defense loan program, they'd be cut out of the student loan business entirely.[47]

Ultimately, Congress was moved: by concerns about students walking away from their debt if colleges managed collections, by an interest in keeping costs to the government relatively low, and by the idea that even low-income students should have some kind of personal financial investment in their education. They decided to create a system for financing higher education that tweaked commercial loan products and involved commercial lenders to suit both the lenders' and policymakers' aims.

Expanding Access to College on Certain Terms

At the same time that the government opened the college-financing system to organizations concerned with their own profit, policymakers were looking to expand access to college to those who historically hadn't had it. In a sense, expanding the college-going public beyond the largely white, male population became intertwined with these organizations' drive to earn money through the student loan program.

The Higher Education Act of 1965 was one part of Johnson's suite of initiatives aimed at reducing economic and racial inequality. Johnson told the crowd gathered to watch him sign the bill at his alma mater, Southwest Texas State College, that his experience teaching at a "Mexican school" in Cotulla, Texas, as a college student was part of what inspired his quest to bring a decent education within reach of every American.

"I shall never forget the faces of the boys and the girls in that little Welhausen Mexican School, and I remember even yet the pain of realizing and knowing then that college was closed to practically every one of those children because they were too poor," he said. "And I think it was then that I made up my mind that this Nation could never rest while the door to knowledge remained closed to any American."[48]

Although Johnson invoked the idea of providing opportunity to Americans of different races when signing the bill, he also had students like himself in mind when making the nation's biggest investment to date in higher education. Johnson told the crowd of his time at Southwest Texas State: "I shaved and I showered in a gymnasium that was down the road. I worked at a dozen different jobs, from sweeping the floors to selling real silk socks. Sometimes I wondered what the next day would bring that could exceed the hardship of the day before. But with all of that, I was one of the lucky ones—and I knew it even then."[49]

Other policymakers involved in the design and passage of the Higher Education Act saw the prospect of helping younger versions of themselves in the legislation too. Senator Wayne Morse, of Oregon, told his colleagues during testimony that he wouldn't have attended the University of Wisconsin without help from a high school biology teacher. "I had no chance of going to college, but she took out a life insurance policy on me and some other boys and girls, and she used those as security to put us in college and keep us there as we needed to borrow money from time to time," he said.[50]

And indeed, at the time the lawmakers decided it made sense for the government to subsidize students' college education, colleges were largely filled with people like themselves. In 1964, the year before the law passed, 12% of white men who were twenty-five had completed four years of college or more compared to 7% of white women, nearly 6% of Black or other races of men and nearly 4% of Black or other races of women, according to government data.[51] (By 2021, 38% of white 18- to 24-year-olds were enrolled in college, compared to 38% of Black Americans of that age, 60% of Asian Americans in the same group, and 33% of Hispanics. Roughly 33% of men in this age group were enrolled in school, compared to 43% of women).[52]

Just five years before Johnson signed the Higher Education Act into law, the US Commission on Civil Rights found that some colleges, mostly in the South, had explicit policies against enrolling Black students. The commission also found evidence that even in the northern and western United States, schools used tactics, including asking students to submit a photo with their application, to suss out an applicant's race and may have had unannounced quotas on the number of Black students they would take even if the potential students' academic credentials qualified them for admission.[53]

Even though Johnson and other lawmakers' rhetoric signaled that their ambitions for the Higher Education Act were for it to address educational inequality among races, the image of a college student at the time they made this historic investment was likely white and male—in large part because that's who could be found on campus.

Ultimately, lawmakers decided on a program that aimed to provide the funds to expand access to college to students other than their younger selves—but on certain terms. Although the role of higher education as a way to achieve national priorities was still present in some of the discussion during the development of the Higher Education Act, that emphasis on expanding access to individuals assumed a benefit for those individuals that policymakers decided they should be required to pay for.

The design of the program, where students would cobble together resources, including some subsidies from the federal government and their own funds, began to offer an answer to Rivlin's 1961 question. The taxpaying public would shoulder some of the burden, but students would largely be on the hook.

Using government funding to subsidize and guarantee loans appeared to have other benefits as well. It followed an already well-established model in states and through USA Funds. It also avoided some of the collection challenges colleges faced with the National Defense loans, and as Rivlin noted in her 1961 book, a guarantee plan could cost the government "virtually nothing" because the debt wouldn't technically be on the government's books—although the taxpayers would be on the hook in cases where students defaulted on their obligation.[54] In addition, by providing middle-class families with some way to relieve the pressure of college costs, the guaranteed loan program staved off momentum that had been building in Congress around offering tax credits to families paying for college, which would cost the government directly and provide little benefit to poorer families who didn't have a tax liability.

Despite their initial hesitation, financial institutions and the state and nonprofit guarantee programs started to embrace the guaranteed loan program. Less than a year after Johnson signed the Higher Education Act, the American Bankers Association launched a campaign, including a twenty-four-page promotional brochure, to convince its members to lend to students—in part to keep the government out of the business of lending to students directly, the *New York Times* reported in 1966.[55] That was a goal shared by policymakers.

Under the American Bankers Association plan, states and nonprofit groups would guarantee the loans, and the federal government would subsidize the interest. "The Johnson Administration hopes the association's plan works because it would prefer not to have to begin a general program to lend students money," the *Times* reported. "Such a program would be a budget cost to the Government at a time when the President is trying to hold the budget down."[56]

The plan would open the door to a decades-long relationship between commercial banks, quasi-public or nonprofit organizations, and the government—with implications for students—that's still being untangled.

"A Tough Day, but a Proud Day"

As MaNesha Stiff turned to leave her parents, she began in earnest the journey toward some of the lofty ideals espoused by the architects of the Higher Education Act. Decades earlier, Johnson and other policymakers extolled the ability of education to change a student's or even a family's trajectory. That, in part, was why they had vowed to eliminate financial barriers to otherwise qualified students faced with attending college.

For Stiff, attending North Park offered the opportunity to get out of economically depressed Hammond, not just for the four years of school but also for good—and her parents knew it. "It was a good day, a tough day, but a proud day," Stiff said of the day her parents dropped her off.

But to get to that day, Stiff had to contend with the particulars of the college finance system—the "practical realism" as Johnson's secretary of health, education, and welfare Celebrezze had put it—policymakers had designed.

Although today an entire media and rankings industry urges students and families to shop around for the best educational and financial fit, it's more common for students to approach the college process like Stiff did. They apply to one school, relatively close to home.[57] That's still true today after more than a decade of coverage of the explosion in student debt since the Great Recession. Back in the late 1990s, Stiff and those guiding her were even less focused on ensuring that she had affordable college options to choose from.

"My high school advisers were just trying to get us out of high school," Stiff said. "Back then they were like, 'Let's just make sure you don't go to summer school your senior year.'"

So Stiff was left with one option for attending college, and she was determined to go, regardless of the price tag. "I certainly was not going to put myself out there to not be able to succeed or have a chance in life after I got accepted," Stiff said.

When North Park's financial aid offer arrived in the mail, a package that included the Pell Grant—the money the federal government provides to low-income students to attend college—Stiff's mom opened the envelope, and teenage Stiff sat down at the dining room table with the paperwork in front of her. Her mom pointed to the places where Stiff had to sign.

"I signed, I signed, I signed and signed again," Stiff said. As far as she was concerned, there were no other options. "Either you're going to sign this and go to school, or you're not and you're not," she remembers thinking.

"My parents did not have the money," she said. Nonetheless, they also looked for ways to contribute. Stiff's mom applied for a parent PLUS loan, the government loan program that parents can use to pay for their children's college education, knowing—and hoping—her credit score wouldn't qualify her for the debt. Under the federal loan program, students could borrow beyond the undergraduate loan limit if their parents were denied a PLUS loan. That meant that if Stiff's mom was rejected, it would leave room for Stiff to borrow more herself. "Thank God she wasn't able to get it," Stiff said of the debt.

Once Stiff started classes as the first in her family to go to college, she came up against her lack of familiarity with the peculiar workings of higher education. When Stiff decided she didn't like a class and didn't want to stay enrolled, she just stopped going. "I didn't know that you had to drop a class officially to drop a class," Stiff said. That mistake, which she made more than once her first semester, put her on academic probation and in danger of losing her financial aid.

"I knew that I could not go home, because if I went home, I was not going to finish school," Stiff said. So she wrote to appeal the decision and renewed her focus on staying on top of her schoolwork and administrative deadlines.

Although she was no longer in danger of having to leave school for academic issues, Stiff's position at college was still tenuous because of finances. It wasn't uncommon for her to scramble at the end of each semester to make arrangements to pay or settle her bill so that she'd be able to register for the following term.

"Basically everyone who looked like me, we were in the same situation," Stiff said of other Black students at the school. "In the dining area or in the lobby we would be asking each other, 'What are you going to do? What are you doing next semester?'"

Back in Indiana, Stiff's family was finding room in their budget so she could continue her education uninterrupted. Even after grants and student loans, Stiff still faced a gap. So her mom would consider whether her daughter might need anything before buying a new package of underwear. Once Stiff's sister got married, she and her new husband moved into an apartment on the second level of Stiff's family home to help her parents with expenses, given that so much of their funds were going toward helping Stiff stay in school.

Stiff's family showed their financial commitment to her education in other ways too. Toward the end of her college career, Stiff was in danger of not being able to sign up for classes because of an outstanding balance on her account—that could have put her at risk of not graduating. Instead of mailing the check, her mom thought she could deal with the situation faster if she just drove the hour from Hammond to North Park.

Stiff walked across campus to meet her mom at Old Main, the century-old tan-brick building that housed financial aid and other administrative offices, to deal with the balance together. The financial aid staffer working with Stiff—whose name she still remembers decades later—"got kind of cheeky" with Stiff's mom. It was around that time that Stiff started realizing the sacrifices her family was making for her to attend school, even outside the money she was borrowing through the student loan program. "There were still times that we had to come out of pocket and make up the difference," Stiff said. "If we had to come out of pocket, that means that someone is going without back home."

"My mom took time out of her day, maybe even took a day out of work, to write a personal check to make sure that I was able to stay in school and be ready for my classes—how dare you?" Stiff remembers thinking. She sat in traffic on Lake Shore Drive; she paid for gas—all seemingly dismissed by the financial aid officer's tone. Stiff walked her mom to the door of the building, watched her cross the parking lot, and then turned around and walked back into the office and yelled at the financial aid staffer, threatening that if she ever talked to her mom that way again, "We all would just be in a mess."

Stiff walked out the door without giving the staffer time to respond and registered for her classes. For the rest of that day and the next, Stiff worried someone would come to her room to discipline her over the outburst, but they never did.

Despite the financial challenges of paying for college, once Stiff overcame her initial academic hurdles, she thrived at North Park. She joined student organizations and put to work what she was learning as part of her communications degree by writing grants to increase funding for first-generation college students. As part of her involvement in those activities, Stiff observed as administrators interacted with students and strategized logistics for major events. By the end of her sophomore year, Stiff knew she wanted to make a career in higher education, ideally as a dean.

When she graduated, she returned to work briefly at TRIO, the program she'd participated in growing up. But Stiff wasn't earning enough to cover her student loan payments or to live on her own. She moved back to Hammond to live with her parents and put her student loans into forbearance, a status that pauses payments but allows interest to still accrue. In the years leading up to her graduation in 2003, the interest rate on federal student loans fluctuated between more than 8% and roughly 4%. During that period, Stiff tried to pretend the loans didn't exist.

But a little more than a year after she graduated from North Park, Stiff returned to work there in her first full-time job. The $28,000 or $29,000 a year she was making felt like enough to rent an apartment and start making progress toward repaying her loans. So she called up her student loan company and encountered some of the same skepticism toward her commitment to the debt that had so worried lawmakers in the 1960s. "The representative asked me, 'Was I ever planning on paying them back?' And I was livid," Stiff said. "I'm like, What the hell do you mean, 'Do I ever plan on paying them back?' As if I have a choice in the matter."

A Program for Students Tweaked to Meet the Needs of Lenders

In the years and decades after the Higher Education Act was signed into law, policymakers continued to interrogate the nation's approach to financing college—debating the program's goals as well as who it should be for and at what cost—and molding the initiative to suit their aims. They also tweaked the program to meet the needs of the lenders, guaranty agencies, and other organizations participating in it that would threaten—in both subtle and less veiled ways—to leave the program if it didn't suit their bottom line, creating a credit crunch for families and students.

As in the 1960s, policymakers of the early 1970s couched their approach to higher education in language of access. Just one example: then secretary of health, education, and welfare Elliot Richardson described the Nixon administration's proposals as aiming to fulfill the administration's belief that "no qualified student who wants to go to college should be barred by lack of money."[58] But lawmakers weren't willing to commit to that access at too high a cost for taxpayers. Instead, they facilitated that access by continuing to mold commercial loan products to meet the needs of the organizations financing education.

Middle-class students who needed loans to pay for college were being turned away from banks, officials lamented, because they were competing for capital from these institutions with more profitable loan options. Poorer students, whose families didn't have connections at banks, were in an even worse position, they said.

To create more liquidity in the student loan market, the Nixon administration proposed launching a private agency backed by the full faith and credit of the US government that would buy, store, and sell student loans created by colleges and banks. The funds lenders received from the corporation in exchange for their loans would allow them to create new ones. The Student Loan Marketing Association, which came to be known as Sallie Mae, would be structured similarly to another institution used to encourage access to a different pillar of the American dream, homeownership. Officials envisioned an institution like Fannie Mae, the Federal National Mortgage Association, which through a similar model provided liquidity to the housing market.[59]

The structure allowed the government to encourage financing for college without assuming the high cost that it would take to actually finance college. Senator Claiborne Pell, after noting Nixon officials' "very strong emphasis on keeping the cost of education off the national budget," asked Richardson in 1971 hearings whether "these budgetary factors play a role in [his] emphasis on loans over grants?" "It undoubtedly plays some part," Richardson told the senator, adding that the administration believed "it is appropriate, and effective, to call upon the private sector."[60]

The creation of Sallie Mae added one more institution into the mix of commercial sector lenders and nonprofit or quasi-state-run guaranty agencies that had a stake in the future of the way Americans pay for college. But using these nonfederal government actors to technically keep the cost of the federal government's investment in higher education off the books didn't protect it from incurring costs. In fact, it contributed to it.

In 1975, lawmakers probed the factors behind potentially $1 billion in defaults on guaranteed student loans as part of hearings before the Senate's permanent subcommittee on investigations. What they found is that lenders, which were supposed to take aggressive steps to recoup payments from delinquent borrowers before turning to the government to collect on the guarantee they were promised in case of default, weren't trying very hard to collect their money. And why should they? Unlike commercial loans, student loans came with little risk of losing money in case of default.[61]

Despite these practices, the threat of creating a liquidity crunch loomed over any possible change to the guarantee. When asked by Georgia Democrat Sam Nunn what would happen if the federal government were to guarantee 90% of a lender's loss instead of 100%, Gregory F. Lancaster, assistant vice president of security at Pacific National Bank in Los Angeles, responded: "We would not be in it . . . We would not make these loans."[62]

At that time, there were some guaranteed student loans that didn't have 100% of the government's backing. These were insured through state and nonprofit intermediaries, known as guaranty agencies, instead of through the federal government directly. If a borrower defaulted on one of these loans, the lender would turn the loan over to the guaranty agency to collect, and the federal government reimbursed guaranty agencies for only 80% of their losses in case of default. These loans had a lower rate of default for two main reasons, lawmakers suspected. The first was that state and nonprofit guaranty agencies generally wouldn't back loans made directly to students by institutions, which since the 1972 amendments to the Higher Education Act had included for-profit schools eager to offer financing if doing so meant enrolling more students.[63] The other major factor: states and guaranty agencies shared, in part, in the risk of default.[64]

Nonetheless, concerns about liquidity once again pushed lawmakers toward offering the 100% guarantee on a larger swath of loans. Lenders that made loans that were insured by the federal government directly were dropping out of the program, and at the same time guaranty agencies were clamoring for access to the 100% backing. Lawmakers obliged, looking to encourage the creation of more state and nonprofit guaranty agencies.[65]

Entities Earning Money Off the Student Loan Program Influence Policy Surrounding It

That decision to have the government cover the costs of default for guaranty agencies led to an explosion in the number of these organizations participating in the program, creating a powerful, entrenched group with financial interests in a program of funding college through government-backed loans. In this way, the fate of students interested in pursuing a college education, as well as the fate of the government's goal of increasing access to it, was further intertwined with organizations that relied on issuing and collecting loans for their revenue.

Before the government began offering the 100% guarantee on loans to these state and nonprofit institutions, the number of them in existence was somewhere between seventeen and twenty-six, depending on the year. Between the 1976 amendments and 1981, the number of guaranty agencies grew to fifty.[66]

It would be one of many episodes over the next few decades when the financial interests of the nonprofits, state agencies, and commercial companies that earn money off the student loan program would influence the policy surrounding it and borrowers' experiences.

In the early 1990s, the Clinton administration and some members of Congress sought to mitigate the influence of these entities on the student loan program and limit their costs to the government. An accounting change in 1990 had made it more palatable for the government to lend directly to students instead of using commercial lenders and guaranty agencies as intermediaries. Whereas before any money the government loaned out was simply a hit to the Treasury, the Credit Reform Act, signed that year, had allowed the federal bean counters to account for the notion that the loans were supposed to be repaid.[67] Suddenly, bank-based lending, with its ability to keep loans largely off the government's books, didn't look quite as attractive.

In addition, while campaigning for president, Bill Clinton ran on the idea that his administration would create an opportunity for student loan borrowers to repay their debt as a percentage of income. They and other proponents of a pay-as-you-go system believed it would be possible only if the government lent directly to students, because only the Internal Revenue Service had ready access to income information and could deduct borrowers' payments automatically. So they went to work trying to implement what they called direct lending as a way to replace the bank-based system.

The student loan industry mobilized in response. USA Group, the parent company of USA Funds, paid $20,000 a month to a lobbying firm with ties to the Democratic Party to try to influence lawmakers' thinking on the plan.[68] Student loan organizations also used their sway over college financial aid officers—often these companies were the ones providing these offices with access to new software or sponsoring receptions at their conferences—to convince them to lobby lawmakers against the direct lending program. In some cases the connection was so obvious it was difficult to ignore; a group of letters opposing direct lending faxed from financial aid officers to lawmakers' offices had Sallie Mae printed on the top.[69]

Ultimately, the efforts were successful. When Congress first authorized the direct loan program in 1993, it was intended to be phased in over five years, but when Republicans took control of Congress in 1995, they threatened to scrap direct lending entirely. In response, Secretary of Education Richard Riley agreed not to promote direct lending. A competition between the two programs to win over schools began.

The programs were required by law to have "the same terms and conditions." But according to Thomas Butts, a longtime advocate of direct lending who worked for decades on federal student aid policy in various roles at the University of Michigan, the Department of Education, and higher education associations, the direct loan program could have offered borrowers cheaper terms because of the government's low cost of borrowing and because it didn't require the government to pay lenders and guaranty agencies special interest allowances and fees.[70] That requirement for a level playing field meant that features of the bank-based loan program became part of the direct loan program, according to Butts. These provisions, like certain interest capitalization events, partially explain why in some cases, even in recent years, borrowers' balances exploded beyond the principal amount they borrowed, even when they're making payments, Butts told me.[71] Interest capitalization is when interest is added to the principal of a borrower's loan. That creates a bigger pot from which more interest can accrue.

The outside parties benefiting from the student loan program also played a major role in a policy change that helped to accelerate student loan borrowing during the 1990s and early 2000s. Before the early 1990s, only students from families earning below a particular income cap could borrow from the federal student loan program. While these students were in college, the government paid the interest on their loans. But as part of the 1992 reauthorization of the Higher Education Act, Congress expanded the loan program, offering an option for borrowers at any income and in which interest accrued while students were in college.[72]

Charlie Eaton argues in his book *Bankers in the Ivory Tower* that financial executives created the conditions that pushed families and lawmakers to look for more resources to pay for college and took advantage of those conditions. Crucially, Eaton pins the push toward expanding access to student loans on the financial sector, which brought schools along in their lobbying efforts, rather than on the schools themselves.[73]

Throughout the 1970s and 1980s, business and financial executives "undermined," as Eaton put it, jobs that didn't require a college degree by busting unions and moving factories. That made college more attractive because it became Americans' best shot at a decent financial life. At the same time, Eaton argues, business and financial leaders pushed for tax and spending cuts that meant the government provided less funding for students to go to college.[74]

With more students looking to go to college and limited resources available to them, associations representing both lenders generally and organizations participating in the student loan program more specifically proposed a loan program without an income cap. In testimony during hearings to reauthorize the Higher Education Act in the early 1990s, Stephen Biklen, a vice president at Citibank who was testifying on behalf of the Consumer Bankers Association, said his organization endorsed a proposal for unsubsidized loans for middle-income students put forward by the National Council of Higher Education Loan Programs, an association of guaranty agencies, lenders, and other organizations involved in the loan program.

"Increases in college costs have exacerbated the problems faced by students from middle-income families attending the institution of their choice. More assistance needs to be offered to these students, but at a lesser cost to the federal government than is needed for those programs targeted to low-income students," he said in written testimony.[75]

Congress ultimately heeded the financiers' suggestions. Following the changes to the loan program, which drastically expanded eligibility, total student loan volume accelerated. During the 1992–1993 academic year, before the existence of the unsubsidized loan program, annual total student loan volume stood at about $24 billion in 2022 dollars. By ten years later, it had grown more than five times to nearly $131 billion, and unsubsidized loans accounted for more than half of that volume.[76] Although other factors—including growth in enrollment and college costs, as well as the impacts of the recession—played a role in the growth in student debt during this period, the availability of loan dollars also likely helped fuel the rise.

It makes sense that organizations involved in the student loan system worked hard to derail speedier adoption of direct lending and to find ways to expand student loan volume, given how much they were earning off the bank-based loan program. By the mid-1990s, despite its libertarian origins, USA Funds was benefiting enormously from its government-funded business. The organization earned so much from government fees and collection payments that it recorded, as the *Washington Post* put it, "an 'excess'—the nonprofit word for profit," of $67 million. By 1996, USA Group, USA Fund's parent company, was telling shareholders in its annual report that "more borrowers, schools, states and lenders rely on us for more education loan-related products and services than any other company in America." The company's top executive was earning a salary of $1 million (roughly $2 million today).[77]

In the background of this growth, USA Funds officials began strategizing ways to ward off challenges to the organization's nonprofit status. In a 2007 report, Edward Schmidt, the organization's general counsel who chaired a task force focused on the issue, described that the organization's expansion in the 1990s meant that it was offering "a wide range of services that arguably no longer fit comfortably within the nonprofit corporate model," Schmidt said.

"The company was rapidly expanding, adding hundreds of employees annually and generating sizable revenues. Our concern was that the government might eventually come in and challenge the continuation of our tax-exempt status," he continued.[78] USA Group eventually solved this problem by selling most of its assets to Sallie Mae and using the proceeds to fund a private foundation (now the Lumina Foundation) focused on education issues.[79]

The decisions made in the early years of the student loan program—to facilitate access to higher education through a consumer finance product—created a web of companies and institutions interested in keeping the loan business afloat and policymakers available to help them do it. "This [is a] classic 'iron triangle,'" Jon Oberg told me, regarding the relationship between interest groups, bureaucrats, and policymakers, which had become so strong that, during the 1990s, subsidies for all players in the federal student loan program dominated higher education policy discussions.[80] In other words, the iron triangle motivated those working on the issue to sink more into the existing system instead of searching for broader reform.

As a Department of Education staffer in the early 2000s, Oberg warned the Bush administration that organizations that were initially established to ensure that the bank-based loan program had enough liquidity to fund students were taking advantage of the program.[81] In the mid-1970s, around the same time the number of guaranty agencies began to balloon, states were also increasingly establishing organizations that would raise money by selling tax-exempt bonds and then using the funds to buy up loans from other lenders or lend to students themselves. In 1980, Congress passed a law that would ensure that such organizations would earn a 9.5% rate of return on student loans. At the time, the idea was to provide the lenders with a set minimum return during a period of high interest rates.[82]

In 1993, Congress ended the program for new loans but grandfathered in old ones. During the low-interest-rate environment of the early 2000s, these entities started washing new loans through their pre-1993 bond estates so they could continue to capture the subsidy. One former Department of Education staffer once described this process to me as "you would put a dead dog in the freezer with filet mignon and sell the dead dog as filet mignon."[83] For years, Oberg had tried to warn bureaucrats at the Department of Education and policymakers that some lenders were still illegally receiving the subsidy. But Congress and the George W. Bush administration failed to heed Oberg's warning, even as their ranks and election war chests were filled with staff and funds from the student loan industry.[84]

Although for decades policymakers had bent the student loan program to encourage outside entities to participate in it, when the economic environment became challenging, the government had to bail them out. In 2008, as investors started to hesitate to provide lenders with capital to make new student loans—despite the federal guarantee—the government bought up some of the loans in these lenders' portfolios so they would have capital to make new ones.[85] "That was the death knell for a bank-based loan system," David Bergeron, who worked for decades at the Department of Education, told me. "They killed themselves."

And indeed, in 2010, as part of the legislative process that created the Affordable Care Act, or Obamacare, lawmakers ended the bank-based loan system for new federal student loans. Once again, the student loan industry lobbied to stop it, but when it couldn't, its members insisted on having a foothold in the direct loan program.[86] In recent years, many of the student loan servicers, the companies that are borrowers' first point of contact when repaying their student loan, and which borrowers and advocates have charged with not providing enough information or the right information for borrowers to repay their loans successfully, worked as guaranty agencies or secondary markets in the bank-based system.

Even twelve years after the government ended the bank-based program, the interests of the institutions that participated in it were still shaping policy in other ways too. In 2022, as the Biden administration proposed canceling $10,000 in student debt for most borrowers, opponents attempting to block the plan through the court system invoked the risk to the bottom line of these entities posed by cancellation as part of their argument for why it was illegal.[87]

Johnson Tyler, a legal aid attorney who works with student loan borrowers often facing the most devastating consequences of the system—including having their tax refunds and Social Security checks offset to repay their loans—described the student loan program as having a strange feel to it, "which is 'we're here to help,' but we're not." Government officials, especially since the Obama administration, have tried to impress upon borrowers that if they're struggling, they can turn to generous repayment plans to make payments more manageable. But the entities actually responsible for enrolling borrowers in those safety nets have priorities outside of just helping borrowers, including their bottom line, he said.

"It's a weird way to run a program that's designed to improve people's lives that all these taxpayers are paying for," Tyler told me.

Student Loans Opened Doors, but at What Cost?

In some ways the money MaNesha Stiff borrowed did for her exactly what lawmakers thought and hoped it would do: enable her, a student whose family didn't have the funds to pay for her to go to college, to attend the school of her choice and get a degree that would open doors to a career she wouldn't have had without it.

After graduating, Stiff continued to believe in the power of higher education as a tool to move her career forward. About three years into her post-college job, Stiff decided to get a master's degree, taking advantage of a program offered by her employer and alma mater that would pay for her continuing education at the school. The degree helped her switch to a new job that paid her more money, but after a few months, Stiff looked around at her colleagues and their credentials and realized that, if she wanted to be a dean or in upper leadership in some capacity, she would need to get a PhD.

Even though she struggled at times to pay down her debt for her undergraduate degree, Stiff was excited to have financing available to pay for graduate school. This time around, she felt savvier than that eighteen-year-old filling out student loan paperwork at the dining room table, but the notion that she needed the degree to move ahead and the debt in order to get the degree was a familiar one.

As was the case for college, the money Stiff borrowed for graduate school did, in a sense, what it was supposed to do—facilitated her access to a degree that got her a better-paying job. But the terms under which Stiff received that access blunted the impact of the opportunity on her life.

Every time Stiff has earned more money, she worried about how it would affect her student loan payments, which she was paying as a percentage of her income. In 2017, Stiff lost her job, a fate her degrees weren't enough to protect her from. "I was just so in shock," she said. "Here I am with a PhD, and it was hard for me to find something afterwards." She took what part-time jobs she could and didn't tell her parents for a year. "I was devastated. I was embarrassed," Stiff said. After three years of searching, Stiff ultimately landed a full-time role in higher education during the COVID-19 pandemic, when student loan payments were paused. Each time we spoke, as the deadline for payments to resume loomed, she expressed anxiety about making her student loan payments on her new salary.

"I'm nervous," Stiff said in December 2021. "I don't want to be defeated by my student loans."

Although Stiff's experience with student debt took place decades after policymakers first designed the student loan system, she has experienced its consequences years later. Lawmakers were interested in expanding access to college to students who hadn't traditionally had it, but they wanted to keep costs to the government low. Crucially, policymakers were confident that students would benefit financially from their education, which justified the idea that students should be investing in it themselves instead of relying exclusively on government grant aid to pay for school. But the students weren't good credit risks, and so they tweaked a traditional loan product, inviting in an entrenched sector of private actors who regularly used the threat of pulling their liquidity to wrench concessions from policymakers.

For Stiff, attending college and receiving her PhD allowed her to grow intellectually and personally. "I would not trade my PhD in for the world," she said. But she questions whether the credentials did much for her financially. "There's a part of me that still wonders if I would have been able to do anything without a degree, or a PhD, or a master's." She'd continued to sink time and resources into an education she'd already invested in, even though it wasn't clear it would make her better off financially.

In the late 2010s, scholars started to coalesce around a term for what the group of students like Stiff have experienced, students who entered higher education in the decades following the launch of the student loan program—largely less white, less wealthy, and less male than the college students before them: *predatory inclusion.* Or as Louise Seamster, a scholar of sociology and African American studies at the University of Iowa, describes it, "a turn from former exclusion of a marginalized group, to inclusion, but on terms that negates the benefits."[88] In the decades since the student loan system was first devised, companies have used it to engage in literal examples of predation, exemplified by various scandals. But for many borrowers, like Stiff, the predation is more subtle.

Black borrowers in general and Black women in particular, like Stiff, tend to borrow more to attend college because of centuries of racist policies that have blocked their access to wealth building. At the same time, they often need the credentials more than their white peers do because of discrimination in the labor market. That same labor market discrimination makes it more difficult for them to repay the debt.[89]

These and other borrowers buy into the rhetoric underpinning America's approach to funding higher education—invest both time and money in yourself, and your life will be better. But they're met with the reality that the "better life" is facilitated through a con-sumer loan product, just like any other, with interest rates and profit-making institutions fueling its growth.

Stiff thought that borrowing for college would help her achieve a middle-class life. Although she got one traditional marker of suc-cess, a home, the loans made her hesitant to have children because it would be hard for her to afford both her student loan payments and all the bills that come with a child. She also avoided luxuries like travel because of the debt. Stiff's experience with student loans has also made her waver on how she should advise her niece and nephew as they consider their own post-college plans.

"Some days I say this, and some days I take it back," she told me the first time we spoke in 2021. We'd connected because she responded to an article of mine about student debt, detailing how scared she was for when payments would resume after the pandemic pause. "Most days, if I had to do it all over again, I don't know if I would. . . . We're all in school trying to achieve the American dream, and then when we graduate that's the last thing that we're able to achieve because we have student loan debt just hovering over everything."

3. The Pell Grant

What Happens When the Federal Government Cuts Support for College

While growing up in northwest Philadelphia, Justice Passe was surrounded by reminders of the importance of college. In the house he shared with his mother, four aunts, five siblings, and his grandmother, the latter matriarch lined the walls of the living room, dining room, and her bedroom with books she was always encouraging him to read.

Throughout Passe's childhood, he watched as his relatives juggled jobs and classes. When they graduated, he would attend the parties in their honor. These events were so revered in his household that other family members would be sure to take the day off work, or at least a few hours, to attend.

Friends and relatives gathered at the house for soul food and a graduation cake.

When he was eleven years old, it was Passe's mom's turn to bask in the accomplishment. After years of taking courses at the Community College of Philadelphia while she raised children and worked, she graduated with her associate's degree. Passe picked out a stuffed bear wearing a graduation hat and handed it to her when she finished walking across the stage.

All this made Passe certain from a young age that he would attend college. By the time he entered high school, he'd set his sights on Harvard. "I wanted to shoot big," Passe said of his goal. Plus, he'd heard that a school like Harvard would provide generous aid to students with financial need. So he worked hard to keep his grades up and joined his school's swim team, student government, and more. He applied and was accepted into a program that brings about a dozen students from across Philadelphia to the city's science museum for exposure to science, technology, engineering, and math career fields and college prep.

For six months of his freshman year, Passe learned how to create a business plan and pitch a start-up to investors as part of an entrepreneurship competition. His success in that contest got him an invite to a summer start-up boot camp at Drexel University. These tastes of the business world piqued his interest in pursuing a career in the field; the experiences—along with conversations with his adviser in the STEM (science, technology, engineering, and math) program—also started to gnaw at his convictions about college. Passe still planned to go, but he realized that if he wanted to pursue a career in business, he likely wouldn't learn much of what he needed to through his classes, which were often taught by academics instead of practitioners.

He'd decided that the college experience his relatives so prized—getting some independence and the chance to better understand yourself outside of the household you grew up in—was just a by-product of the true purpose of higher education. "I just thought it was a way to position yourself in the trajectory for upward mobility for a job," he said. Once the time came to actually apply for college, Passe's list turned more practical than that initial Harvard dream. The schools he chose were close to home. And although he'd learned through his STEM scholars program that he'd get some help paying for college through the federal government's Pell Grant and a state financial aid program, he knocked any college off the list with an unreasonable price tag.

A realization about his family's financial circumstances during his senior year made Passe determined not to borrow for college. One afternoon Passe was chatting with his mother in the living room when he joked that he might not go to college. "She took it very seriously," he said. His mom started to lecture him about all the benefits she and her sisters got from college and about how he'd greatly improve his ability to get a job with a college degree. After her "spiel," as Passe described it, he wondered out loud, "Just curious, how much student debt do you have?" When she told him about $180,000, Passe was shocked.

The debt was a combination of loans from her time in school, both at the Community College of Philadelphia and Temple University—a degree she was never able to finish because she was too busy raising her kids and working—and loans she took on to pay for Passe's two older siblings to attend college. And although this was the first time Passe heard the number, he knew his mom had trouble managing the debt on her postal worker's salary. She worked thirteen-hour days, sometimes making herself sick to ensure that Passe and his siblings were taken care of. "Did she really get the return on investment for college?" Passe asked himself, adding, "It pains me that she's working so hard. She doesn't really have time to relax and enjoy herself because she's trying to put food on the table."

Passe knew he didn't want to add to that burden, and he also didn't want to take it on himself. After the conversation with his mom, Passe decided: "I refuse—I refuse to pay for student loans."

A Plan for Poor Families Developed by American "Royalty"

If it had been up to Claiborne Pell, students like Passe wouldn't have had to even consider taking on loans. Pell's route to and through higher education looked very different from Passe's. But his name and tenure of more than three decades in the Senate would come to be much more closely associated with experiences like Passe's than his own. Pell championed the government's largest scholarship program, now known as the Pell Grant Program, which was designed to help low-income students avoid burdensome debt. Instead, since the mid-1970s, cuts to the program and rising college costs have eroded its ability to protect low-income students from difficult-to-repay student loans.

Claiborne Pell was born in 1918 into a family whose lineage stretched all the way back to the founding of the nation.[1] And the family had the money and trappings to go with that ancestry. A charter of land to the Pell family from England's King George III in the eighteenth century blossomed into a fortune, Pell attended prep school and then Princeton, and at the age of twenty-one, he received a trust so large that, if he managed it correctly, he likely would never have had to work again.[2] "They were a form of American royalty," Bill Clinton said of the Pell family, a fact Clinton first realized when reading up on the Pells after he found himself as a college freshman looking down from his Georgetown University dorm room onto the dinner parties and society functions in the backyard of the Pells' Washington home.[3]

Pell's posh upbringing was apparent in the way he carried himself; his voice had an almost British lilt. He was frequently referred to by contemporaries as elegant, patrician, and eccentric, and he was known to go running in a tweed sport coat.[4] Although Pell and his family could pay for private education and higher education several times over, he became committed to ensuring that lack of funds wouldn't get in the way of a student attending college.

That commitment likely dates back at least to Pell's experience in the Coast Guard, where he enlisted months before the bombing of Pearl Harbor.[5] There, for the first time, Pell worked toward a common goal with people of much-lesser means. He was struck by how they were limited not by their talent, but by their financial circumstances. "He saw, particularly during the war, a bunch of very, very smart people who had more talent probably than some of his colleagues at Princeton but they would never have the resources [for a college degree] or that the universities would never be receptive," said Rhode Island senator Jack Reed of Pell.[6] The GI Bill, which furnished a college education for millions of World War II veterans, served as inspiration for his proposal: grants provided by the federal government to low-income students to pay for college.[7]

As early as 1969, then senator Pell introduced legislation that would give every student $1,000—about $8,000 in today's dollars—for the first two years of college.[8] At the time, the cost of attending a four-year college averaged about $1,800.[9] But he started to sense that providing that much funding to every student would have consequences on the government budget that he knew lawmakers wouldn't realistically be willing to absorb.[10] Pell came up with a solution to the issue while skiing in the Alps, a place physically and spiritually removed from the middle-class and poor households struggling to pay for school. His idea was to use a formula to target the funds to the students with the most need. He drafted the plan on a place mat and gave it to his staff when he got back home.[11]

The idea of providing a need-based grant directly to students appealed to some in the think tank and philanthropic set as well. In 1968, a panel convened by the Carnegie Foundation recommended a federal role for higher education that included these grants, work-study, and loans.[12]

By the early 1970s, the grants sketched out on Pell's place mat and in commission reports were closer to becoming a reality, and Pell was committed to bringing them to fruition. He was facing a challenging reelection campaign in 1972, partly for his slim legislative record up until that point.[13] In hearings surrounding what would ultimately become the 1972 reauthorization of the Higher Education Act, Pell provided his rationale for a basic grant program. He told his fellow lawmakers and members of the Nixon administration that "philosophically" he believed the federal government "should provide a floor of assistance, as a matter of right," to students who want to attend college.[14]

Pell also sought to differentiate his approach from the Nixon administration's proposal, which officials were touting as removing financial barriers to a college education for low-income students but that heavily relied on an institution—what would ultimately become Sallie Mae—to facilitate more student loans. Under the administration's plan, loans would make up a significant portion of the assistance offered to even low-income students.[15]

Ultimately, the legislation incorporated Pell's proposal, providing students with a basic grant of up to $1,400 that would shrink based on how much a student's family could afford to contribute to their college costs.[16] But lawmakers would have to appropriate the money every year—it wasn't guaranteed. That meant that from the beginning, the reality of the program differed from Pell's vision of a source of funds that low-income students could count on to pay for college.[17] Sallie Mae, the institution meant to facilitate an increase in student loans that Pell was so worried about was approved by Congress as well.[18]

Subsidies for the (Relatively) Well-Off Battle Grants for Low-Income Students

Pell succeeded in getting his program of grants enshrined into law. But another approach was competing with the idea that the federal government's role in addressing college affordability should be to remove barriers to low- and middle-income college students through grants and loans. Some policymakers preferred providing relief to families paying for college through the tax system. That strategy would provide a subsidy to families who could afford to pay for college up front and wait for a tax credit or deduction. It would be of little help to those who didn't have the means to pay for college in the first place. Although tax breaks would certainly cost the government money, their budgetary treatment—they weren't an outlay in the same way that government spending on scholarships would be—meant that they didn't appear as expensive as spending directly on students or colleges.

When lawmakers debated the Higher Education Act that created the first broad student loan program in the 1960s, the Johnson administration was also fending off proposals to use tax credits to help families pay for college tuition. The Johnson administration's preferred program of subsidized loans won out, but savvy families looking for relief from college costs found ways to use the tax system to their advantage. The *Boston Globe* reported in 1967 that in twenty-three states, families could set up parent-controlled savings accounts for their children and avoid paying income tax on the account's earnings.[19] For students like Passe, who live in households where every dollar is going to cover the bills, using these kinds of accounts wasn't an option.

In the years following the 1972 reauthorization of the Higher Education Act, which established the Pell Grant Program, demands for some kind of preferential tax treatment for families paying tuition grew louder as middle-class households struggled to keep up with spiraling college costs. Those costs had grown from an average of $1,878 for a year at a four-year school in the 1971–1972 academic year to $2,355 in the 1976–1977 academic year.[20] The push by lawmakers to turn tax credits from idea into reality—and the Carter administration's response—illustrates the power of the (real and imagined) middle class to drive both political and social conversations surrounding the government's approach to financing higher education. Policymakers, pundits, and others presume that a staple of middle-class life is access to funding to pay for college—something they do not always assume of those who are poor. Historically, when that access has been put in jeopardy and it appears the college finance system isn't working for middle-class families, policymakers have taken it as a signal that the nation's approach to paying for college isn't working generally and have stepped in to try to fix it.

As Shirley Chisholm, the first Black woman elected to Congress, put it in 1978 in an op-ed opposing the tax credit proposals: "Today middle-class families find the cost of sending their children to college almost overwhelming. In other words, the middle class is realizing for the first time what has been a fact of life for many poor and minority group families for generations: Higher education may become the exclusive privilege of the wealthy unless the federal and state governments can provide financial assistance for those costs."[21]

In an effort to thwart the tuition tax initiatives in Congress, the Carter administration proposed expanding the federal student aid program to make more middle-income students eligible for Pell Grants and to provide subsidized student loans to a larger swath of students. The initiatives would mean that more than 60% of the country's college students qualified for government college aid, the *Washington Post* reported at the time.[22] As he announced the proposal, Carter said it would "provide more real help than any tuition tax credit," which he asserted was wasteful because of the benefits the credit would accrue to upper-income families.[23]

In presenting the plan to congressional lawmakers, Joseph Califano, Carter's secretary of health, education, and welfare, explained that while the administration remained committed to helping low-income students afford college, "the time ha[d] also come to provide assistance to families who do not now receive benefits but who also need them." Califano linked the challenges middle-class families were experiencing in paying for college to the administration's willingness to support a dramatic expansion in the government's role in financing higher education. Setting up a clash between using tax credits or the grant and loan program to subsidize middle-class families' higher education costs, both Carter and Califano warned that the president wouldn't sign a bill that contained both proposals.[24]

Pell supported both the administration's ambitions and officials' approach to achieving them, describing the goal of the hearing in which Califano appeared as figuring out "how we can help middle-income America, which pays its taxes and does the work and gets scant thanks for it—and is suffering at this time."[25] But other lawmakers were still skeptical of the Carter administration's approach to providing aid to the middle class. Lawrence Coughlin, a Pennsylvania senator who sponsored one of the bills on tax credits for tuition, said that the White House's proposal "smacks of a welfare-like program."[26]

Even as the Carter administration's plan worked its way through the legislative process, tax credit initiatives continued to gain momentum. The measures were so popular among lawmakers that the House refused to push the Carter proposal through, despite pressure from leadership.[27] Meanwhile, New York state lawmakers passed their own version of tuition tax relief and a plan to encourage tax-deferred college savings accounts. The proposals sailed through to success so quietly that education lobbyists, Washington officials, and one of the banks that would administer the savings account were all caught by surprise, the *New York Times* reported.[28]

Despite pressure to use the tax system to help middle-class families afford college costs, Carter's proposal to subsidize middle-class students through the grant and loan program ultimately won out on the federal level. In the late 1970s, low-income students benefited from the concerns over how middle- and upper-middle-class families would afford college costs as lawmakers expanded the Pell Grant Program to cover more students and a historically large share of college costs.[29] But as the decades wore on, the notion of helping low-income students through increased spending often competed directly and indirectly with using subsidies in the tax code to help middle- and upper-middle-class families afford college. That meant that in some cases, the interests of families who could afford to pay for college as long as they had a bit of liquidity—or could afford it outright but were still concerned about the costs—won out over the interests of those who truly needed assistance paying for school.

A Rhetorical—and Actual—Shift

The years following the Carter administration's expansion of the student loan and grant program to middle-class families were plagued by notoriously high inflation, putting government funding to subsidize college at risk of being cut. That meant that the government's cost of the college-financing program ballooned, not only because millions of new households entered it but also because high interest rates meant that the government had to pay more to provide student loan companies with their "special allowance," or the guarantee that they would receive returns a certain amount above the rate of Treasury bills.[30]

But it wasn't just economic conditions that began a decades-long pattern of squeezing Pell Grants such that they covered less and less of the cost of a four-year public college. At the same time, Ronald Reagan's administration shifted the rhetoric and philosophy surrounding the student loan program during the 1980s, which helped to push Pell Grants to lose value, which they never quite recouped.

Shortly after taking office with promises to cut taxes and government spending, Reagan-era officials set their sights on rolling back the Carter administration's drastic expansion of the federal student loan program amid a broader effort to dismantle the then newly created Department of Education.[31]

In the first year of the Reagan administration, officials used the regulatory process to quietly propose that the share of discretionary income that families be required to contribute to their child's college education before qualifying for a Pell Grant go from 10.5% to between 40% and 55%.[32] That would mean that a family of four earning more than $15,860—or about $57,000 in 2024 dollars—wouldn't qualify for the grant, the *New York Times* reported. At the time, families earning up to $25,000—or $90,000 in 2024 dollars—qualified for some relief. The American Council on Education, the leading education lobby, estimated that the proposal would slash eight hundred thousand students from the rolls of the Pell Grant Program. Even for those who were still eligible, the changes could create uncertainty in the amount of money they would receive—chipping away at a fundamental purpose of the grant: to push low-income students to enroll in college by providing them with a reliable source of aid.[33]

As they were building the case for these cuts, Reagan-era officials publicized data suggesting the government was providing grants to undeserving students. In 1981, then secretary of education Terrel Bell touted a study of a sample of Pell Grant applications conducted by an outside firm, indicating that the government was overpaying Pell Grant recipients by as much as $452 million. "The root of the problem is that, unlike most other need-based Federal programs, we generally accept on faith the information provided by students and parents on student aid applications," Bell said, announcing the findings. "The vast prevalence of over-awarding is proof that we must strengthen dramatically our procedures for verifying the accuracy of student information."[34]

In a memoir of his time as a member of Reagan's cabinet, Bell was less subtle about how the administration viewed students who used government grants and loans to pay for school. David Stockman, Reagan's budget director, saw these students, along with welfare recipients, Medicare users, and others, as "tax eaters" and a "drag on the economy," Bell wrote. "We were going to pull those leeches off the backs of decent, hardworking people," Bell wrote of the administration's mission.[35]

These "tea leaves" of political rhetoric that officials shared publicly helped career staff like David Bergeron understand the administration's priorities as they crafted budget requests. Bergeron's own path to Department of Education staffer began with a Pell Grant that allowed him to attend the University of Rhode Island with just $50 in help from his parents. In addition to the administration's public statements, the behind-the-scenes questions Bergeron and his colleagues were receiving from the Office of Management and Budget signaled a new skepticism about federal assistance to college students.

"It became clear that something had shifted," said Bergeron, who started at the department during the Carter administration, shortly after he graduated from college. The shift he was witnessing: a change in how the government defined what success for the Pell Grant Program would mean. Instead of trying to ensure that low-income students received access to higher education, officials were concerned with making sure that only those they viewed as studious, moral, and truly needy received the funds. "We could see it coming, we could hear it coming, we could see it in the politics, and we were getting lots of pressure to figure out ways to document the effectiveness of programs," Bergeron told me.[36]

A few years into Reagan's first term, Bergeron and his colleagues began working to build a large-scale survey that could prove the impact that student aid programs, in particular, the Pell Grant, were having on low-income students' persistence and attainment.

At the same time that Bergeron was working with a team to prove the Pell Grant was getting results, his Education Department colleagues were under pressure to minimize the level of fraud in the program. Although policymakers' concern about fraud and abuse was growing, and extended to a broad array of government programs, any suspected improper Pell Grant payments drew particularly intense scrutiny, Bergeron said. The Pell Grant Program's size meant that even if a small share of the grants were awarded improperly, it would amount to a large dollar figure, he said.[37]

Concern about improper payments "had a very substantial impact" on Bergeron and other Department of Education staffers' ability to convince the White House Office of Management and Budget to allocate more money for Pell Grants, he said. The first question Bergeron and his fellow staffers were asked in meetings with Reagan-era budget officials was what they were doing to address any Pell Grant payments made in error. "That became a really key question we were always asked, then it was questions about performance that came along with it," he said.[38]

The fear among policymakers and bureaucrats that the government is wasting federal financial aid funds on undeserving students persists to this day. It is a notion that can undermine low-income students' access to the funding they're entitled to and the college education it's supposed to encourage. Every year, the government selects a percentage of students who apply for federal financial aid for "verification," akin to an audit by the Internal Revenue Service. As part of the process, families are required to submit extra documentation to prove that the information on their Free Application for Federal Student Aid, or FAFSA, is accurate.

Verification disproportionately affects Black and Latino students applying for financial aid. The *Washington Post* found in 2021 that for every 100 families from a white neighborhood subject to verification, 140 were selected from majority Latino neighborhoods and 180 from majority Black neighborhoods.[39]

Getting selected for verification can pose real risks to students, particularly those whose families may not have experience with the college process or are balancing work, school, and other responsibilities. The process can be so onerous that some students fail to complete it, putting at risk their access to Pell Grants and other financial aid. In other cases, the verification process can dissuade students from enrolling. In the 2019–2020 academic year, about 7% of students selected for verification didn't receive financial aid as a result of the process, according to the Department of Education.[40]

The comments from Reagan's first secretary of education, Terrel Bell, that the accuracy of information submitted by students and parents about their financial need was putting the integrity of the Pell Grant Program at risk are part of decades of rhetoric that influenced policy requiring that financial aid recipients prove that they're poor. While there certainly is fraud in the financial aid program, the large-scale, headline-grabbing fraud tends to come from unscrupulous schools or companies, not the students themselves. Still, in defending proposed cuts to student aid funding in the early 1980s, Bell said of the Reagan administration's beliefs, "We think we're still a bit too generous," charging that without slashing the program, thousands of students who didn't need financial aid would get it. At the same time, his agency requested $2 million from Congress to verify income data submitted by Pell Grant recipients.[41] That same $2 million could have been used to give $5,000 in aid a year to four hundred poor college students.

The Reagan administration's portrayal of aid recipients as taking advantage of government generosity didn't stop with Bell. Shortly after becoming secretary of education during Reagan's second term, William Bennett defended proposed cuts to the student aid program, including increasing the percentage families would be required to contribute from their first $5,000 of discretionary income before qualifying for a Pell Grant to 11% from 18%, by saying that the changes "may require, for some students, divestiture of certain sorts—stereo divestiture, automobile divestiture, three weeks at the beach divestiture."[42]

Reagan administration officials also used language from previous policymakers to describe the role of the government in financing higher education. The Johnson, Carter, and even Nixon administrations had brought proposals to Congress that they argued would eliminate financial barriers for students interested in attending college. But to Bell, college tuition was "primarily the responsibility of the family," with the role of government as a final backstop to help "those who would not otherwise be able to obtain a college education."[43]

Bennett argued that asking students to shoulder more of the cost of their college education made sense, given the increase in earnings provided by the degree. Officials echoed that notion in White House budget documents: "Students are the principal beneficiaries of their investment in higher education. It is therefore reasonable to expect them—not taxpayers—to shoulder most of the costs of that investment."[44]

That marked a change from previous administrations, which had viewed investing in students' college attendance as a potential boon to the economy and the country as a whole. It was also a departure from the rationale used to justify the GI Bill and student loan programs, which assumed the country would benefit in some way from subsidizing college attendance. The philosophical shift in the government's role in funding students' college education also came with a shift in policy proposals. Whereas the Carter administration pitched large increases in federal financial aid funding to stave off calls for using the tax code to finance higher education, the Reagan administration shilled tax-free savings accounts that families could use to pay for college at the same time it proposed cuts to student aid. The programs, which came as part of a suite of initiatives, including vouchers for low-income students to use at private schools, made clear "the limited role of the federal government" the Reagan administration envisioned in higher education, as well as its goal to "wherever possible restore more choice and control to the family," Reagan told Congress at the time.[45]

The shift in requiring more contributions from families to pay for their children's college pushed education advocates and policymakers to find ways to make those contributions more manageable. Some state lawmakers began proposing educational savings accounts similar to Individual Retirement Accounts, which would allow families to save tax-free for college. In states like Michigan, policymakers were experimenting with initiatives that allowed families to contribute funding to a trust at birth that they could redeem for four years of tuition when the child turned eighteen.[46] Like the tax credits proposed by some during the Johnson and Carter administrations, these initiatives provided an advantage to those who could afford to pay for some of their college costs out of pocket, or to save, but they would do little to replace the government funds that low-income families used to afford college.

Although Congress didn't always acquiesce to the dramatic cuts in aid that Reagan administration officials sought, by the end of

Reagan's administration, the rhetoric and proposals had succeeded in shifting the balance of paying for college from grants toward loans and other means. Between 1980 and 1986, the share of entering freshmen using Pell Grants dropped from 32% to 17%, according to a survey from the period by University of California, Los Angeles. The share of students using loans rose from 21% to 25%.[47] The changes hit certain types of students particularly hard; for example, the share of Black students in New Jersey public colleges dropped from one in every eight students to one in every nine.[48] And a whole industry began to emerge to counsel students on the best way to manage their loans.[49]

Over the course of the Reagan administration, policymakers largely starved the Pell Grant Program of funding increases. But in addition to the cuts themselves, administration officials used their bully pulpit to create skepticism about those who used government funding to pay for college, and they nurtured the notion that families should be contributing much more to the cost of their children's education. That language also helped to fuel the embrace of the idea that the government would assist families in paying for college—as long as they could afford to help themselves.

Knowing about a Pell Grant Isn't Enough

By the time Justice Passe was preparing to attend college, it had been nearly fifty years since Claiborne Pell had envisioned a system in which low-income students wouldn't have to worry about how they would pay for school. During that time, policymakers chipped away at that notion in part by emphasizing that a college education required some sort of up-front investment from families.

Passe internalized the notion that affording college would be his responsibility and not the government's. Even though he qualified for roughly the maximum Pell Grant, Passe knew the funding wouldn't be enough to pay for the bulk of his four-year degree, so he took it upon himself to find the money elsewhere. Twice a week, he took a train and a bus across Philadelphia to the city's science museum to participate in standardized test prep and other college-readiness programming—he knew it would boost his chances not only of getting into school but also of earning some money to attend.

When Passe found himself suddenly stuck at home like the rest of the world in March 2020, he used the time to search for more college funding. While scrolling through Instagram one day, he came across an account called the Scholarship Plug, where a woman was encouraging viewers to apply for one hundred scholarships.

With no club meetings to attend, Passe decided he had time to take her up on the challenge. He developed a system that included a Google Doc with basic information like his name, address, and school that all scholarship applications required, as well as five essays that responded to common prompts. Once the system was in place, Passe would sit on the couch or on his bed or at his desk in the room he shared with his three siblings and apply—copying and pasting the standard information and crafting essays from his templates to meet the requirements of each program. He enlisted high school teachers and his college adviser to help edit the essays, which covered things like how he planned to use his education to build wealth that he would ultimately return to his community. Every time Passe finished an application, he'd log his progress in a spreadsheet. Over the course of about six months, Passe applied to 110 scholarships. He won seven of them, for a total of $50,000.

The scholarship haul, plus federal and state grants, still weren't enough to cover college costs at some of the schools Passe was considering—he had to be discerning. Initially he'd planned on attending Albright College, a liberal arts school about sixty-five miles from Philadelphia. But after talking with some of the school's graduates, Passe became skeptical. Some were working in jobs that didn't align with their career goals, and others were getting paid very little. Students who used federal student aid to attend Albright earn $55,578 on average ten years after entering school and leave with about $27,000 in federal student debt.[50]

He decided to attend his mother's alma mater, Community College of Philadelphia, instead. The anecdotal information Passe collected about Albright, combined with assurances from his college adviser that CCP would help him find work and transfer opportunities, convinced him it was the right choice. Passe started college during the pandemic, taking online courses asynchronously while interning in the financial services industry and working for the 2020 Census, organizing files. He met his fellow students in person only as part of student government meetings and events.

Passe took advantage of a system that allowed Community College of Philadelphia students to transfer to some Philadelphia-area colleges relatively seamlessly. Initially, he'd been attracted to Drexel because of its co-op program, which incorporates work experience as part of the curriculum. But the cost—roughly $60,000 a year in tuition and fees without scholarships—and the limited financial aid the school offered him pushed Passe toward Temple instead.[51] At Temple, Passe would benefit from discounted tuition as a Pennsylvania resident, but he still worried about the price tag, which could have been nearly $30,000 with meals and housing.[52] So he delayed transferring in order to keep working and build up funds to avoid taking on loans.

Middle Class Entitled to Tax Break While Lawmakers Squeeze Low-Income Students

Pressure from competing programs and philosophical approaches to how—and whether—the federal government should subsidize college attendance squeezed the Pell Grant Program. But the original design of the grant also created a situation in which the initiative often didn't deliver on its promise. Theoretically, the Pell Grant was supposed to ensure that all Americans, regardless of income, had access to a college education, but members of Congress didn't fund it as an entitlement, like Social Security. That meant that lawmakers could tweak the size of the grant or the number of students eligible for it in order to meet their budget needs. The back-and-forth over the Pell Grant in the 1990s exemplified this dynamic.

As part of the process of reauthorizing the Higher Education Act in 1992, the Senate overwhelmingly passed a bill that would, in theory, allow for increases in Pell Grants, but to achieve that broad support, senators eliminated a proposal that would have turned the grant into an entitlement. That approach meant that students could get up to the amount Congress authorized, but it wasn't guaranteed. Instead, each year, the lawmakers in charge of appropriating funds—a different group of policymakers from those focused on education who had shepherded through the Pell Grant increase—would actually decide how much the government would spend on the grants.[53]

Ultimately, lawmakers did pass a higher education law that raised the maximum Pell Grant by $600, but the increase was in name only. The House Committee on Appropriations passed legislation *decreasing* the maximum award for the upcoming academic year by $100. By increasing the amount authorized for the grants, both then president George H. W. Bush and Democratic lawmakers could take credit for delivering on a noble cause without actually funding it.[54] In reality, lawmakers were anticipating broader support for—and planned to use their actual and political capital on—programs helping the middle class, not the poor.[55]

The pattern of underfunding wasn't limited to Republican administrations. Shortly after Bill Clinton took office as president, his secretary of education, Richard Riley, announced that the deficits in the program were so large—about $2 billion—that officials were considering reducing eligibility for the grant or providing less money through the grant per student.[56]

Meanwhile, Clinton also became a vocal advocate for using the tax code to subsidize college costs—an initiative that was designed to appeal to the middle class, amid pressure from the right to minimize taxes. As part of a "middle-class bill of rights," Clinton pitched making $10,000 of college tuition tax deductible.[57] In explaining the rationale for the plan, David Longanecker, assistant US secretary of

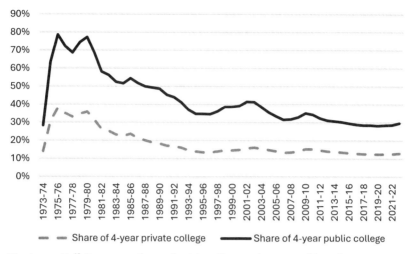

Maximum Pell Grant as a share of tuition, fees, and room and board
Note: Author calculations based on data from the Institute for College Access and Success and the College Board.

higher education, said it didn't come from some kind of education funding philosophy but instead was a reaction to Republicans' success in the midterms.[58] And indeed, Newt Gingrich, the architect of the so-called Contract with America—the suite of policy proposals that fueled Republicans' electoral success—expressed Reaganesque views on college financing. Gingrich told a ballroom of college presidents that he preferred to fund programs like work-study instead of initiatives like the Pell Grant that gave money to students with no strings attached.[59]

During his campaign for reelection, Clinton continued to emphasize the role of subsidies through the tax system, pitching the $10,000 tax deduction, in addition to a $1,500 tax credit for the first two years of college, and allowing families to withdraw funds to pay for college from their retirement accounts without tax penalties.[60]

The idea for the HOPE Scholarship, as Clinton dubbed the $1,500 tax credit, was an effort to counter proposals from his Republican opponent, Bob Dole, to drastically slash individual tax rates and capital gains taxes, according to Robert Shireman, who worked on education policy for decades in Congress, the White House, and the

Department of Education.[61] Clinton was aware of the success of the scholarship—"which was not a tax credit, but was an actual scholarship," Shireman said—in Georgia, a program the state launched in 1993 to provide students with certain merit- and need-based qualifications access to two years of free college, Shireman said, and he liked the sound of it.[62]

By designing his program as a tax credit instead of as a grant, Clinton could appeal to voters who might worry about increased government spending and provide himself with the opportunity to "hammer away" at the message that he was making two years of college tuition-free, Shireman said. "Unfortunately in the case of higher education policy," tax credits are "a pretty awkward fit," according to Shireman. Because there's a delay between when a household spends the money and when it receives the credit, these kinds of tax policies tend to be more beneficial to those households that actually have to pay taxes. As Shireman put it, "Tax credits tend to favor higher-income people rather than lower-income people," who in many cases aren't required to pay taxes.[63]

Despite this perspective—"I'm intentionally sounding somewhat politically cynical about the use of tax policy," Shireman said, as we discussed it—Shireman found himself as a staffer first in the Clinton administration's Office of Management and Budget and the National Economic Council, advocating the tax credit program in meetings with other areas of government, like the Internal Revenue Service, and helping to implement it.[64]

"What do you do when you have a job where part of your job is something you don't totally believe in? You try to convince yourself that it's a good thing," Shireman said. He thought that perhaps the tax credit satisfied some of the middle-class desire for a program to help with college costs. He also wondered whether, by providing some assistance to pay for college to the middle class, the tax credits helped create strong political will for providing assistance to pay for college to low-income students.[65] Indeed, many of the most popular and enduring initiatives providing economic assistance, like Social Security, are popular in part because they are universal (or at least close to it) and therefore have the buy-in of the politically powerful middle and upper middle classes and, in some cases, the wealthy.

And to bring the education establishment on board with the tax credit and deduction plan, Clinton did propose an increase in Pell Grants.[66] The plan both upped the maximum Pell Grant amount and expanded the number of students eligible for the grant.

Meanwhile, tax-deferred college savings plans were becoming an increasingly attractive way for state lawmakers to appeal to vocal middle- and upper-middle-class constituents concerned about college costs.[67] Some states had been experimenting with prepaid tuition programs and savings accounts for college since the 1980s, but their tax treatment was uncertain for the first several years of their existence. Then in 1994, a federal court ruled that income from Michigan's prepaid tuition plan wasn't subject to federal taxes.[68] In 1996, congressional lawmakers created Section 529 of the internal tax code, which allowed account holders to defer taxes on earnings from the accounts as long as they were used for higher education.[69] Those changes pushed state lawmakers across the country to offer the plans.[70] In 2001, Congress made the money withdrawn from the accounts tax exempt, as long as it was used for college costs, sparking another rash of growth for the accounts.[71]

By the end of the Clinton administration, the focus on middle-class tuition relief since the late 1970s, both from the White House and from states, combined with less emphasis on keeping the Pell Grant in line with inflation and college costs, meant that the gap in college attainment between poor and wealthy students had grown.[72] During the George W. Bush administration many of the same factors, like keeping program costs low, continued to pressure Pell Grants. In 2004, officials quietly changed the formula for calculating Pell Grant eligibility in such a way that roughly eighty thousand students were knocked out of the program.[73] Without the formula change, budget officials worried that the program, which was already experiencing a shortfall, would cost an extra $300 million.[74]

But another move from the Bush administration highlighted a factor other than budgetary concerns that was squeezing Pell

Grants: the funding the government was providing to entities involved in the student loan system. In 2005, officials proposed cutting subsidies to private student lenders and using the savings to increase funding for Pell Grants.[75] "You could never make up the ground that was lost in terms of the investment in Pell Grants because it's competing with other needs," said Bergeron, the former Department of Education staffer, like the subsidies needed to convince commercial entities to continue participating in the student loan program.[76]

The Obama administration illustrated the trade-off between Pell Grants and subsidies to student loan companies in an even starker way. In 2010, as part of the Affordable Care Act, lawmakers ended the bank-based student loan program. Going forward, the government would loan directly to all federal student loan borrowers and use the savings to increase Pell Grant funding. "We've expanded Pell Grants for millions of people, including millions of young women, all across the country," Obama said, touting the move during a 2012 presidential debate. "We did it by taking $60 billion that was going to banks and lenders as middlemen for the student loan program, and we said, 'Let's just cut out the middleman. Let's give the money directly to students.'"[77]

The Obama administration tried to redirect government funds toward assisting low-income students in paying for college in other ways too, but the political commitment to helping middle- and upper-middle-class families got in the way. In 2015, the White House proposed curtailing some of the tax benefits of tax-advantaged college savings accounts, known as 529s, and using the funds to expand the American Opportunity Tax Credit, which provides a credit to families, with an income limit, for paying college costs.[78] The idea was to take benefits accruing largely to wealthier families—in 2010, less than 3% of households were using a college savings account, and those households had twenty-five times the assets of families who weren't using them—and put those savings toward a more targeted tax break.[79] But the small constituency who used the accounts was a vocal one, and the plan sparked an uproar from parents and law-makers on both sides, including prompting a personal appeal from Nancy Pelosi aboard *Air Force One* to drop the proposal.[80]

How Colleges Eroded the Pell Grant's Value

Federal policymakers' interest in supporting other approaches to financing college—including subsidies to student loan providers and tax cuts—over the Pell Grant helped to shrink its value over time. But colleges played a role too. The structure of the Pell Grant Program requires the government to provide funding to schools while placing little responsibility on the colleges themselves to make tuition affordable for low-income students. That's meant that over the years, in many cases, colleges have been able to focus their own resources on luring middle- and upper-middle-class students who are more attractive financially because they require less aid than Pell-eligible students do. Because of their inequitable access to things like standardized test prep and advanced coursework, these wealthier students may also bring the kinds of grades and test scores that can raise a college's prestige.

Lawmakers' decision during the early 1970s to create a voucher-like student aid system, where the funds follow students to the insti-tution of their choice, instead of an institutional aid system, where the colleges receive the funds if they meet certain conditions, has allowed schools to use their own money in ways other than subsi-dizing low-income students. "There's no responsibility on schools to either keep their costs down or to spend their institutional aid dollars to supplement" the Pell Grant, Stephen Burd, a senior writer and editor at New America, a think tank, told me.[81]

Almost immediately after the new source of federal funding be-came available to colleges in the 1970s, in the form of Pell Grant money, some started looking for ways it could supplement other ar-eas of their budget. At the time, Jon Oberg was working in Nebraska's state government as a budget and management analyst and was engaging with institutions in the state as they determined how they were going to use the Pell Grant funds. Many said they'd pull the assistance they were offering to low-income students because the Pell Grant could provide for those students instead, he remembered.[82]

"I said, 'No, this is not the way this is supposed to work; the Pell Grant Program is supposed to add on to the benefits for the low income,'" Oberg remembers. "They said, 'Well, that's not the way it's set up.'" The two sides ended up compromising, with at least one school using the funds to provide facilities and other services to students but not directing them toward helping low-income students afford the cost of college, he told me.[83]

In the following decades, an entire industry known as enrollment management began advising colleges on how to use their incoming classes and the incentives—or disincentives—they offered particular students to achieve strategic goals. Innocuous examples of these strategies include providing a scholarship to a high schooler with a talent for playing the cello because the orchestra's lead cellist is about to graduate. But more sinister approaches involve designing incoming classes to maximize funding that colleges receive on students' behalf, either from their families or the government. For example, schools will observe how an applicant interacts with their website, as well as other data, to determine exactly how much financial aid they need to offer to the student to convince them to attend. Critics of these tactics, like Oberg, say they squeeze the amount of money colleges actually spend on low-income students. In a 2001 letter to college presidents, Richard Riley, then secretary of education, hinted that policymakers shared similar concerns. In the letter, he asked college officials to ensure that their schools used Pell Grants to actually bring the cost of college down for students, instead of using them in place of funds the school had already planned to provide those students.[84]

This practice persists: American colleges still use government money to avoid subsidizing low-income students with their own funds. A 2017 working paper from Lesley Turner, an economist at the University of Chicago, found that, on average, about 15% of Pell Grant funds go to schools' coffers instead of students'. At selective nonprofit colleges, schools tend to decrease the institutional aid they offer to Pell Grant recipients because the students have government funding available to them.[85]

Through his research, Burd, of the New America think tank, provided more detail on how colleges' drive for particular types of students has undermined the Pell Grant. Burd has been a close observer of student loan policy since the 1990s, when he was a reporter at the *Chronicle of Higher Education*. "I had always thought the Pell Grant was great," Burd said. For much of his career, there was a sense among think-tank wonks and policymakers that Pell Grants provided enough funding for low-income students to attend college without borrowing and that student loans were used largely by middle-class families as a liquidity tool—or as a way to pay for college over time if they didn't have the cash up front. "I saw that that was totally untrue, or no longer true, in any way, even at publics," he said, referring to public colleges and universities.[86]

That observation pushed Burd to investigate the ways that colleges' policies were making the Pell Grant less valuable. He initially focused on private colleges, for which the data was "totally convincing." The schools were asking Pell-eligible students to contribute a significant portion of their household income—sometimes as much as half—to their college costs while providing discounts to wealthier students in order to lure them to the schools.[87] For the colleges, the approach made sense economically; a student from a wealthy household who got a 20% discount still paid 80%, whereas a student from a poor household could wind up spending more than half of his or her family's income to pay for college but still barely make a dent in the full price of tuition. Although the evidence at private schools was "glaring," Burd became increasingly concerned about strategies public colleges were using to mold their classes. That's because these schools, Burd reasoned, educate many more students than private colleges and, theoretically, have a mission of serving their state's low- and middle-income students.[88]

Burd learned that the situation at public colleges wasn't much better. During the 2015–2016 academic year, Burd found that 52%

of the public colleges he analyzed expected students from families earning $30,000 or less annually to contribute at least $10,000 per year to their college costs.[89] That was in large part because the colleges were spending their own resources to draw students from wealthier families. Squeezed by state budget cuts, public colleges were looking for other sources of revenue, which they found in luring students from wealthier families at the expense of subsidizing poorer ones. By providing some families with a small discount, which they framed as a scholarship for good grades or standardized test scores, the schools could get families to pay the rest of the tuition funds. Burd's research found that between 2001 and 2017, more than half of the public schools he analyzed doubled the amount (adjusted for inflation) they spent on aid for students who didn't have financial need, and roughly 10% of schools increased it by more than ten times.[90] Because these students were also more likely than Pell-eligible students to grow up with access to resources like well-funded public schools and SAT tutoring, they not only brought money but also had the kind of characteristics that would help them score well on college rankings.

"Colleges were taking the Pell Grants for low-income students, but then spending their institutional dollars more on nonneedy students," Burd said.[91] That schools were never required to subsidize their Pell Grant students and were able to spend their money elsewhere meant that even when policymakers increased Pell Grant funding, it wouldn't be enough to cover college costs.

Despite (or maybe because of) the flaws in the Pell Grant's design, which has allowed its value to erode, policymakers and schools are still committed to the idea that students should be able to take their government aid wherever they want, even if the school doesn't commit to funding them. That was clear in the 2021 battle over a proposal to make two years of community college free in President Joe Biden's social spending package, known as Build Back Better. The initiative was one of the first dropped by the Biden administration as it negotiated with Democratic senators Joe Manchin and Kyrsten Sinema in an attempt to convince them to vote for the bill.[92]

One of the reasons officials slashed the provision: lobbying organizations representing private colleges (among others) advocated for increasing the Pell Grant instead of making community college free, the *Wall Street Journal* reported at the time. The proposal from the White House and congressional Democrats would have provided federal dollars to states that agreed to kick in their own funding to bring tuition down to zero, unlike Pell Grants, which require no commitment from states or colleges. What's more, private and public four-year schools would have gotten nothing from a free community college plan, so they focused their efforts on Pell Grants, a source of funding, yes, for low-income students but also for the colleges themselves.[93] In this way, higher education leaders convinced policymakers to sacrifice broader reform in favor of continuing to invest in the existing system. In other words, they fell victim to the sunk-cost fallacy—they decided to continue to invest in an existing system because they'd already poured time and money into it, instead trying something new.

"Institutional approaches are embracing and acknowledging the idea that for disadvantaged students to be well supported you have to rely on the institution to commit to that and hold them accountable for that," Shireman said. "Voucher approaches do not accomplish that."

A Subtle Advantage

In the middle of writing this book, I experienced the impact of these policy choices firsthand. Almost immediately after giving birth to a baby boy, blankets, rattles, and board books started showing up at my apartment. So did checks along with notes from aunts and uncles and family friends designating the funds for my son's future. In between googling how to get a baby to nap in the crib, I started researching the best ways to invest this money on his behalf. But I shouldn't have sweated the exact type of account I planned to use—regardless of what I chose, he would already be at an advantage.

For me and for many other parents who experience it, the leg up is so subtle that it may almost fail to register. Growing the money into enough to pay a decent chunk of tuition by the time my son is eighteen years old will require some work (see: middle-of-the-night googling) and saving on my part. But the tax-advantaged treatment of the account I choose to use and the policies going back decades that allowed my family to build wealth that they could then gift to us will drive its increasing value while I do very little.

What's more, when it comes time for my son and his peers to apply for financial aid, our family is likely to receive another quiet government subsidy. The Free Application for Federal Student Aid, or FAFSA, does not take assets like home equity and retirement savings into account when calculating how much help a family might need to pay for college. That means that households that have the benefit of these cushions could qualify for a similar amount of financial aid as other families who may have the same income but do not have the ability to fall back on home equity or retirement funds to pay for school in a crunch. Given the gap in wealth between Black and white families in the United States, which is itself one of the most persistent legacies of slavery, white households are much more likely to gain from the FAFSA. Economists have estimated that white families who could benefit from this situation get an "implicit subsidy" that's worth $2,200 more per year than what Black students receive.[94]

The combination of barely acknowledged advantage with some effort required is part of what makes these policies, which provide more of a benefit to the well-off, so hard to get rid of or slash. In many cases, members of this vocal constituency may not recognize that they've received a government benefit—in the form of tax-advantaged savings accounts or the government's decision to ignore certain assets when calculating financial aid—even as they decry larger government subsidies to low-income students and borrowers or at least fret about the implications of such policies for taxpayers.

The subtlety of these advantages also contributes to a narrative that students and families should be saving to pay at least a portion of their college costs, although the reality is that such a wide swath of Americans live paycheck to paycheck, without extra money to contribute to a college fund.⁹⁵ That in turn reinforces the idea that higher education is primarily an individual benefit that individuals should pay for—a long distance from the idea espoused by then senator Pell that students' ability to attend college shouldn't be limited by their financial means.

Justice Passe embraced the media's and policymakers' messaging that it is students' and families' responsibility to avoid student loans, even though when he was growing up, his family didn't have the extra funds available to contribute to a tax-advantaged account that would help save to contribute to college tuition. During high school, he entered a series of business competitions, and one topic kept coming up. "When I came across personal finance, I was like, Why do I keep seeing this? I was like, 'This is really important. Why is it not taught in school?'"

Passe became so bullish on the notion that following strategies for budgeting, saving, and investing could change people's circumstances that he organized financial literacy fairs in high school. He brought in experts who encouraged students to budget and to save money where they could, like brewing their coffee at home every day instead of buying it on campus. He didn't want other people's parents to work thirteen-hour days and still be worrying about the next paycheck.

During a competition in 2019, Passe put the lessons he'd learned about personal finance to use. He sat in a conference room in Temple University's student center pretending to be a financial adviser and explained to a judge role-playing as his client how to manage $30,000 in student debt on an entry-level salary and still achieve the client's financial goals. Passe told the client about budgeting strategies like finding discounts for groceries.

He won the competition and received a scholarship. If Claiborne Pell had had his way, Passe would have at least had his education at a public college paid for. That Passe had to provide a budget for a theoretical student loan borrower in order to receive a scholarship to pay for a state college indicates the gap between the US college finance system today and Pell's vision. Recent college graduates are expected to skimp on groceries to afford their student loans, and low-income high schoolers need to cobble together a variety of funding sources if they hope to attend college without taking on debt.

Passe recognizes the inequality baked into the system. He knows his chances of getting into an Ivy League school with a generous financial aid policy would have been slim given the high school he graduated from. And he also knows that not attending an elite private school could hinder his chances of netting a dream job that could change his financial circumstances, which to Passe is the point of higher education: "All that college really is, in my opinion, is trying to have a better trajectory in a job that's going to be paying you more than your current social class." When Passe looked through the profiles of employees at a prestigious strategy consulting firm where he one day hoped to work, he saw they all had attended Ivy League schools.

But he never banked on the chance that policymakers or higher education leaders would smooth the path to these types of jobs for students like him. And indeed, since the government began investing in students' higher education, both through grants and loans, policymakers have waffled on how much government assistance is justified and who deserves it. In addition, other actors involved in the higher education finance system, including colleges, have used the design of these programs to their advantage.

So Passe has hustled to find several contacts at his target firms in hopes of bypassing official recruiting channels that he believes gatekeep jobs from students without fancy degrees. Once Passe achieves his goal of starting his trajectory into the upper middle class, he plans to use a 529 or other vehicle to save for college for any of his future children: "I think my income would offer me the luxury to be able to do so."

4. States Pull Back

What Happens When States Cut Support for College Too

Often embedded in both the public and the personal conversations surrounding student debt is the idea that it can be avoided by making the right personal choices. Headlines like "How to Pay for College without Student Loans" and "6 Alternatives to an Expensive Undergraduate Degree, and What Exactly to Do to Avoid College Debt" coax students toward strategies like starting off at community college to stave off taking on loans.[1] These suggestions may come from journalists, members of Congress, or well-meaning observers whose experience researching college options and compiling a list of schools at a variety of price points confirms the idea that it is possible to avoid or minimize student loans by approaching the process of applying to college strategically. At the same time, their knowledge of so-called budget options like trade school or short-term training programs and their costs—these courses often require students to spend thousands of dollars either out of pocket or through loans—is likely less intimate.

It's no wonder, then, that this advice and its implications often miss an important reality: for many students, even the cheapest higher education option available requires taking on some debt. During the 2018–2019 academic year, more than half of community colleges were unaffordable for students receiving a Pell Grant.[2] This is in part a result of declines in state subsidies for higher education that became particularly notable in the wake of the Great Recession. The approach of the federal government and third-party actors involved in the student loan system is in part to blame for the rise in student debt, but state policymakers played a role in making it difficult for families to afford college without taking on loans.

It wasn't always the case that it was difficult for families to find a college option with manageable tuition. Some baby boomers remember being able to pay for college through part-time and summer work. At the time they attended school, most students could indeed afford college without loans. The idea that college is affordable as long as students do their research still persists. But public colleges, which are often the most affordable option, were also fundamentally different in two key ways: many states subsidized their schools so heavily that students could attend for free or a relatively low fee, and more than four out of five students were white.[3]

That the share of white students at public colleges declined in tandem with state funding could be a coincidence. If it is, it's concerning that today's collegegoers, who are more likely to be students of color, don't have the same access to an affordable higher education as previous generations of students who were more likely to be white. But the history of higher education funding in California illustrates that the trends are likely related.

During the mid-twentieth century, California's well-resourced and prestigious public institutions were the envy of many across the country. Today, the state is still arguably one of the most committed to funding higher education to make it more affordable. Still, it hasn't been immune to the nationwide forces over the past several decades that have pushed some policymakers to question the value of low-cost public college and to pull back from funding it—all while the state's population has increasingly become less white.

A Master Plan for Affordable College

In the late 1950s, California policymakers convened a panel of experts to determine how higher education institutions and the state would cope with what they assumed would be growth both in the number of students attending college and in the number of colleges themselves. Clark Kerr, the head of the University of California system at the time, was the driving force behind the panel and led its efforts.[4]

In the decade leading up to the group's convening, spending on higher education in California had more than tripled due to a variety of factors, including increasing enrollment, inflation, and the expansion of California public colleges' offerings.[5] Going forward, Kerr wanted to ensure that the three state college systems— the University of California, the California State Universities, and the state community colleges—had a coordinated plan to absorb increased enrollment without threatening the University of California's role as the premier research institution in the state. Preventing the systems from duplicating their efforts would also save the state money.[6]

In the years leading up to what would come to be known as the California Master Plan for Higher Education, the state played a major role in funding the University of California. From 1911 to 1960, between 55% and 70% of the institution's budget came from the state, and student fees provided a small contribution.[7] That

commitment to funding higher education came in part from a notion called the California idea, argues Simon Marginson in his book
*The Dream Is Over: The Crisis of Clark Kerr's California Idea of Higher
Education.* Marginson describes the concept as a mix of access and
excellence in service of the state, society, and the economy.[8] It drew
from the California progressives, Marginson writes, a group of political reformers who believed that all high school graduates should
have access to higher education and that the state should expand its
public college system to meet those demands.[9]

By the 1959–1960 fiscal year, the state was devoting 11% of its
budget to its colleges, which the authors of the master plan described as "a greater amount than is spent by any other state in the
nation for public higher education."[10] That money accounted for
more than half the funds that California public colleges spent that
year.[11] But because the state had a large and growing tax base, each
individual taxpayer was devoting far less to funding public colleges
than taxpayers in other states were.[12]

With the schools relying heavily on the state for funding, they
were able to minimize the money they needed from students. As
part of the master plan, the authors recommended that the state
maintain its nearly century-long commitment to tuition-free higher
education. In making the recommendation, they invoked a recent
speech from James L. Morrill, then president of the University of
Minnesota, who called raising tuition at public colleges "an incom-
prehensible repudiation of the whole philosophy of a successful
democracy premised upon an educated citizenry."[13]

Reagan Battles Campus Unrest and Free College

Less than a decade after the state published the California Master
Plan for Higher Education, Ronald Reagan began the long process
of unwinding the state's commitment to tuition-free higher education. This was years before his administration would express wari-
ness about the Pell Grant and those who used it. Still, his state-level

approach foreshadowed some of that skepticism. During his campaign for governor, Reagan sowed and capitalized on distrust of colleges and their students following campus protests over the Vietnam War. In 1966, Reagan lamented that the University of California, Berkeley, "started going downhill" a year earlier "when the administration began appeasing student demonstrators."[14] He told reporters at a press conference that campaign audiences frequently asked him about the state of affairs at the University of California. "There are things going on that just don't belong on a campus," he said.[15]

But it wasn't just student behavior and protests generally that had Reagan concerned—he specifically highlighted the role that protests related to race played in changing the character of the state's public colleges. On the campaign trail, he urged his rival, then governor Pat Brown, to condemn a planned Black Power demonstration on the Berkeley campus. "California must not become a hotbed of racial riots," he said. "We cannot have the university campus used as a base from which to foment riots."[16]

During the period that Reagan served as governor, activists also agitated to change the demographics of who benefited from the schools. In the 1960s, students, spurred in part by the civil rights movement, started to demand an end to racial discrimination on college campuses across the country.[17] One of the most notable actions took place in California, where protesters at San Francisco State College convinced the school to create the nation's first college of ethnic studies and admit more students of color.[18] At the same time, California legislators were also working to increase the number of nonwhite students at the state's colleges by allocating funding for grants, loans, work-study, and counseling through a new initiative called the Educational Opportunities Program.[19]

But Reagan came into office with a particular view of the college experience—something markedly different from a diverse campus where students and faculty explored research and political interests. Reagan once told a "high state official" that his idea of college was "four years on a campus with red brick walls and you leave with a tear in your eye," the *Los Angeles Times* reported in the early 1970s.[20] The *Times* noted he attended one of those "tear in your eye" schools, Eureka College, a small, Christian, liberal arts school whose student body in the early 2020s was 70% white.[21] "The Eureka College model seems to have stayed with him for 40 years," the paper wrote.[22]

Once he took office, Reagan pushed for public four-year institutions to charge tuition—$400 at the University of California schools and $200 at the state colleges—in part as a way to transform the colleges into institutions free of political activity. Just days after his inauguration in 1967, Reagan told reporters that charging tuition at the schools would "get rid of undesirables."

"Those there to agitate and not to study might think twice before they pay tuition," he added, "they might think twice how much they want to pay to carry a picket sign."[23] In advocating for the schools to charge tuition, Reagan also argued for a shift in the state's role in funding individual students' education. "There is no such thing as a free education. There is a costly education. The question is 'Who shares the cost?" he told reporters.[24] In his first budget proposal, officials pitched cutting the budgets of the University of California and California State systems by 10%, despite rising inflation and the state's growing population.[25]

That first proposal from Reagan's officials to charge tuition ultimately wasn't successful, but the battle over how to fund the state's public colleges had consequences. Reagan officials convinced the University of California's Board of Regents to release $19 million from its special reserves, pushing it to put forward the system's own funds to supplement the more limited appropriation from the state that Reagan was pushing for.[26]

In addition, both the University of California and the California State systems temporarily halted their admissions processes as they evaluated the proposed budget cuts. Kerr threatened that both his system and the California State colleges could cut admissions in response to decreased funding, pushing more students toward community colleges, which were funded by local taxpayers.[27] Just weeks after Reagan offered his tuition proposal, the University of California's Board of Regents voted to fire Kerr, the architect of the master plan, considering him an obstacle to Reagan's plans for the state's colleges and universities.[28]

Meanwhile, Reagan kept the threat of a tuition charge alive. If the University of California's Board of Regents didn't institute a permanent tuition charge in the following year, Reagan warned in March 1967, "we're going to have to review our entire approach to the financing of the university based on the funds that are available." He added that the schools could afford to slash "intellectual luxuries" for a year or two.[29]

Throughout the following few years of Reagan's governorship, he battled with legislators and higher education officials over how much the state would contribute to California's public colleges and tuition. The fight over finances would continue to run in tandem with Reagan's efforts to clamp down on behavior at the state's colleges that he viewed as not befitting campus life. He proposed charging tuition but allowing low-income students to use a combination of loans and grants to pay for it.[30] Amid the governor's push for tuition, the University of California regents began to study the idea, and in 1968, a regents' committee proposed raising the incidental fee charged at University of California schools and calling it a university registration fee instead. The proposed change was more than semantics. Under the committee's plan, money from the fees would go toward funding operations, like the office of the dean of students, which would be covered by tuition at other colleges.[31]

During this period, the governor's approach to funding state colleges and universities was so extreme that after he vetoed millions of dollars in funding the state was set to send to the UC system, University of California regents urged the lawmakers to override his veto.[32]

At the same time, Reagan spoke forcefully against campus activity that he deemed unacceptable. Reagan didn't directly tie his criticism of events like a lecture from Black Panther Party leader

Eldridge Cleaver to funding for the state's colleges. Still, the language he used indicated that he viewed students' access to higher education very differently than the authors of the California Master Plan for Higher Education did: they saw providing residents with tuition-free higher education as fundamental to democracy. In a 1969 letter, Reagan asked state lawmakers to help him get rid of the "criminal anarchists and latter-day Fascists" on college campuses, writing to legislators that "higher education in our state colleges and universities is not a right, it is a privilege."[33]

By amplifying the unrest on college campuses, Reagan also likely made it easier for voters and lawmakers to accept cuts in state funding to California's colleges. Amid a back-and-forth in late 1969 over the most severe slashes to public higher education Reagan had proposed in his three-year term, the *Los Angeles Times* noted that the University of California "may find it difficult to generate support for any increase because the university, plagued by student unrest and a variety of other problems, never has been more estranged from the general public."[34]

The following year, after four years in office and debate over whether to charge tuition at the state's public colleges, Reagan got what he wanted. The University of California Board of Regents voted in 1970 to add an educational fee—"as tuition is called," the *Chicago Tribune* reported at the time—to the activities fee the school already charged. At the time, the increase put the fees at the University of California among the highest for public universities nationwide. The move marked a shift away from the master plan's notion that the state should provide higher education to all high school graduates. The university "must accept the general concept that the student is economically responsible for a part of his education costs," Reagan said.[35]

Throughout Reagan's second term as governor, he continued to battle the state's higher education leaders over both the schools' budgets and students' behavior on campuses. The campus unrest and the governor's response to it, which drew national attention and at times disrupted classes and other basic university functions, harmed the schools less than Reagan's proposals to slash university funds, according to Charles Hitch, then president of the University of California system. Hitch warned in a 1971 statement that Reagan "has achieved with the stroke of a pen what bomb threats, pickets, intimidation, and aggression could not. We have repelled those attacks but we have no way of countering fiscal blows like these."[36] But Reagan's "fiscal blows," as Hitch described them, were made easier by tying them to those bomb threats and pickets; as the *Los Angeles Times* noted in 1973, Reagan's "harsh political rhetoric" toward California's colleges, particularly the UC system, had "persuaded a part of the public that tax dollars spent on higher education are a waste."[37]

"It Was a Lot Then, but Now It's So Unrealistically Out of Reach"

As Reagan, state lawmakers, and the higher education community fought over how much the state should subsidize the cost of college and whether to ask families to increase their contribution, more than one million students enrolled in college in California.[38] Kathleen White was one of them.

Growing up in San Francisco in the mid-twentieth century, White's parents, who never attended college, were "overenthusiastic," as she put it, about the idea that she and her two sisters would go. For White, the oldest of the three, it wasn't too much of an ask; she'd always felt comfortable in school and was pretty good at it.

When it came time to apply to college, White took on the task herself. At home she thumbed through college promotional booklets, pulled the applications out of the middle of the packet, and filled them out by hand. She received several positive letters back, but she couldn't afford the travel and living costs at more far-flung schools. Ultimately, White adjusted to the cheapest option.

She graduated from high school at sixteen and promptly moved out of her childhood home to live among friends in San Francisco who had done the same. White took courses at a community college during what would have been the last semester of her senior year. The following semester, White enrolled at San Francisco State, part of the California State University system (around this time, Cal State was charging about $118 in fees, or about $879 in 2024 dollars).[39]

Although Reagan's proposals to slash college budgets and charge tuition marked a shift in state policymakers' approach to higher education in California, at the time White, who entered college in 1973, attended these schools, the state still subsidized them at a level higher than today. In the mid-1970s, the state spent roughly 18% of its budget on higher education, compared to 11% during the 2018–2019 academic year, according to the Public Policy Institute of California.[40] At California State University campuses, one of which White attended, the state spent about $11,678 per student during her time there, compared to $8,962 following the Great Recession. At UC schools the funding drop was even more dramatic, going from $26,062 in the mid-1970s to $14,509 during the 2009–2010 academic year.[41]

While White was in school, it wasn't only the state's college subsidies that helped to keep her costs low. She also lived in San Francisco during an era of affordability that would be unrecognizable to today's young adult residents of the Bay Area. You could find housing at a reasonable price—the median California rent in 1970 was $126 a month or about $1,045 in 2024 dollars—and White and her friends did whatever it took to hunt down resources available to them.[42] They'd drive their cheap and often nearly inoperable cars to North Beach at the northeastern tip of the city for student specials like spaghetti dinners for a dollar or two. Through word of mouth White and her friends learned to navigate the social safety-net system to access affordable health care and other resources. "This is coming out of the Haight-Ashbury period," White said, referring to the San Francisco neighborhood and major hub of the 1960s counterculture movement. "You had a lot of young people without money wandering around the city."

Although she was able to hustle her way to resources, White worked too to pay her expenses. She patched together jobs such as dispatcher at the campus police department, waitress, and nanny. She also had other responsibilities. In college, White got married and had her first child. After she graduated, White decided to continue on to graduate school, thinking it would help to open more doors. By the time White earned her master's degree, she was pregnant with her second child.

The years White spent in college and graduate school were marked with juggling and the feeling that the precarious balance between her and her husband's lives as students, parents, and workers was one emergency away from collapsing. When her husband's veterans' benefits ended, he stopped attending college—one semester short of earning a degree—so that he could work full-time and help provide for the family. For three years when her children were young, White worked full-time during the day, and her husband worked full-time at night so they could afford basic necessities and make sure their children were taken care of. The couple sent their son to a campus-based childcare center that operated as a co-op, with parents taking on shifts. White and her husband would trade off fulfilling their co-op duties, and it was often the case that other parents wouldn't show up. "There were absolutely days where we would have to bring kids to class," White said. "I don't even know when I did homework, I can't remember, I had no idea, I was probably asleep," said White, who was in her sixties when we started talking.

Even with work and the relatively cheap tuition and housing, White still had to take on loans to get through, always opting for the maximum amount she was eligible for. It wasn't just that she needed money to afford her basic expenses; by going to school, White was trading in the opportunity to work more and earn more money immediately for the promise that she could afford a better life in the future. Once she finished school for good, White constantly felt as if she were digging herself out of a hole. Despite all of the hours she and her husband spent working, they struggled to afford to meet their expenses, including her student loan payments. They rotated which bills they would pay late, and it was always at least one of them.

Although the period when she and her husband were finishing up their studies, raising young children, and then beginning to pay back her student loans was challenging, if she'd tried to do it today, she believes it would have been impossible. "It was a lot then, but now it's so unrealistically out of reach for people who have middle-class jobs," she said.

Taxpayers' Revolt

While White was studying, working, and raising children, resentment over high taxes among California property owners blossomed into a political movement, the results of which ultimately made the state's budget so volatile that stakeholders, including in higher education, couldn't count on it as a reliable source of funding.

The proximate cause of what would come to be called the taxpayers' revolt was the impact of late-1970s inflation on homeowners and commercial property owners in California. Suddenly, properties were being reassessed at higher values, which came with higher property taxes.[43] And incomes weren't rising fast enough to keep up.[44] Howard Jarvis, a businessman and political activist who had been pushing for years to significantly cut state taxes and end public funding for basic services, was able to capitalize on residents' anxiety surrounding these changes.[45]

It wasn't just high property values that made Jarvis's arguments convincing, according to Manuel Pastor, a professor of sociology and American studies and ethnicity at the University of Southern California. The campaign came at a time when there was a shift in the Californians who would benefit from the services taxpayers fund. Nonwhite young people were becoming a demographic force, growing from 30% of the youth population in 1970 to 44% by 1980, according to Pastor.[46] At the same time, in the early 1970s the faces of students in public schools were shifting, and a decision by the California Supreme Court challenging the state's school-funding scheme meant that, as Pastor put it in an interview with me, "rather than you being able—if you were paying high taxes—to make sure they were just going to your children, your high taxes were going to everyone's children."[47]

Growing up, Pastor benefited from the public services that California's higher taxes provided to its residents, including the decent public schools he attended as a child and affordable access to the UC system, which he described as "a jewel."[48] Even with that investment, Pastor still struggled to keep financially afloat while in college. In his first year, financial aid covered all of his expenses, but at the end of that year, Pastor was called into the financial aid office after his father earned more than he'd initially predicted. Financial aid officials wanted Pastor's family to contribute $100 more to his education. "I think I cried. I certainly was pretty emotional that I couldn't get $100 more from my family because we didn't have it," Pastor told me.[49]

Pastor found ways to pay for school without seeking more financial aid or student loans, including by working summers as a painter, stopping and starting college a few times to be able to earn money, and using funds from a trust that he had gotten after being hit by a car as a child. Although finding the money to pay for school without debt as a working-class Latino student was challenging, Pastor sensed that the change Jarvis was pushing for, known as Proposition 13, might make it nearly impossible for future generations.[50]

When he graduated from UC Santa Cruz, Pastor was selected by his fellow classmates to give a speech at graduation, and his address warned about Proposition 13's impact. At twenty-two years old, Jarvis's proposal looked to Pastor like something that "wasn't about taxes," he said. "It was about locking in a permanent advantage for an older and whiter generation. It was about short-changing the resources the state needed."

California residents voted in 1978 through a ballot referendum for the law by an overwhelming margin, 65% versus 35%. The result was to tax property at 1% of its value at the time of purchase. The law also returned property values to their 1975–1976 levels for tax purposes. These measures provided a larger benefit to legacy home-owners while also limiting the property tax funding the state could use for education and other services for California's more recently arrived residents. It also gave state lawmakers—instead of local officials—the power to allocate property tax revenues and required that at least two-thirds of lawmakers approve any increases to the state's tax revenue.[51]

As a scholar, Pastor saw how California voters' decision to lock in the advantage of legacy homeowners who were more likely to be white and locked students and families of color out of the benefits he'd received growing up.

Proposition 13 helped to shift the notion of what the state was ex-pected to provide to its residents. In the 1950s and 1960s, the era of the California Master Plan for Higher Education, the state invested in its future through things like higher education, said Pastor, who is the author of *State of Resistance: What California's Dizzying Descent and Remarkable Resurgence Means for America's Future.* By the time Jarvis was building support for Proposition 13, the faces of the peo-ple using those resources were changing. In few sectors was that shift more obvious and contentious than in higher education. The same year voters passed Proposition 13, the US Supreme Court ruled that an admissions program at the University of California, Davis, medical school, which reserved 16% of spots in the incoming class for minority applicants, was unconstitutional. The ruling was the result of a lawsuit filed by Allan Bakke, a twice-rejected applicant to the medical school who charged that the set-aside policy was the reason for his rejection and amounted to reverse discrimination.[52]

"When it became clear that the state was starting to change de-mographically and that more people wanted in on the California and American dream, the state began to pull back its welcome mat," Pastor said.

Although the politics of Proposition 13 were specific to California, over the next several decades, the older, whiter generation's permanent advantage, as Pastor put it, would be locked in across the country. In 1980, when more than 83% of students attending public colleges were white, states spent $9,068 per public college student on average, accounting for inflation.[53] During the 1980–1981 academic year, students at four-year public colleges were charged, on average, the equivalent of $2,970 in 2023 dollars in tuition and fees.[54]

In the aftermath of the 2008 Great Recession, when the share of white students had dropped to slightly less than 63%, states spent on average $7,780 per public college student.[55] That same year, 2010, the average price of tuition and fees at a four-year public college was $10,700.[56]

In the years since the downturn, the share of public college students who are nonwhite has continued to tick up—in 2020, white students accounted for nearly 53% of public college students—as has the level of funding. In 2020, states spent on average $8,715 per public college student. Still, that's about $359 less than in 1980.[57] Tuition in 2020 hovered at $12,490.[58]

That public colleges became more diverse and more expensive at the same time may be a coincidence. Even if that's the case, the notion that students of color have to incur greater financial risk to access the American dream is something that policymakers should want to reckon with—and in some cases, they are. But as the battle over Proposition 13 and Reagan's efforts to cut state funding to California colleges illustrates, the lawmakers' decisions to pull back state support for higher education—and other government services—is often linked with changes in who is using those resources.

Little Slack When a Downturn Hits

In the immediate aftermath of Proposition 13, California pulled back on its investment in its colleges as competition among a variety of priorities for the now more limited state funding grew. The result was a system of colleges and universities that enrolled growing numbers of students but for which a lack of state investment meant the campuses' physical infrastructure suffered.[59]

But some of Proposition 13's biggest impacts on state funding for colleges came decades later. Because California relies so little on property taxes to fund its operations, any fluctuation in the amount the state brings in personal income taxes can have a major impact on its budget. That dynamic amplifies the pressure that recessions place on state coffers, because residents' income and the state's revenue from income taxes tend to drop during those periods.[60]

During the early 1990s, the administration of California's then governor Pete Wilson cited an increase in the state's "tax receiver groups—students, welfare recipients, prisoners and Medi-Cal eligible," that was growing more quickly than the group of people paying taxes as a main factor in the state's budget woes. The uptick, his administration speculated, was due largely to an increase in the number of children in the state, fueled in part by immigration.[61] In her book *The Color Bind: California's Battle to End Affirmative Action*, Lydia Chavez chronicles how the Wilson administration's anti-immigration stance helped to keep him in power for a second term and ultimately demonstrated the political potency of white rage, leading voters to pass a ballot initiative that would hamper affirmative action efforts at the state's public institutions, including colleges.[62]

Policymakers were growing concerned about the availability of public funding for priorities like higher education at the same time that they and voters worried about who would benefit from that funding. In the wake of the early 1990s recession, the leaders of the state's three higher education institutions warned that the state's pattern of investing less and less in California's colleges and universities—as measured by a percentage of the state's revenue—was putting the master plan's promise at risk.[63] That notion was particularly troubling, said Barry Munitz, then chancellor of Cal State, because the demographic mix of students was changing. "We are in danger of changing the rules" for the increasing droves of nonwhite students looking to attend California public colleges, Munitz said. "This is a potential nightmare for the state."[64]

And indeed, the drop in state funds and corresponding shift of the costs to students and families pushed nonwhite and nonwealthy students away from higher education. Between 1992 and 1993, the number of students enrolled in the California Community College system dropped 9%—the biggest decline since 1978, the *Los Angeles Times* reported, the year Proposition 13 became law.[65] The reason behind the decrease, according to a report prepared by system officials: money. The fees had more than doubled, and the state did not have enough funds to offset them. The increase in fees hit students already enrolled at the colleges and nonwhite students particularly hard, according to the report.[66]

Following the bust of the dot-com bubble in 2000 and the ensuing recession, California's public colleges once again suffered from large cuts in state funding as residents' lower income resulted in less tax revenue for the state. More recently, the Great Recession and its slow recovery pushed state lawmakers to drastically cut funding to California's public colleges. In 2008, in the midst of the Great Recession, California spent $11,234 per full-time student enrolled in its public colleges. By 2013, that number had dropped to $9,374.[67] At the same time, the amount of money the public colleges were getting from students and families grew; in 2008, their tuition revenue per full-time student was $2,293. In 2012, it was $4,040.[68] During that period the amount in-state students and their families paid also grew; during the 2007–2008 academic year, undergraduate tuition for California residents at Cal State schools was $2,772. By the 2011–2012 academic year, it had jumped to $5,472.[69] At the University of California, Berkeley, in-state students paid $8,383 in tuition and fees to attend during the 2007–2008 academic year, a sum that had grown to $14,460 by the 2011–2012 academic year.[70] The Great Recession and its slow recovery also marked a period of growth in the number of nonresident students at UC schools. In 2012, they made up about 13% of students compared to 9% in 2008.[71]

Perhaps because of its historical commitment to funding higher education, California has done a better job than some states at mitigating the impact of tuition increases on students from poorer households. California is one of a handful of states that provides generous financial aid to low- and moderate-income students. In 2014, California spent more per low-income student than the federal government spent on Pell Grant recipients in the state.[72]

Still, finding the funds to afford expenses outside of tuition, including housing, books, and other costs, can make it difficult for students to afford college without taking on debt. The complex interplay of state, federal, and institutional aid programs can also make it difficult for some students to actually access funds to help them cover rising college costs, said John Aubrey Douglass, a senior research fellow and research professor at the Center for Studies in Higher Education at the University of California, Berkeley. That's particularly true for low-income students who attend schools with fewer resources to help them navigate the financial aid process, he said.

Although students in California are more likely than those in many other states to find a high-quality, affordable public college option, state disinvestment has had harsher consequences for the schools that serve a larger share of low-income and nonwhite students. As Laura Hamilton and Kelly Nielsen document in *Broke: The Racial Consequences of Underfunding Public Universities*, the state's pullback from funding higher education has most affected the University of California, Merced, the university system's newest school, where 55% of students are Hispanic and more than 60% of students qualify for Pell Grants.[73] It has pushed Merced toward coping strategies that put both students and the school itself in a precarious position. While older and whiter campuses in the system can more easily turn to tuition-paying out-of-state and international students, philanthropy, and large endowments—for example, Berkeley's endowment per student is thirty-one times that of Merced's—to compensate for a lack of state funding, a school like Merced has fewer options.[74]

University administrators there have looked toward enrolling more students to increase revenue, even though the school's infrastructure is already strained. Hamilton and Nielsen describe the push to increase enrollment even as an already-crowded campus forced students to find odd spaces, like an unused elevator, to study, and wait for hours to see an academic adviser.[75] To build more facilities for these new students, the school engaged in a large-scale public-private partnership, mixing the school's and its students' futures with the goals of PepsiCo, a for-profit company.[76]

Across the country, colleges like UC Merced are serving students who have traditionally been underrepresented in higher education. And like Merced, they're doing this work in an era when the state government resources available to public colleges are much less than when these underrepresented students were largely absent from college campuses. As a result, instead of turning to state coffers, public colleges are relying on soda companies to keep their doors open.

Feeling the Impact of State Budget Cuts and a Complicated Loan System

Decades after Kathleen White finished her studies at California public colleges, she felt the pressure that recessions and the limits on tax revenue created by Proposition 13 were placing on those institutions as she started to help her children prepare to enter higher education in the late 1990s.

White took almost the opposite approach of her parents, who were hands-off both in the application process and financially. "I was like a helicopter," she said of her involvement with her children. White assisted her children, the first of which entered college in 1999, in part because she had knowledge they didn't. "I taught at a college so I knew a lot about the application process, and the deadlines and the options," she said. But she had other motivations too: "I wanted to make sure they went."

Her youngest son, Sean, confirmed that it took some nudging from Kathleen to get him to a four-year school. He described himself as "anxious" to get working and said that if his mom hadn't pushed, he probably would have tried to go straight to work out of high school. Throughout the application process, Sean seriously considered only state schools. Although he wasn't sure exactly how much his family would have to pay and borrow—Kathleen and her husband monitored those details more closely—"I knew generally to try and keep the cost down," Sean said. He enrolled at California State University, Northridge, in Los Angeles in the fall of 2009 and picked up shifts working retail and selling ads for the college newspaper to make extra money. He learned to live cheaply, buying Walmart mac and cheese and other microwavable foods to stay satiated (a fact that spurred his mom to squeeze her eyes closed and purse her lips when he shared it on a Zoom call), but Sean could sense that in the world outside his school, households were being forced to take similar steps, and not just as part of a college rite of passage.

Sean watched as coworkers from the sporting goods store he worked at in high school got laid off, and he saw several radio stations fold even as he was taking classes in radio production. He worried about which career to pursue. Sean had been considering real estate and had even studied for the real estate licensing exam in high school, but he cast it aside as the industry was bringing down the whole economy. Like the roughly 40% of college students who don't finish in six years, Sean took a meandering path to graduating.[77] He underestimated the challenges of living without his support network close by, and after a particularly lonely experience in 2012 watching the San Francisco Giants win the World Series by himself, he transferred to San Francisco State.

While he was still in school, Sean was offered a job in agriculture technology sales, and he took it. He was ready to start enjoying

San Francisco as a twentysomething, and balancing work with school—he called the process of commuting to campus and parking the "silent schedule killer"—was making that difficult. It was ultimately the combination of tiring of playing video games during the early months of the COVID-19 pandemic and the loss of a retail business opportunity that pushed him to finish. By then it had been seven years since Sean had left college the first time, and he'd had to navigate the bureaucracy of things like getting credit for courses he had taken that weren't even in the current course catalog.

Throughout this time, Sean wasn't worried about repaying his student loans—because his mother worried and paid for him. Whereas White cobbled together student debt, work, and whichever other resources she could find to pay for college and living expenses, she wanted to provide her children with more of a cushion. Because White set the expectation that her children should go to college without giving them much say in the matter, she felt like it was her responsibility to finance their degrees. "Everyone in my family saw how hard it was for my mom. She didn't have much help from my grandparents," Sean said. "She promised herself that she wouldn't make her kids go through the same thing. We're definitely grateful for that."

A Loan Program That Creates Options but Feels "Crappy"

All three of White's children chose to attend public colleges in California, which, while affordable compared to many college options, were at times roughly five times as expensive as when White was going to school.[78] During college and after, her children also coped with living expenses, like housing, that were much higher than during her own young adulthood. Throughout her whole career White worked extra hours and in the summer to help cover the cost of raising three children in San Francisco, including saving up for their college. But it still wasn't enough. In addition to the student debt that White's children took on and her commitment to help them pay, she borrowed in her own name through the PLUS loan program, which allows parents to take out government loans to pay for schooling for their children. Although White appreciated having options to pay for her kids' tuition other than out of pocket—which she couldn't afford to do—she felt "crappy" when it was time to take on the debt.

White estimates that she spent fewer than ten years free of student loans during the time between when she paid her own loans off and the time she took on debt to pay for her kids' college. And the second time around, the loans proved much less manageable. For one, White had to borrow a lot more—roughly $100,000—because college costs had increased so much since she went to school. In addition, in the intervening years the student loan system had become increasingly unwieldy, making the experience of paying the loans back more complicated. Like millions of other people, White ended up on the hook for tens of thousands of dollars through a loan product that was far more complex than the idea that Lyndon Johnson espoused in the 1960s—that the government would give those who couldn't afford college a boost in paying for it. Her experience also illustrates how a combination of federal policies, state decisions to cut funding for higher education, and the rising cost of living in general pushes families toward student debt that can be a strain. That's even the case when they're looking at colleges that are among the cheapest ones.

For years, advocates and researchers have worried that the PLUS loans White used can trap parents with unsustainable debt loads for decades. Congress created an avenue for parent borrowing in 1980, conceiving of the program as a valve to alleviate the cash crunch that contributing to college costs might create for some families.[79] Lawmakers also hoped that the program might relieve some pressure from students to borrow.[80] In its original form, Congress capped parents' PLUS loans, which had an interest rate of 7%—well below the high interest rates of that inflationary period.[81] But a little more than a decade later, lawmakers removed the cap on the loans, allowing parents to borrow up to the cost of attendance as long as they didn't have an adverse credit history—or essentially no major negative credit events, like a default, bankruptcy, or a relatively large delinquent loan balance.[82]

The decision came amid a push from the third parties involved in the student loan program and colleges to give middle-income families more room to borrow to pay for school. Throughout hearings surrounding the 1992 reauthorization of the Higher Education Act when the cap was lifted, witnesses bemoaned the challenges these families faced paying for college.

Lawrence Hough, the chief executive officer of Sallie Mae at the time, told lawmakers, "In today's college market, the aggregate $20,000 available under PLUS does not buy a 4-year college education at most schools."[83] Carl Donovan, the president of the National Council of Higher Education Loan Programs, a trade group for servicers, lenders, and guaranty agencies, said, "College costs are increasing annually, and middle-income families are finding it exceptionally difficult to finance college expenses."[84] And indeed, Congress ultimately took these organizations up on their suggestion to create an unsubsidized loan program for students with no income limits.[85]

Some of these loan groups floated increasing the limits on parents' PLUS loans, but it was college representatives who suggested removing them entirely.[86] Patricia Smith, the director of legislative analysis for the American Council on Education, a higher education lobby, told lawmakers that her organization was particularly supportive of the PLUS program in part because it allows parents to borrow "and thereby minimizes student debt."[87] She framed her recommendation that parents be allowed to borrow up to a school's cost of attendance minus other financial aid as a measure that would "reduce the need for students to borrow." Thomas Butts, then the associate vice president for government relations at the University of Michigan, speaking on behalf of the National Association of State and Land Grant Colleges, also advocated removing the limit on how much parents could borrow, saying it would "significantly" improve the PLUS program's ability to serve as a loan for middle-income students.[88]

For Butts and other advocates, allowing parents to borrow up to the cost of attendance less all other student financial aid fit in with what they believed were the philosophical underpinnings of the student loan program. The government subsidizes low-income students with grants. It was expected that middle-income students pay for college through some combination of aid from their school, earnings from a summer job or other work, and a parental contribution. The PLUS program was meant to provide cash flow to parents to meet their obligation, Butts said. "That works in theory if a student gets the parent contribution and the student contribution and enough aid to meet the whole cost," he told me. "What happened historically is that aid packages did not meet the whole cost."[89]

As part of the financial aid application process, the government calculates how much a family should be expected to put toward college costs on the basis of their income and some of their assets. Theoretically, colleges should be offering financial aid packages that meet a student's total cost of attendance less that expected family contribution, according to Butts. In reality, schools' financial aid packages often still leave a gap.[90] That's created a situation in which schools are sending students financial aid offers that indicate that if they want to attend the school, they'll have to find some avenue for contributing more than they can afford, perhaps including through PLUS loans.

"I don't recall much discussion about the problem of parents being essentially forced to take out PLUS loans," Butts said.[91] "That appeared to happen, and it was an unintended consequence of making that policy change." At the time, lifting the PLUS cap made sense, because otherwise many middle-income families would need to turn to riskier loan products to finance the cost of a student's education, Butts said.

Butts, who spent some of his career working at the Department of Education, said there are ways the government could have put constraints on how much colleges charge, by, for example, asking schools to tie their cost of attendance to what they've charged in the past instead of projecting it going forward.

"That, as you probably know, has never happened," he told me.

At the time Butts made the recommendation to lift the cap on parents' PLUS loans on behalf of the associations, he was more focused on pushing through another effort he believed would save students and the government a significant amount of money. For decades, Butts lobbied Congress to move toward a direct-lending program or one in which the government made student loans to students without private lenders, state guaranty agencies, and other intermediaries getting their cut.

The recommendation to lift the PLUS cap was a couple of paragraphs in a roughly thirteen-page testimony outlining a direct-lending program. In fact, it came as an answer to a question he posed about the role that those intermediaries could still have in the student loan program in a direct-lending system. The relatively low cost of the PLUS program and "the more natural relationship between credit worthy parents and lenders makes policy sense" for lenders and guaranty agencies to be involved, he wrote at the time.[92]

During the two-decade fight to implement direct lending, one common source of pushback was that the policy change would result in job losses at lenders, guaranty agencies, and other third parties, Butts said. These entities were often politically powerful, in some cases because they had direct ties to state government.[93] "Rather than advocate for making the whole thing direct lending, including PLUS, the focus would be on students," Butts said. "Offering to the loan industry the PLUS program, which would seem to be a more natural kind of thing for them, was a way to help save jobs and so forth."[94] This was an early proposal, and ultimately the PLUS program lived on as part of direct lending.

When Butts and others made the recommendation to lift the PLUS loan cap, the program "was meant for middle-income students" whose families could manage the loan burden, he said. Still, the loans didn't require a typical credit check, which would have allowed lenders to get a sense of whether a household's income was enough to afford the payments.

The combination of essentially unlimited loans for parents and a minimal credit check created a situation in which many low-income parents became saddled with federal student debt they couldn't afford. The PLUS program and certain other student loan initiatives "were never intended to be programs for low-income students," Butts said. "Folks didn't keep up the contract between who benefits most from the education, society or the student. It's a partnership, if you will, because both parties are benefiting. I think we're losing sight of that."

Indeed, the PLUS program in its current form illustrates the risk that families are being asked to assume for students to gain access to a college degree. With nearly 4 million households owing a total of $104 billion in parent PLUS loans, they make up a small share—about 6%—of the overall student loan portfolio.[95] But the data surrounding the debt paints a troubling picture.

According to a 2022 report from the Century Foundation think tank, more than half of households using parent PLUS loans also received a Pell Grant, a sign that they're low income.[96] And families have trouble paying the PLUS debt down. After ten years, more than 55% of the loan's initial balance still remains, and after twenty years, parents still owe 38% of the loan on average.[97]

Black households, who have less funding to draw on to pay for college as a result of decades of policies that have blocked them from wealth building, feel the impact of parent PLUS loans disproportionately. The share of Black parent PLUS borrowers who the government has determined can't afford to contribute anything to their children's college education increased from 15% in 2008 to 42% in 2018.[98] Put another way, about 33% of Black households using parent PLUS loans in 2012 were from households with families earning less than $30,000, according to an analysis from New America. For white families, that share is about 12%.[99]

Colleges have helped to fuel the challenges parents face in managing these loans. Roughly 15% of schools described the loans to households as "awards," according to a 2018 analysis of financial aid offers from the New America think tank and uAspire, a college-advising organization. That can mislead families into thinking that the loans are a form of grant aid or a more generously subsidized loan.[100] Some reporting has indicated that colleges that are relatively wealthy but not wealthy enough to offer generous financial aid packages, steer families toward the loans to finance expensive tuitions, even if they can't afford the debt.[101]

But a battle over the eligibility requirements for the loans during the early 2010s illustrates how in some cases, families' and schools' relationship to the debt is more nuanced. In 2011, the Obama administration briefly tightened the credit requirements for parent PLUS loans. One result: the number of families receiving the loans at historically Black colleges and universities, or HBCUs, dropped by 45% over the following two years. Some HBCU leaders worried that by making it more difficult for families to borrow under the PLUS program, students would be forced to drop out.[102] Three HBCUs closed.[103]

In other words, without parents' PLUS funding, students from low-income families struggled to afford to attend colleges that lacked the funds to provide generous financial aid. In both cases, decades of policies that fueled the racial wealth gap were in part to blame for the reasons these families and schools were so reliant on the PLUS loans. The Obama administration ultimately reversed course on the credit standards.[104]

Critics of the PLUS program have argued that the loans should be capped once again, to prevent colleges from pushing debt on families that they can't afford to repay.[105] But as the history surrounding PLUS loans and HBCUs illustrates, without increasing grant aid, that could leave already-disadvantaged students struggling for funds to pay tuition at disadvantaged schools.

In addition, it will do little to help borrowers currently repaying PLUS loans. Right now, they're shut out of some of the biggest benefits of the student loan program, including most of the options that allow borrowers to repay their debt as a percentage of their income.

It's hard to say why lawmakers haven't done much to change the PLUS program so it's less onerous for low-income families. But one possibility? The program typically makes the government money, partly because parent borrowers don't have access to the generous repayment terms available to students.[106]

Regardless of the reason, as college costs have increased—the price of a four-year public college more than doubled between when Congress eliminated the cap on PLUS loans and the 2023–2024 academic year—these loans have become more of a burden.[107] They're also fueling growth in student debt among older borrowers. In 2020, Americans older than fifty held 22% of the nation's outstanding student loans, some of which was the result of debt they took on as parents for their children's education.[108]

In part because the government treats Parent PLUS loans differently, they were particularly challenging for White to repay. Most federal student loans offer myriad options for repayment to make them more manageable, but parents borrowing through the federal government have one option to repay the debt as a percentage of their income, and it's the least generous of these income-driven repayment plans. The Biden administration also initially left parent borrowers like White out of one of its signature student loan policy initiatives—making a loan forgiveness program for public servants easier to access. In addition, parent borrowers won't be able to access a repayment program that the Biden administration has touted as transformative without using a confusing workaround.[109]

White worked for the state for decades as a teacher and administrator in the California Community College system. So when she heard about Public Service Loan Forgiveness, an initiative launched in 2007 that wipes away the remaining federal student loan debt of public servants who have made payments on their loans for at least ten years, White assumed she'd qualify. But she applied twice and was rejected. White wasn't alone. In the first year that borrowers were eligible for debt relief under the program, roughly 99% of applicants were denied.[110] Often these rejected applicants met the spirit of the program—they, like White, had worked in public service for at least ten years and made payments on their federal student loans during that time—but they were rejected on a technicality. They didn't have the right type of federal loan or were making payments on the wrong type of payment program. In 2021, the Biden administration announced a temporary expansion of the program to help these borrowers qualify for relief, but it did not extend to parent PLUS borrowers.

"It's like, 'OK, we have great news here for some people,'" White said on learning of the program's expansion in 2022. "Not me."

The era of state budget constraints that followed Reagan's rhetoric and Proposition 13 in the 1970s had left White vulnerable in the late 2010s to the challenges of navigating an increasingly complex student loan system. Paying for college and teaching college students during this period also exposed her to the ways that college costs and student loans interact with other expenses students face during school and beyond.

As a community college teacher and administrator, White saw in her students echoes of her own struggle to balance parenting, work, and school, but a confluence of factors made their path even riskier to navigate. In some cases, students would come to her office to try to enroll but couldn't because they'd defaulted on federal student loans they'd borrowed to attend a for-profit college. When White was in school, for-profit colleges existed and made efforts to lure students, but they had become much more successful. In the 1990s and 2000s, they used internet and television advertising to recruit and enroll students. This caught the eye of many people who, during the Great Recession and the years following it, were suddenly out of work and looking to retool. It was much harder for her students to avoid them than it had been for her.

White also encountered students who didn't fall prey to unscrupulous colleges but whose previous attempts to get a degree created an obstacle to their continuing schooling. High housing and childcare costs meant that some students attending or looking to attend White's school had to take on two or three jobs just to afford basic needs. Indeed, across the country, 45% of nearly eighty-six thousand college students surveyed before the COVID-19 pandemic by the Hope Center for Student Basic Needs at Temple University said they had struggled to get regular access to food in the previous thirty days; more than 50% said they were housing insecure, and 17% reported having been homeless in the previous year.[111]

Those challenges, in addition to the cost of college itself, can make it difficult for students to persist. And when they leave a school without paying the bill, colleges will often block them from reenrolling before they pay up or will withhold their transcript, an obstacle to students' ability to transfer. These students came into White's office too, trying to sign up for courses, and she'd have to tell them they couldn't. "The only word I can think of is *heartbreaking*," she said.

Because White's children had her financial backing and knowledge of the college process, they didn't have to worry about an emergency derailing their college career or being lured into taking on debt for a worthless degree. Still, rising costs—of college and everything else—meant that they and White questioned the economic value of the education they received. "It's not like you see people suddenly with degrees in their hands who can afford to live here," White said of San Francisco, where in May 2024 the median rent was $3,199 a month, and the typical home was valued at nearly $1.3 million.[112]

White looks at the difference between what it cost her to attend college and what her students and children are expected to pay. She knows that the added cost hasn't translated into increased value. "What was the difference between what I got and what they're getting?" she asked.

In fact, almost immediately after finishing college, her son Sean decided that his degree didn't give him the value he needed, so he enrolled in graduate school. "I saw how competitive it was in the job market," Sean said. "A BA doesn't really cut it." He chose an online master's degree in strategic brand communications at the

University of Illinois at Urbana-Champaign. After he'd completed a free certificate program offered by the school through Coursera, an online platform that partners with universities to offer courses and degrees, the university offered him the opportunity to apply to one of its degree programs. "It worked pretty good from their marketing perspective," he said.

And indeed, part of the aim of Coursera's free offerings was to lure students into paying for degrees. Degree programs like the ones offered by University of Illinois in partnership with Coursera have become increasingly common over the past decade. In these deals, colleges often give the company a portion of the revenue that each enrolled student brings in exchange for marketing and technological expertise.[113] Coursera says that its fees tend to be among the lowest in the market for degrees of this kind and that colleges retain a relatively large share of the revenue for their programs. Still, public universities' use of these deals has become particularly controversial because they represent these schools' privatization of a portion of the educational experience, and because they require the schools, which may already be strapped due to state funding environments, to give up a portion of tuition revenue.[114] But that same lack of resources from the state also puts pressure on these schools to look for revenue elsewhere, including from students across the country and around the world, whom they can more easily access with the help of online program managers.[115]

Unprompted, Sean picked up on his program's corporate-style marketing techniques. "I noticed how they pushed the brand like a company. It worked on me, I guess," he said. When we first spoke, he was a few months away from graduating and still had an outstanding balance for his final semester. Kathleen reminded him he would need to pay it to graduate—an occasion the family was planning to fly to Chicago to celebrate so Sean could toast with his classmates in person. About a month later, Sean had decided to take on a loan to complete the degree. "It's bittersweet," he said. "I just couldn't swing tuition." Ultimately, Sean graduated with about $28,000 in student debt. He did land a job at a start-up, but he's not sure his degrees helped him much with that. He sent out hundreds of applications before finally getting hired.

When Kathleen's generational peers complain on Facebook or in person about mass student debt relief, she knows they likely don't have the experience she's so familiar with through her children, her students, and her own student loan journey. Like millions, in part because of state funding cuts, her family had to finance college through loans that policymakers, responding to families' and schools' concerns, made increasingly complicated. And like so many across the country, they worked to pay them back in an uncertain job market and amid high housing and childcare costs. "Everyone who is saying they paid theirs," White said, "it's not the same—the costs are not the same. If they're old enough to be saying that, it's not the same."

5. Credentialization

The Ever-Decreasing Value of a College Degree

When reports leaked that President Joe Biden planned to cancel student debt en masse, the reaction from some Democratic economists was swift—and negative. Larry Summers, who served as the director of the White House National Economic Council, when Biden was vice president, called the proposed policy "unreasonably generous" and worried it would contribute to the already-high inflationary environment.[1] Jason Furman, another top economic adviser in the Obama White House, warned, "Student loan relief is not free. It would be paid for. Part of it would be paid for by the 87% of Americans who do not benefit but lose out from inflation."[2]

Once the policy became official—Biden indeed announced he planned to discharge $10,000 in debt for borrowers earning $125,000 per year or less, and an extra $10,000 for those who had received a Pell Grant in college—the criticism continued, with Furman charging that the plan was "reckless" and would pour gasoline on "the inflationary fire that is already burning."[3] That was despite indications from other economists—and Goldman Sachs—that the forgiveness would have a minimal impact on inflation, particularly because the administration planned to combine it with the resumption of student loan payments after two years of a pandemic pause.[4]

The intensity of some economists' obsession with the idea that student debt relief would supercharge inflation was "bizarre," noted Nobel Prize–winning economist Paul Krugman. "So bizarre that I can't help suspecting that in many cases they're coming from people who would rather take a cheap shot than lay out their real reasons for opposing this program."[5]

But if you take a step back to realize what mass student debt relief represents to the economics profession, it suddenly seems less bizarre for people like Summers and Furman to be so concerned. Instead, to use a word often employed by economists, it's *rational* for them to react strongly to the proposal. By forgiving some student debt, the president of the United States essentially acknowledged that a fundamental economic model did not work as predicted—that it no longer made sense to continue to sink resources into something that wasn't working.

America's student loan system is premised in large part on human capital theory, or the idea that people can increase their productivity—and therefore earnings—by investing in their education and skills. If it were true under the current system, then borrowers' investments in themselves would largely pay off. In his speech announcing the debt relief, Biden noted that hadn't been the case for decades. He called education "a ticket to a better life" that has "become too expensive for many Americans." "An entire generation is now saddled with unsustainable debt in exchange for an attempt, at least, at a college degree," he said. "The burden is so heavy that even if you graduate, you may not have access to the middle-class life that the college degree once provided."[6]

By canceling some student debt, Biden signaled that the theory of a payoff from investing in oneself through higher education was in need of some updating. That was an affront to those who had bought into and promoted it. As Tressie McMillan Cottom, a sociologist whose research and writing exposed the way the higher education system, and particularly for-profit colleges, haven't worked to meet Americans' needs for improving their economic prospects, put it: "If you forgive some student debt, you admit that a key assumption of economic policy failed. These are priests arguing for their god."[7]

That a college degree was no longer an automatic ticket to a middle-class life, as Biden noted, was partly related to state disinvestment that pushed college costs up and partly due to changes to the loan program that made it difficult for students to pay off their debt. But it was also a result of shifting demands from employers, which used their power to insist on certain credentials from workers, in some cases without compensating employees for their boost in education.

Kendra Brooks didn't need the president to tell her that the promise of higher education wasn't working out exactly as planned. In fact, by the time Biden, flanked by Secretary of Education Miguel Cardona, took to a White House podium to announce his administration's student-debt forgiveness plan, Brooks had been trying to tell him for more than a year that the nation's student finance system wasn't working.

Brooks, a member of the Philadelphia City Council, authored a city resolution calling on Biden to cancel all student debt in the first hundred days of his presidency, describing it as "only one step toward the establishment of an equitable, accessible higher education system."[8] The resolution was largely symbolic, essentially a way to show the president that student debt relief was a priority for Philadelphia's residents.

Part of what motivated Brooks to call for mass student debt relief was the stories she heard from her constituents—at rallies, other events, and even out with friends on vacation. They complained to her about how their debt was keeping them from buying a home or starting a family. But her advocacy also stemmed from personal experience. Several times in her life, Brooks, fifty years old when we spoke, did exactly what human capital theory would suggest she do: invest both time and money in herself to improve the financial circumstances for her and her children. And it never quite paid off.

"The Only Option I Could Think Of"

When growing up in North Philadelphia, Brooks planned on going to college. But when it came time to attend, she didn't have the money to do so. But Brooks was so committed to the idea that she joined the military, knowing it would be the only way she could afford school.

"I was a pretty bright young woman but also very rambunctious," she said.

But when Brooks reported to her entry physical, she found out she was pregnant. In order to ship off, she would have had to give her mother custody of her daughter. So instead of enlisting, she decided to stay home with her parents and young child. A year later, when her daughter was a year old, Brooks was wondering what to do next, as she wasn't making much money as a certified nursing assistant— even working overtime. "The only option I could think of was to go to college," Brooks said.

Brooks enrolled at the Community College of Philadelphia in 1991 and balanced her classes with working full-time as a certified nursing assistant. Sometimes she would go to her job at a nursing home during the day—where she worked with bed-bound residents, feeding them, changing their diapers, and turning them every couple of hours so they'd have a good range of motion—and then travel to class at night. During other periods at CCP, Brooks would set up her work schedule so she could be off on Tuesdays and Thursdays to attend a full day of school.

And of course her daughter and her partner's three children required care. If Brooks's daughter had a day off school, she'd sometimes have to take her to class. There was a period when the juggling got so stressful that Brooks's partner convinced her to stop working so she could focus on her studies. "We had to make some tough decisions going down to one paycheck in order for me to hurry up and finish school," Brooks remembered.

Another tough choice: toward the end of her time at CCP, Brooks's classes got more technical—she was studying nursing—and between the time required to be successful in those courses and all her other responsibilities, she was "completely overwhelmed," Brooks said. To take some of the pressure off, Brooks's daughter went to live with her mom in Florida for about a year. Overall, it took Brooks seven years to complete her associate's degree.

Throughout that period there was one overarching thought that pushed her to get beyond the stress and disruption to her life created by her schooling: "I just wanted to make sure I was able to provide a better life for my daughter," Brooks said. She loved working with her nursing home clients, which was the job she had before she started college and that she continued to work while in school, but "it wasn't paying the bills." Brooks earned $4.80 an hour doing that work, or about $11.18 in 2024 dollars.

Despite all of the effort she put into completing her associate's degree, Brooks knew it wouldn't be enough for her to land the kind of decent-paying job she'd hoped for, so she enrolled at Temple University to earn a bachelor's degree. By then Brooks had decided she couldn't stomach the bandages and wound care often required of a nurse—and the time commitment and cost the career path would mean for her family. Brooks thought about pursuing another health profession, physical therapy, but opted against it because it would require her to earn a master's degree or doctorate to start practicing. "I needed to hurry up and finish school and begin to make money," she said.

Instead, she chose to study recreational therapy, for which a bachelor's degree would be enough for her to work right away— and her plan worked. When Brooks graduated, she began working at two jobs in her field that required the degree, but the roughly

$31,000, she was earning wasn't enough to make it affordable for her to repay several thousands of dollars in debt. Eventually, after she and her partner separated and her expenses increased, managing her student debt became so challenging that Brooks defaulted on her loans and experienced some of the harshest consequences of the system—the government garnished her paycheck and seized her income tax refund for years to repay the loan.

After Brooks got back on surer footing, she decided it was time to return to school. At the time, she was working in a more administrative role as director of camping and recreation at a nonprofit, and she felt she needed to earn another degree so she could advance her career and make more money. "Frankly, as a young Black woman trying to climb a corporate ladder or a nonprofit ladder, you have to be the best and the brightest—no one was giving me a break or any real opportunities," Brooks said. "If I wanted a raise, I had to prove I needed the raise."

Brooks felt the credential could help her do that, and the data backed her up. With labor market discrimination, Black women on average need advanced degrees to get close to parity with their white and male peers—although a higher credential still isn't typically enough for them to reach it. In 2023, Black women with advanced degrees were paid $41.89 an hour, according to the Economic Policy Institute, a worker-focused think tank, more than $10 less than white men with a bachelor's degree.[9]

So Brooks found a local program where she could take courses to complete her MBA at night and on weekends, and she borrowed to attend.

Access to Education Tied Up with Other Interests

The path Brooks followed—get more education to improve your circumstances and those of your children—is so ingrained in American society that it's difficult to question. The student loan system is in part premised on the idea that, by increasing access to education, the loans can create opportunities for more Americans to have a better life. But throughout American history, policies aimed at increasing access to education haven't always been as neutral as we think of them. Instead, the push toward these policies by businesses, educational institutions, and advocacy organizations has often been tied up with those organizations' own interests.

In his book *The Credential Society: A Historical Sociology of Stratification and Education*, the sociologist Randall Collins argues that the expansion of the American educational system and the proliferation of educational credentials required for jobs reveal the ways that increasing access to education has always been about more than providing students with the knowledge and skills to participate in democracy or compete in the labor market. For example, he notes that the driving force behind the expansion of mandatory elementary education during the nineteenth century was a fear among the country's largely Anglo-Protestant elite that an influx in immigration from Eastern Europe would alter the character of the nation. To counter that potential influence, Protestant reformers urged that students be required to attend elementary schools, which would become sites of indoctrination in certain values.[10] Laws mandating that students attend elementary school spread in the states where immigrants were arriving in the largest numbers, according to Collins.[11]

Supporters' arguments for expanding public secondary schools were based on similar ideas, Collins argues. Although they pointed to the benefits of public high schools to the industrializing economy, "on occasion," Collins writes, advocates largely referred to "good citizenship, political stability and moral qualities," as they pushed to increase the number of public high schools.[12]

Business interests also helped to drive the expansion of public high schools in the early twentieth century, Cristina Viviana Groeger argues in *The Education Trap: Schools and the Remaking of Inequality in Boston*. With businesses increasingly seeking employees to do paperwork and other administrative tasks, private and public schools raced to provide training for white-collar workers, fueling an expansion in public high schools.[13] The new pool of skilled white-collar workers allowed businesses to rely less on unions to provide trained employees, thereby increasing management's control over their workers.[14]

The expansion of public and mandatory elementary and secondary education certainly provided benefits for students. Those included making it much more difficult for families to send their children to work and, in the case of public high schools, providing immigrants and women with the training—in both work and a certain set of social norms—that allowed them to increase their economic mobility.[15] But as Collins's and Groeger's research illustrates, expanding access to education wasn't solely—or in many cases, even primarily—about providing students with opportunities. Instead, it served as a way to preserve the power and control of those who already had it, whether the Protestant social elite or management in the business world. In some ways, the expansion of higher education served a similar purpose.

Throughout the early nineteenth century, colleges popped up across the country, creating an oversupply. By the 1850s, many schools were contending with financial crises, Collins writes.[16] In an effort to lure students to cope with the financial difficulties of college, the schools began to transform their curriculum and social environment. Schools developed many of the markers of today's college experience in the popular imagination, such as fraternities and football games.[17] This dynamic helped to turn colleges into a place that cemented economic status, not one that necessarily provided for economic mobility. "The collegiate culture took the function of bringing together the children of the upper middle class, forming them into groups of friends bound together by sentiments of college activities and eventually intermarrying," Collins writes.[18]

Throughout the late nineteenth and early twentieth centuries, colleges sold the idea that they were places that minted success in order to attract students who were already likely to be successful with or without the colleges' help. This created a "self-fulfilling prophecy," according to Collins.[19] "Having attracted most of the upper-middle and upper classes, and then the middle class and the most ambitious and intelligent members of the lower class, they could point out that the elite positions in American society were increasingly filled by college graduates," he writes.[20]

Groeger highlights some of the specific tactics that colleges, in conjunction with employers, used to cement the idea that the pathway to professional success ran through certain schools. On the front end, elite college officials would pick and choose who deserved to be in their incoming classes. In 1860, roughly half of Harvard's students came from families whose estates would be worth about $3.5 million in 2020 dollars, according to Groeger.[21] Later, in 1900, elite university leaders formalized their definitions of merit through organizations like the College Entrance Examination Board, now known as the College Board, founded in part by then presidents of Columbia and Harvard to standardize admissions requirements. They used other tactics to zero in on a certain type of student. For example, in the late nineteenth century, Harvard Law School began to screen out applicants who graduated from Catholic colleges, Groeger writes.[22] On the back end, alumni and officials of these schools would work with companies to create certain professional standards, Groeger notes.[23]

This dynamic is still in place today at many of the nation's most elite colleges. Because the schools are so selective, they rarely take a chance on a student who would need a quality education to acquire the skills and knowledge to land a decent job. Instead, it's what students bring with them to the college—networks and an understanding of professional social norms in the case of wealthier students, intelligence and hard work in the case of the relatively small number of middle-class and poor students at these schools—that almost guarantee their success. In this way, elite colleges essentially function as a finishing school for many students.[24]

The professionalization of business provides one of the starkest examples of the way colleges and elite professionals worked together to cement a degree as a tool to gatekeep the access to suc-cess of women, low-income people, and people of color. During the first forty years of the twentieth century, corporate America trans-formed from a place where less than one-fifth of leaders had a col-lege degree to one where more than half did.[25]

Universities and employers worked together in the early twen-tieth century to ensure that corporate employees and leaders fit a specific profile, one that had more to do with certain social qualifiers than skills. Groeger cites correspondence between college officials and Procter & Gamble noting that the consumer goods giant sought a sales employee who was the "'dominant type' with an 'impressive appearance.'"[26] In describing students to potential employers, col-leges would use words like "chap" to signal that a future graduate was from a lower class.[27]

Employers scanned résumés for membership in a fraternity or social club—a sign that students were coming to their company with a Protestant and likely wealthy pedigree.[28] By the early twentieth century, "the path from elite boarding school, to membership in Harvard's final clubs, to jobs in finance, was a well-worn channel," Groeger writes.[29]

The partnership between colleges and employers to turn busi-ness into a field that required at least a bachelor's degree and in some cases a master's to advance was in part a response to the influx of women into white-collar work and the programs that trained them in public high schools, proprietary schools, and elsewhere, accord-ing to Groeger.[30]

Before the late nineteenth century, when men largely served as secretaries, the position was one that worked almost like an appren-ticeship, with the ability to ultimately move into the boss's job. As women began to take over the position, it turned into an entirely separate professional sphere.[31] College degrees, which were largely available only to white men, helped in that effort, allowing their re-cipients to chart a career path unavailable to the women performing administrative tasks.[32]

During the nineteenth and twentieth centuries, more Americans got access to education. At the same time, a growing number of employers and professions started to require it. The result was a situation in which education became synonymous with success. Indeed, in some cases—for example, women and second-generation immigrants during the late nineteenth century—it was transformative, providing access to opportunities that historically weren't available. Still, educational institutions in cahoots with alumni, professional organizations, and employers also became sites where financial success wasn't necessarily earned but was minted. As Groeger puts it, "At the same time that education became and was increasingly lauded as a means of achieving the American dream, schools became a new foundation for the reproduction of social inequality."[33]

Pockets of American society, notably, the most prestigious corners of corporate America, often still function this way. Business is one of the majors for which the difference in earnings between graduates of different schools is the largest, in part because large companies focus their largest recruiting efforts on elite colleges.[34] In her book *Pedigree: How Elite Students Get Elite Jobs*, Lauren Rivera chronicles economically privileged students' path from selective higher education institution to entry-level role at an elite consulting firm, bank, or law firm. What she found is that those doing the hiring at these high-status employers understand merit in part based on "cultural beliefs that are entrenched in applicants' and employers' own upbringings and biographies," and not necessarily on technical skills.[35] These employers "set the bounds of competition" by limiting recruiting efforts to specific schools where wealthier students are more likely to end up and more likely to succeed.[36]

The relationship between elite universities and companies that pay some of the highest salaries is one I witnessed firsthand. As an MBA student at Columbia Business School, I watched as my classmates spent hours preparing for and attending recruiting events hosted by top banks, consulting firms, and tech companies while often investing much less energy into their coursework. And why would they? Columbia's MBA program, like many elite MBA programs, operates with a policy called grade nondisclosure, which means potential employers aren't supposed to ask about students' grade point averages as part of the recruitment process.

Students who were interested in learning the fundamentals of accounting, corporate finance, or economics could do so through their classes, often taught by leading experts who were devoted to their work and to teaching. But success in these courses and mastery of their concepts weren't necessary to land a prestigious job. Instead, Columbia functioned as essentially a screen for top companies. The hard part was getting in (perhaps made easier if you were an heir to a successful family business or came from a top college that restricted access to low-income students). Once there, you were virtually guaranteed to land a top corporate job (maybe not your first choice but still well paid) regardless of how well you had understood or mastered the material that the degree was theoretically meant to certify.

A Changing Economy

The relationship between elite business schools and elite employers is perhaps one of the most obvious examples of the way an employer's request for a credential is less about skills required for a job and more about the signal the degree sends. With other credentials, the question of whether the degree confers skills an employer needs or simply sends a message is less clear. For example, a bachelor's degree in English may provide a graduate with few of the direct skills needed for an entry-level marketing job, but it does indicate to potential employers that the graduate is likely able to write and think critically at a certain level.

Changes in the economy since the 1980s, including increased reliance on technology and globalization, have changed workplaces so that bachelor's-level skills are required for many of what Anthony P. Carnevale, the founder of Georgetown University's Center on

Education and the Workforce, calls "good jobs," or those that are in the upper third of the wage distribution and typically offer benefits.[37] Part of what accelerated this trend, according to Carnevale, was the Federal Reserve's decision under Paul Volcker in the late 1970s and early 1980s to drastically increase interest rates in an effort to slow inflation. When inflation tamped down, companies accelerated their investments in technology and helped to fuel a new technology-based economy, he said.

Although for decades employers have required workers to have degrees to get the good jobs, the jobs don't necessarily pay them enough to cover the educational investment required. Since the early 1980s, "there's been a shift in economic power" between employers and employees, Carnevale told me, and "employees have been the losers."[38] Unionization—one of the key ways that employees, regardless of their credentials, can push their employers for higher pay—declined.[39] Workers' "share of productivity and growth has been declining since the 1980s, [and] the bosses are making money hand over fist," he said.

The shift in power, as Carnevale described it, reached new heights during the Great Recession and shortly thereafter, which contributed in part to the rapid uptick in student debt. A body of research indicates that slackness in the labor market resulting from the Great Recession pushed employers toward increasing credential requirements, even as the skills required to perform the jobs they were hiring for didn't fundamentally change. A study of online job-posting data by researchers at Northeastern University, Harvard University, and the Federal Reserve Bank of Boston found that the uptick in the number of people looking for work in the wake of the Great Recession accounts for roughly 25% of the increase in skills demanded by employers between 2007 and 2010.[40]

The research project also highlighted other evidence indicating that, in the wake of the recession, a larger share of newly hired workers—even for low- and intermediate-skilled jobs—had college degrees than before the recession.[41] Despite requiring candidates to have higher degrees than in the past, these jobs didn't necessarily pay more. That meant that workers who invested in their degrees had—and in many cases continue to have—trouble repaying their loans. Every percentage-point increase in the local unemployment rate between 2007 and 2009 corresponded to a $370 increase in borrowers' outstanding student debt in 2019. As such, the increase in the average local jobless rate between 2007 and 2009 of 3.8 percentage points translated to an uptick in student loan balances of $1,400, other researchers found.[42]

The findings suggest that the recession-induced increase in student loans has to do with workers' need for credentials to get a foothold in the labor market—but at lower pay. What's more, the recession pushed workers to reenroll in higher education at the same time that states were pulling back funding from public colleges, pushing up the price of higher education and the level of student debt.[43] An earlier version of the research found that other types of debt, including credit cards and auto loans, behaved differently than student loans during the recession—they all dropped. This added fuel to the notion that the increase in student loan balances had to do with workers' need to earn more degrees.[44]

In this way, the Great Recession exposed the weakness in human capital theory, the philosophy underpinning the student loan program and the nation's belief in the power of education. The idea that an educational investment in oneself is worthwhile because it increases earning potential and payoff was thwarted by employers' capitalizing on a slack labor market to scoop up educated workers without having to pay them more.

Policy Changes Plus Students' Hunger Allow Schools to Capitalize

A significant body of research indicates that employers took advantage of students' and workers' belief in the notion that a degree is a worthy investment that confers higher pay. But there's evidence that schools have also capitalized on students' hunger to get a leg up. Perhaps nowhere is that clearer than in the market for graduate education, and in particular, master's degrees. Over the past several years, colleges have expanded the number of master's degrees they offer. Between 1995 and 2017, the number of fields granting at least a hundred master's degrees per year grew from 289 to 514, according to a 2018 report from the Urban Institute.[45] By the 2015–2016 academic year, colleges were awarding about two master's degrees for every five bachelor's degrees they gave out.[46] Between 2000 and 2022, the share of adults between the ages of twenty-five and fifty-four with a master's degree grew from 6% to 12%. That dynamic has been the major driver in the growth of graduate degree attainment overall, according to the Department of Education; the share of adults in that age group with a graduate degree has doubled since 2000, the department found.[47]

This growth in graduate degrees has been accompanied by an increase in graduate school debt, which has fueled the growth of student debt broadly. Between the 2010–2011 academic year and the 2017–2018 academic year, graduate school borrowing grew by over $2 billion, according to the Center for American Progress. During the same period, undergraduate borrowing dropped by nearly $15 billion.[48] During the 2021 to 2022 academic year, the Department of Education disbursed $39 billion in federal student loans to graduate students, or about 47% of the loans the department disbursed overall—the highest share of federal student loan disbursement going to graduate students ever. Still, students borrowing to attend graduate school accounted for 21% of borrowers overall.[49]

It's not just aggregate debt for graduate school that's increased; individual debt loads are higher too. Between 2000 and 2016, the amount borrowers who completed graduate school used to finance their education grew from $53,140 to $66,502 in 2020 dollars.[50]

Some of the growth in debt for graduate school is certainly tied to price increases at professional schools that offer the most expensive degrees, like dental and medical schools.[51] But there are limits to how much revenue such programs can generate for universities; they're costly to operate and can educate only a small number of students. What's more, although student debt has consequences for today's medical professionals—for example, they may choose more lucrative specialties or to practice in an area where they can earn more money—their earnings are generally enough to manage the debt.[52]

Master's degrees, in contrast, offer universities an attractive way to enroll large numbers of students. Their admissions standards are often opaque, meaning that schools can make them appear selective and desirable even while they aim to attract as many students and tuition dollars as possible.[53] And unlike professional degrees, master's degrees in subjects like international relations and communications have a much more tenuous tie to the labor market. That makes it more difficult for students to reap enough of an earnings benefit to comfortably service their debt. Even though the debt that students take on for graduate degrees has increased over the past two decades, the earnings premium for having a master's degree has held steady during the same period, suggesting that students aren't getting as much of a return on their investment in advanced training as they used to, according to the Department of Education.[54]

College leaders have acknowledged in the media that these programs generate money for their schools. They may likely continue to be an attractive source of funds as colleges work to cope with demographic trends that are fueling declines in undergraduate enrollment.[55] Julie Kornfeld, then Columbia's vice provost for academic programs, told the *Wall Street Journal* in 2021 that "master's degrees 'can and should be a revenue source' subsidizing other parts of the university."[56] In 2017, Helen Drinan, then the president of Simmons University in Boston, told the *Hechinger Report* that as she searched for ways to shore up the school's finances, master's degrees became an obvious option. "We said, 'This is where we're going to make more money,'" she told the outlet.[57]

The uptick in master's degrees and graduate school–related debt didn't occur in a vacuum from the labor market. Over the past few decades, jobs have increasingly required graduate-level education to get hired at all—for example, the number of STEM jobs for which workers need at least a master's degree grew by approximately 6% between 2004 and 2015, according to the Indiana Business Research Center—or at least require the degree in order to qualify for a certain salary.[58] That dynamic certainly fueled student demand for degrees. But a few decisions by policymakers made capitalizing on that demand particularly attractive for universities, and even likely fueled it.

The Free Lunch That Wasn't Free

In 2006, Congress lifted the cap on how much graduate students could borrow, suddenly allowing students pursuing master's, professional, and other degrees to take out loans up to the cost of attendance. At the time, the choice seemed rational, according to Jason Delisle, who was working on Capitol Hill as a staffer for a Republican lawmaker on the committee overseeing education in the House of Representatives.[59]

Lawmakers and policy wonks were concerned about how much students were relying on private loans, which often have higher interest rates and fewer protections, to finance their education.[60] During the 2005–2006 academic year, students borrowed the equivalent of nearly $26 billion (in 2022 dollars) in private loans to pay for undergraduate and graduate education, according to the College Board. That was up from $13.4 billion during the 2002–2003 academic year.[61]

In part to deal with that concern, lawmakers expanded the PLUS program to include graduate students. At the time, the program allowed only parents to borrow from the federal government up the cost of attendance.[62] These loans carried higher interest rates than those for undergraduates. What fueled the decision was, just like when lawmakers lifted the cap on the loans for parents, an interest in helping households avoid private student debt, combined with the idea that expanding loan capacity would actually save the government money.[63]

Republicans controlled Congress at the time, and they were looking for ways to save money as they prepared their budget bill. Lifting the cap on loans to graduate students looked like a "free lunch," Delisle told me. "You could get people to take out government loans" instead of using private debt, "and it didn't cost the government anything, and in fact it made the government money," he said.[64]

At the time, there wasn't much reason to be concerned that graduate students would struggle to pay back their debt and stick the government with the bill. For one, this was before the expansion and more widespread adoption of programs that allow borrowers to pay their debt as a percentage of their income and then ultimately have the remainder forgiven. But in addition, the narrative—and reality—surrounding higher education, and graduate school in particular, at the time was different, he said. "If you asked the average Republican congressional staffer what they thought about grad school" at that time, Delisle said, "it was great."[65]

And indeed, during the period lawmakers were considering the bill, the bulk of graduate degree programs were what Barmak Nassirian, who has worked in higher education for decades, including for many years at a public college trade association, called "recognizable."[66] They were offered by public colleges and private nonprofit universities with large research budgets and in fields like business, medicine and education, which have a long history of requiring graduate education, he said in an interview with me.[67] Given the high quality of the programs, at the time, only a small share of borrowers who attended graduate school appeared to be struggling to repay their loans. In 2000, the five-year default rate of graduate borrowers was 3%, and students who left graduate school in 2000 had paid down about 16% of their loan balance five years later.[68] That meant that it didn't look risky for students or the government to expand the financing available to graduate students.

"There really wasn't any debate about it whatsoever," Delisle said. Instead, he said, it was thrown last minute into a budget bill through the reconciliation process, which allows lawmakers to expedite budget-related legislation. In a world where the students who took on high debt loads to attend graduate school were going into professional programs like dentistry, extending credit to them that was limited only by how much schools charge didn't "look like some kind of terrible policy move," Delisle said.

"Today if you presented that policy as a brand-new policy" to Republicans, "they would say, 'Are you crazy?'" he commented.[69]

There's some evidence to suggest that the new loan availability pushed education prices up, depending on the program. For degrees where private loan funding was generally available, like medicine, law, and business, the introduction of graduate PLUS loans isn't correlated with an increase in prices, according to research from Robert Kelchen, a professor of higher education at the University of Tennessee.[70] Students who were using private loans for those programs turned to the federal program instead, Kelchen found.[71]

Other research on graduate borrowing more broadly indicates that expensive programs where students were already borrowing up to the limit on federal graduate loans increased their prices following the introduction of PLUS loans for graduate students. Students at these programs also generally borrowed more from the federal government after the change, according to a study by economists at Vanderbilt University, Columbia University, and Brigham Young University.[72]

These studies don't directly get at whether the increase in the amount graduate students can borrow pushed universities to create more graduate programs. But unlimited borrowing, combined with two other policy changes, likely helped incentivize colleges to offer more graduate degrees. At the same time there was little to ensure that the new credentials offered good outcomes for students.

In 2005, Congress repealed a rule that banned all federal funds to programs for which more than 50% of students or courses were online.[73] That meant institutions could offer large online degrees for which students could still receive federal financial aid. Graduate credentials were a particularly attractive option for this kind of program, Nassirian said, because it's easier to sell students on the idea that they can complete a master's degree in a short period of time online than to argue the same for a bachelor's degree.[74] In addition, the demographic often interested in graduate programs—working adults—appreciated the option to earn their degree in a way that fit in with their schedule, he said.[75] That enabled some of the worst actors to take advantage.

In the wake of both the expansion of financing for graduate degrees and the repeal of the limit on the ability of distance education programs to receive federal financial aid funds, the number of graduate degrees offered in the United States ballooned. By the 2020–2021 academic year, American institutions conferred over one million graduate degrees, a 19% increase from ten years earlier.[76] For-profit colleges' expansion into the market was particularly robust; between 1998 and 2018, the schools increased the number of students enrolled in their graduate programs eightfold.[77]

In many cases, these programs leave students with unsustainable debts. About a quarter of graduate programs at for-profit colleges leave students with debt burdens that are so high and earnings that are so low that the programs are considered unaffordable by the Department of Education.[78]

The for-profit college sector's push into the graduate degree space has resulted in unequal outcomes. In 2002, just 5% of graduate students were enrolled at for-profit colleges, and 56% were attending programs at public schools, according to the Department of Education. By 2014, the share of Black graduate students enrolled in for-profit colleges was 30%, up from 5% in 2001.[79]

Four years after graduating from college, Black student loan borrowers with a bachelor's degree had nearly $25,000 more in student debt than white borrowers with a bachelor's degree, according to a 2016 analysis by the researchers Judith Scott-Clayton and Jing Li. Roughly 45% of that gap is due to graduate school enrollment; Black borrowers with a bachelor's degree were more likely to enroll in graduate school. It is also likely partly driven by the disproportionate concentration of Black graduate students in the for-profit sector.[80]

In a particularly egregious example of this dynamic, a class-action lawsuit filed in 2022 alleged that Walden University, a for-profit college, lured Black and female students into pursuing doctorate degrees and essentially trapped them in a cycle of continuing to accrue debt by dragging out the process for actually completing their degrees.[81] As part of the suit, the attorneys representing the students from the National Student Legal Defense Network, a student loan borrower litigation and advocacy organization, and Relman Colfax, a civil rights law firm, alleged that the school engaged in reverse redlining by targeting Black students for a poor product. Walden agreed to pay $28.5 million to settle the suit but denied wrongdoing as part of the agreement.[82]

It's not just for-profit colleges that fueled the rise in graduate programs and graduate student debt. For years, nonprofit and public colleges have leveraged their brands to entice students into attending revenue-generating master's degrees.[83] Another policy choice helped to fuel that dynamic.

Typically, colleges are banned from paying admissions staffers on the basis of the number of students they enroll. But in 2011, the Department of Education made an exception to that rule for third parties that provide colleges with a bundle of services that includes recruiting, marketing, and technology support.[84] This loophole allowed colleges to pay third parties who recruit students on behalf of their university a share of student tuition revenue as long as the companies provide others services as well.

There's an entire industry—in 2021 worth at least $4 billion—that provides these kinds of services.[85] They're called online program managers, and they provide recruitment, marketing, technology support, and other services to colleges that offer online degrees and other programs. In exchange, the schools often fork over a share of tuition revenue that the programs generate. In 2010, Chip Paucek, then the chief operating officer at 2U, the most recognizable company in the space, lobbied the Department of Education to create the incentive compensation loophole that allows universities to pay these companies a percentage of tuition revenue.[86]

"I personally had a lot to do with that," Paucek said of the change in rules in a 2019 *HuffPost* article when he was CEO of the company.[87]

In the years since, the number of colleges working with online program managers and the number of programs offered has ballooned. In 2010, there were at least twenty deals set up that year between colleges and online program managers, according to the Government Accountability Office. By 2020, there were at least 165. During the same period, the number of new online programs with support from an online program manager grew from about 25 to at least 385. As of July 2021, at least 550 colleges worked with an online program manager to offer at least 2,900 certificate and degree programs. The bulk of the schools—about 90%—with these deals are nonprofit and public colleges.[88]

These arrangements have drawn scrutiny from consumer advocates and lawmakers.[89] They've raised questions about whether schools and the companies are transparent enough with students about the online program managers' role in degree programs. Although in many cases instructors from the college whose brand is associated with the program are teaching it, students may be interacting with a company throughout the recruitment and admissions process and taking the class on technology serviced by the company.[90]

Lawmakers and consumer advocates have also expressed concern that the tuition-sharing arrangement incentivizes both the company and the schools to charge high prices and lure as many students as possible into a degree program, regardless of whether students are likely to have a good outcome.[91]

In 2023, the Department of Education announced it would begin weighing updates to the guidance that allows online program managers to get paid on the basis of a share of tuition revenue.[92] But colleges pushed back. Ted Mitchell, the head of the American Council on Education, the leading higher education lobby, cautioned the Department of Education "not to do more harm than good." Mitchell said the online program manager arrangements have provided "increased access to high quality online programs, particularly for underserved populations," and that without the revenue-sharing model, some colleges wouldn't be able to offer them. Mitchell said the department should ensure "appropriate guardrails" to the incentive compensation loophole "are in place to protect student and taxpayer dollars." "This will require a scalpel, not a chain saw," he wrote.[93] In late 2023, the regulatory scrutiny appeared to start to pose challenges to the industry. 2U's stock plunged from a high of $98 in 2018 to roughly $1 in November of 2023.[94]

In some cases, the master's degrees launched by universities following these policy changes are of middling value to students. A 2022 study from Christopher Bennett, an education research analyst at RTI International, a nonprofit research institute, found that a job applicant with a résumé featuring a bachelor's degree was as likely to receive a positive response from an employer as an applicant with an MBA from a for-profit college, primarily online nonprofit or public institution, or a regional university. What's more, that finding held even when employers included a preference for a master's degree in the job listing.

In addition, an MBA wasn't enough to shield applicants from labor market discrimination, Bennett found. Résumés that featured names indicating they were Black men received 30% fewer responses than similar résumés from white men and women.[95] The types of schools featured in Bennett's research aren't typically the focus of attention in the media or public opinion, but they accounted for 67% of MBAs awarded to students during the 2017–2018 academic year.

Still, students who earned master's degrees from more selective institutions with large research budgets weren't immune from the experience of investing time and money into a degree without necessarily receiving a payoff. In addition, because of the schools' reputation, potential students may be more at risk of falling victim to messaging that investing in the degree will be worth it to them.

In 2021, the *Wall Street Journal* exposed how elite universities pushed graduate students toward taking on six-figure debts to complete master's degrees in filmmaking, publishing, and other fields in which decent pay is not guaranteed.[96] That same year, the writer Anne Helen Petersen explored how the University of Chicago was able to use its brand to convince students to take on debt for a particular one-year master's degree program that often left them with middling outcomes.

Students told Petersen of the program that "attendees are often treated as second-class students, and must convince professors to allow them into courses and perform elaborate courting rituals to find one willing to serve as a thesis adviser. Students from PhD programs in other departments told me that it was an 'open secret' that the program was a 'cash cow,'" Petersen wrote.[97]

In his 2011 dissertation, Ozan Jaquette explored how universities used master's degrees for their aims. He found that prestigious universities, especially private ones located in large metro areas, used master's degree programs to generate revenue. Jaquette, now an associate professor of higher education at the University of California, Los Angeles, decided to start researching the topic after, as he puts it, he realized he was "a cash cow myself in a master's program." Jaquette was attending Oxford University, and he started to ask himself, "Why are there so many Americans here and international students that are on one-year master's programs?" People around him speculated that certain changes to the school's approach to its budget and other factors meant that some departments were turning more to American and other international students as a source of funds. "It just struck me as odd and made me want to investigate," he told me years later.[98]

What Jaquette learned is that it's not uncommon for selective colleges, which educate a relatively small share of the country's bachelor's degree students, to be large producers of master's degrees. These schools are hesitant to increase the size of their undergraduate classes or PhD programs because of consequences for their reputation, rankings, and—in the case of PhD programs that typically fully fund students—revenue, Jaquette said. "But those consequences just really weren't there for master's degrees," he said. "You could use your reputation in undergraduate and PhDs to create demands for master's degrees where students think they're kind of getting that, but they're not quite."[99]

Jaquette conducted his research before data existed that allowed students and researchers to better understand the cost of these degrees. Now it's possible thanks to government data to see that Columbia University, Northwestern University, New York University, University of Pennsylvania, and other household-name schools offer master's degrees where the average debt-to-earnings ratio for students four years after they leave school is more than 100%.[100]

As a professor, Jaquette is using this data both to teach his students how to do regression analyses and to steer them away from taking on too much debt to chase prestige. Allowing them to see that, for some fields, the median earnings for a master's degree from a prestigious private university and a nearby public university are similar, but the median debt is double at the private school, has been "kind of eye opening to them," he said.[101] Jaquette said he decided to have his students learn with the data because they're getting advertisements for master's degrees from prestigious schools. "I was them too," he said. "You can be really taken by that."[102]

An MBA Isn't Enough to Protect from Economic Fallout

For Kendra Brooks, the draw to another degree wasn't prestige; it was the idea that getting an MBA would boost her career prospects. She borrowed for the credential on the basis of that premise, but the degree wasn't enough to protect her from a tough economy or the harshest consequences of the student loan system.

When she graduated from Philadelphia's private Eastern University with her MBA in 2010, Brooks had four children, including one getting ready to head to college, and roughly $50,000 in student debt. She did get a raise after earning her degree, but the raise wasn't enough to cover her monthly payments on what she owed in student loans from graduate school. Regardless, a couple of years later, Brooks suddenly lost access to that pay increase or any paycheck when the organization she worked for became victim to state budget cuts to education funding in the wake of the Great Recession.[103] Brooks lost her job—and she started to lose a lot more.

She couldn't afford to pay her student debt or other loans, including her mortgage and car note. Brooks lost her home and her car. "Me and my children were on the verge of homelessness," she said of that period. Her oldest daughter had to come home from Norfolk State University, a historically Black college in Virginia, after just two semesters—including one during which she lived with her grandfather to make expenses more manageable—because Brooks couldn't afford the tuition. Ultimately her daughter had to enlist in the military to finish her degree.

Several years later, sitting in a wood-paneled room wearing glasses with a tinge of red to match her blouse, Brooks was ambivalent about the role the MBA has played in her life. It caused her to take on debt that at some points had been unaffordable, and her education didn't provide her with skills that are particularly useful or necessary for her work. "I think I could have gotten a job and been an elected official without an MBA," she said.

Still, it's hard to know a counterfactual. What Brooks does know is that with her MBA, she was elected to Philadelphia's city council, and it's possible the degree helped create opportunities that led her to that path, including the chance to start a small business when she was laid off that focused on teaching restorative justice and helped push her toward politics. The degree may have also given her credibility among some voters, especially those who were skeptical of her background growing up and the fact that she still lived in North Philadelphia, an area of the city that, at least in headlines, is more associated with crime than politics. Brooks ran for and was elected to an at-large seat on the city council, meaning she had to convince voters outside of her geographic area that she was the right choice for the spot. She started to "degree drop," as she put it, once she could sense that voters questioned whether someone from her neighborhood was deserving of a spot on the city council.

Brooks's experience made her think differently about pushing students broadly and her own children toward college after high school. Her second daughter attended cosmetology school—despite Brooks's initial disappointment—which provided a career path for her daughter that was so viable she could help her mother pay for the cost of her education. In her work, Brooks is focused on ensuring that other young Philadelphians have similar opportunities.

"As an elected official, when I talk about student debt and what does it mean to have higher education, I'm more concerned about postsecondary education as opposed to just a college degree," she said. "How can we invest in young people while they're in high school to transition into good quality union jobs?"

Part of that requires investing in jobs that don't require as many credentials to also provide decent economic opportunity—part of the reason a college degree is so necessary for workers to receive reasonable pay and benefits is that a high school diploma has become essentially worthless.[104] Another approach to achieving that goal is to reward workers who are required to have college degrees with better pay.

"The starting salary for a teacher here in Philadelphia is less than a Philadelphia police officer, and you don't need a degree to be a police officer. You need a degree to be a teacher," Brooks said. The Public Service Loan Forgiveness program, which discharges the debt of borrowers who have worked for the government and certain nonprofits after at least ten years of student loan payments, was supposed to prevent workers in relatively low-paying fields that require advanced degrees from being mired in debt for decades. But in the first few years of the initiative, actually having student debt canceled under the program turned out to be much more challenging than expected.[105]

Meanwhile, the push—both formal and informal—for more credentials continues, even as the investment by government and employers in helping workers pay for those credentials lags. Since the 1980s, employers have required workers to have more degrees, but "we've made the employee pay the price—it's up to you to get the education, get your work experience, and on and on and on," Anthony Carnevale told me.[106]

6. Income-Driven Repayment

Why a Smart and Compassionate Idea Didn't Provide Much Help

By about 1 p.m. Sandra Hinz has already had a full day.

Typically, she and her husband wake up a little bit before 6 a.m. to start taking care of her adult son Dale, who became wheelchair- and bed-bound after a motorcycle accident in 2012. The two give him his first medications of the day, sit him up in his bed, and clean any tracheal tubes—the device in Dale's throat that helps him breathe—that are sitting on the counter from the day before.

Then Hinz and her husband let Dale, who is in his forties, rest, and if he does, they take a few minutes to go back to sleep too. They're up again a little bit before 9 a.m., when Sandra gets the family's breakfast ready. After the oatmeal, yogurt, toast, and chai tea are prepared, she sets up Dale's humidity machine, gets all the pillows out from under him and his sheets off, and checks his vital signs. By the time that's all done, about an hour has gone by, even longer if it's a day when they give Dale a shower. The two load him onto the stair lift, make sure he's comfortable—with a towel by his head, his stuffed animals in his hands to keep them open, and their cat Sharlene on his lap—and he rides downstairs for breakfast.

"We sit there for a while while we're eating and just talk," said Hinz, who is in her sixties. Then they brush Dale's teeth, move him so he's sitting near the counter while they do the dishes, and begin to tackle multiple loads of laundry.

"That's the morning routine that really ends up in the afternoon," Hinz quipped. Sometimes Hinz and her husband are able to close their eyes for only a few hours overnight before starting another morning routine because Dale doesn't fall asleep until 1 a.m. "It's a process," Hinz told me through yawns.

All the chores don't leave Hinz much time for dealing with the paperwork and phone calls that are necessary to meet Dale's needs and take care of other bills. After the family was denied access to a ceiling lift for Dale by their insurance company, Hinz told me, "We're just getting stuck everywhere." They later purchased the lift, used, on their own.

"I need to start getting this stuff taken care of one by one, start getting stuff out of my way so I can concentrate more on what we have to do with my son," she said in September 2021. "I can't have some little glitch coming in the way. I don't want to lose the house and can't even sell it and move because, Where are we going to go?"

And then there are Hinz's student loans. She has about $28,000 in debt that she took on to earn a medical-assisting degree before Dale's accident. When we first met, it was a few months before the COVID-19 pause on student loan interest, payments, and collections was set to expire after an initial extension. For more than two years after we first spoke, officials continued to extend the pause, allowing

Hinz one less bill to worry about paying immediately. But every time I called her during that period, the specter of the payments turning back on haunted her.

"If that were to happen, it would cause some financial distress for sure," she told me in August 2022, a few weeks before the Biden administration announced it would extend the pause again and promised to cancel at least $10,000 in student loans for a wide swath of borrowers.

In the meantime, Hinz called her student loan servicer to see if there was any way to shrink her debt, given the circumstances. "I can't do this," Hinz said through tears, describing how her student loans exacerbated the family's other financial challenges.

"I just don't know what to do. I'm just saying, 'Help me. I need help,'" she said in September 2021. "By now I would have that loan paid off because I would be working somewhere in a medical office doing what I love."

Hinz has written letters to her congresspeople about the debt, but it hasn't resolved her challenges. She's also written to her loan company. "I am writing for an exception to be made for my unique situation as I did not have any control in this matter," she wrote in the fall of 2020. "My wish would have been to be able to work instead of dealing with such a horrendous situation that I was dealt."

A Theoretical Safety Valve

For situations like Hinz's, the student loan program theoretically has a safety valve, a program that allows borrowers to repay their federal student loans as a percentage of their income and have the balance forgiven after a certain number of years of payments. Income-driven repayment, as the program is known, first launched in the early 1990s and has shifted over time in response to policymakers' and borrowers' concerns. Still, these payment plans haven't been enough to protect borrowers from the worst consequences of falling behind on student loans. And as more borrowers have enrolled in these plans, they've become a target for those concerned about the cost to the government of the student loan program.

The philosophical origin of these income-contingent loan programs is typically attributed to the economist Milton Friedman. In the mid-1950s, Friedman noted that the difficulty in financing human capital—basically providing funding for people to expand their knowledge and skills—as compared to physical capital was likely resulting in an underinvestment in students' education and skills.[1]

With no physical asset to seize in case of default and uncertainty surrounding the likelihood of a student's success, investors would have to charge interest rates so high to compensate for potential losses from default that they could conflict with usury laws and make the loans unattractive to borrowers. To solve the problem, Friedman suggested that potential students essentially sell shares in themselves. Investors would front them the money to pay for college in exchange for a percentage of their earnings for a certain period of time after graduating.[2]

"There seems no legal obstacle to private contracts of this kind, even though they are economically equivalent to the purchase of a share in an individual's earning capacity and thus to partial slavery," Friedman wrote. He noted that the government could finance education in this way, as well.[3]

Indeed, other countries finance their students' higher education through this style of loan. For example, in Australia, the government deducts a percentage of borrowers' income, similar to tax withholding, to repay student debt.[4] But these plans differ philosophically from what Friedman proposed. Instead of being self-financing— borrowers who end up earning more would subsidize borrowers who earn less—these programs offered a way for countries that had traditionally fully subsidized their higher education to get back at least some of the money they doled out.[5]

In the years following Friedman's discussion of income- contingent loans, lawmakers and wonks offered several proposals for turning the idea into a reality in the United States. The plans were generally a nonstarter in Congress because policymakers viewed them and loan programs more broadly as a threat to keeping tuition low through more direct subsidies to public colleges.[6]

It wasn't until the early 1990s that the notion of offering federal student loan borrowers a payment plan tied to their income really began to gain traction. At the time, Robert Shireman was working for then senator Paul Simon, an Illinois Democrat, as the Senate's Committee on Health, Education, Labor, and Pensions, of which Simon was a member, was considering updates to the Higher Education Act.

Simon felt like the discussions surrounding the Higher Education Act reauthorization were just fiddling at the edges—focused on things like making small adjustments to interest rates, subsidies to lenders, and the way the government decided how much a student qualified for in aid. He preferred they focus on tackling the bigger questions related to college affordability. Amid these concerns, Simon started going through the *Congressional Record* to prepare himself for the hearing. Shireman suspected that Simon read through one of the paper booklets during the August recess at his home in rural southern Illinois. Scouring the record, Simon came across an August 1991 speech by Senator David Durenberger, a Republican of Minnesota, touting his proposal for a new type of student loan program.[7]

"This proposal would allow students to repay their loans based on their incomes after graduation, not on their personal or family income at the time they enroll. This income-based repayment feature of the IDEA [Income-Dependent Education Assistance] Act means that graduates in lower paying jobs would make lower loan payments. As incomes rise, so would the size of payments."[8] "Senator Simon saw this—he sent it to me with a note to contact Senator Durenberger's staff and learn more about it," Shireman told me.

Shireman and staffers from Durenberger's office and the office of Congressman Tom Petri, a Republican of Wisconsin, got to work trying to develop the mechanics of the program. At the time, they believed that for an income-contingent payment plan to work, the loans would need to be made directly by the government. That's because Durenberger's and Petri's initial proposal called for collecting the payments through the Internal Revenue Service, so they figured the amounts collected would need to be due to the US government.[9]

The idea was to have borrowers with low incomes have their payments reduced to as little as zero dollars a month. The payments would go up as income rises, but borrowers would never pay more than 20% of their income. If the borrower was not able to pay the loan off in twenty-five years through making these payments, the balance would be forgiven.[10]

"You can imagine a situation where there are going to be some people who are poor for a number of years and then they make a lot of money, so from an equity standpoint, it makes sense to have those people fully repay the loan," Shireman said, explaining why borrowers paid more as their financial circumstances improved.[11]

The architects of the plan also decided that if a borrower's monthly payment wasn't high enough to cover the interest, the balance would keep growing. This allowed for a phenomenon that runs counter to how most of us expect to pay a debt, called negative amortization. Typically we expect that when we make a payment toward a loan, it pushes the balance down. But under a plan where payments are tied to income, the monthly bill might be so low that it touches only a portion of the interest, creating a situation in which a borrower throws money at the debt, but the balance keeps increasing.[12]

At the time, the staffers waved away the potential psychological impact of seeing a student loan balance grow. As Robert Shireman wrote in his own history of income-contingent loans, Joe Flader, who had been pushed the government to adopt a repayment program tied to income for years, likened the ballooning balance to "an accounting mechanism . . . since all debts got wiped out after 25 years anyway."[13]

Ultimately, a pilot program allowing a small number of schools to test income-contingent loans wound up in the bill reauthorizing the Higher Education Act that year.[14] But at the same time, Shireman and his colleagues were working through these details, the then governor of Arkansas, Bill Clinton, took an interest in the idea.

On the presidential campaign trail, he touted a proposal that would offer "any American, without regard to income," the opportunity to pay back their student loan "as a small percentage of your income over time after you get out of school and go to work, paid at tax time so you couldn't beat the bill." What he hoped many young Americans would choose instead would be to opt to repay the debt through a year or two of national service.[15]

All the parties seriously considering income-contingent loans concluded that the bank-based loan program couldn't facilitate such a repayment scheme. For it to work, those collecting the loans would need up-to-date income information—data only the Internal Revenue Service had access to.[16] That meant that for Clinton's combined national service, income-contingent loan pet project to become a more widely adopted reality, lawmakers would have to expand the program that allowed the Department of Education to lend directly to students, known as direct lending. That concerned stakeholders, including the lenders and intermediaries involved in the bank-based program—and so income-contingent repayment wound up being inextricably linked to a major battle in Congress over the future of the student loan program.

Meanwhile, Department of Education staffers started to think through the program's particulars. Some favored forgiveness after twenty-five years; others thought it wouldn't be fair to let borrowers off the hook just as they were reaching their earning potential and advocated waiting to forgive the debt until after forty-five years of payments.[17]

Ultimately, Democrats pushed through a plan to phase in direct lending and the option to repay loans as a percentage of income along with it. The plan implemented by the Department of Education looked similar to how the congressional aides originally envisioned it—although congressional wrangling meant that the

Internal Revenue Service collection component of the proposal wound up being axed.

But direct lending became a political target, making the take-up of income-contingent loan repayment difficult. Republican lawmakers led by Newt Gingrich derided direct lending as a Clinton-directed government overreach; Gingrich would later say he was "unalterably opposed" to the program, calling the government "incompetent at almost every direct service it provides."[18]

As part of a deal with congressional Republicans to prevent Congress from killing the direct-lending pilot, then secretary of education Richard Riley agreed not to push schools toward direct lending.[19] Direct lending, which was the only part of the federal student loan program to offer an income-contingent payment plan, became "a partisan boogeyman," Shireman said. That dynamic "killed" the income-contingent repayment plan "in a way because it couldn't be promoted without being considered partisan," Shireman said.[20]

About ten years later, Shireman took a stab at widening the reach of an income-tied repayment plan, this time as the head of a research and advocacy organization focused on college access and affordability that he had founded. Shireman's organization, the Institute for College Access and Success, worked with the decades-old DC-based think tank the Pew Charitable Trusts to do what think tanks do—put out white papers and talk with government staffers— with an aim to draw attention to the idea of paying off student loans as a percentage of income.[21]

As part of this campaign, the groups organized students to show up at field hearings for the Commission on the Future of Higher Education, also known as the Spellings Commission, for Margaret Spellings, then the secretary of education, with T-shirts that read Property of Sallie Mae and a large ball and chain with Student Debt Alert printed on it. But what they didn't mention, Shireman said, was the income-contingent repayment program already on the books. Because it was so partisan, the groups believed that their best shot at more widespread adoption of this type of program was to start fresh.[22]

The groups' initial goal was to push the Department of Education to expand income-tied repayment plans through its regulatory authority to bank-based loans. Instead, congressional lawmakers became interested. They ultimately passed a plan in 2007 that capped payments at 15% of income, but it differed from what Shireman and other advocates had proposed in a few key ways. For one, to keep costs down, they extended the maximum repayment period to twenty-five years (instead of twenty years, as the coalition had proposed) and excluded loans made under the grad PLUS program—which allows graduate students to borrow up to the cost of attendance—from forgiveness under the plan.[23] But according to Shireman, when the Department of Education ultimately implemented the regulations in 2008, it kept in loans for graduate school.[24]

In 2010, the Obama administration officially ended the bank-based student loan program by attaching the provision to the Affordable Care Act, which Democrats pushed through Congress in a special budget process that allowed the act to overcome some of the biggest potential challenges levied by Republicans. Going forward, all student loans would be made directly by the government as part of a program that had an income-based repayment option. As part of the law, the Obama administration reduced the maximum share of borrowers' income that would be devoted to student loans to 10%.[25]

Instead of getting rid of the original, less generous, income-contingent repayment program conceived by Shireman and others in the early 1990s, policymakers layered this other repayment plan on top. That's because, according to Shireman, legal aid organizations and others who were helping borrowers manage their loans with the use of the income-contingent plan were scared to let go of the option they were using successfully. They feared that what replaced it could be worse.[26] "Unknown new things without regulations yet might not be as helpful as the thing they had in hand," Shireman said, explaining the logic.

"It's Never Too Late to Do Anything"

Around this time, when the Obama administration was working to increase access to affordable repayment plans, Sandra Hinz decided to go back to school. By that point, she'd been working in medical offices for nearly two decades.

In the early 1990s she took a job at a group practice copying charts all day, thinking the position would be temporary, but she enjoyed it so much that when that practice moved, she went with it. In the years since, she'd worked for lone practitioners, neurologists, and internists; she and her family had even moved from a rural upstate New York town to outside Buffalo to be closer to the hospitals, surgical banks, and doctors' offices where she could get a job.

An easy talker, Hinz loved chitchatting with patients, whether it was when she walked them from the reception area to the exam room or even just on the phone as she scheduled their appointments. She relished any opportunities to do medical work that she got, like taking blood pressure, temperature, and other vital signs.

So in 2011, feeling adrift following her mother's death a year earlier—Hinz had been her mother's caretaker in her final years and was looking for something to do with herself—she decided to go to school to become a medical assistant. "Even though I worked in these offices for many years, there was still a lot to learn. I didn't know everything," she said. At the time, she was in her early fifties, with a husband and two grown sons, but she wasn't daunted by the prospect of attending college when many others her age would be starting to plan for retirement. "My motto is, It's never too late to do anything," she said.

She also figured that the degree and the job opportunities that came with it would provide her family with a financial boost. Hinz's husband worked in construction, and she and her sons sometimes pitched in to help his jobs move quickly. On weekends or after she was done answering phone calls at the doctor's office, she would often head to one of his roofing jobs and help clean up. The few dollars an hour more that she'd earn as a medical assistant would give her family a little bit of extra cash and stability. "It's not like I was looking to make megabucks," she said on thinking through the decision. "I wanted to do a little bit better than I was doing."

She'd received flyers in the mail from Bryant and Stratton College, at the time a private, for-profit school in Buffalo offering a range of degrees in areas like health care and legal services. Hinz knew people who had attended the school and had a good experience. She appreciated that class sizes would be smaller than at her local community college. She signed up, assuming, or at least hoping, that she would get a scholarship or grant that would help pay the bill.

About a semester in, Hinz realized that there wasn't as much financial help available as she initially thought, but she wasn't going to quit. She loved what she was learning—drawing blood from other classmates, the intricacies of how the brain worked—and she was eager to finish. She'd found a smooth balance between her nights in class and her days working in customer service at a company that distributed oxygen tanks. So Hinz continued on, borrowing modestly and assuming that once she graduated and started earning a slightly higher salary, she'd be able to pay back the debt.

Roughly a year after she started school, Hinz used one of her rare free moments to take a drive with a friend to visit the friend's daughter at the salon where she cut hair. A few minutes into the visit, the friend's husband arrived looking for Hinz with her husband on the other line.

She learned that her son Dale had been hit while riding his motorcycle.

A thirty-one-year-old, who just days before was traveling around the region to play gigs with his band and working with his dad on construction jobs, was now lying in a bed on the trauma floor of the hospital. "We didn't even know if he was going to make it that night," she said.

For nearly eleven months, Hinz and her husband would stay at the hospital until midnight or one in the morning, monitoring Dale's condition and ensuring that he was stable. The following day, Hinz would wake up and go to school. Often, Hinz would bring her laptop and books to Dale's room so she could study while watching him closely. "I had it in the back of my mind—I could hear Dale telling me, 'Don't quit, keep going,'" she said.

When Hinz and her husband brought Dale home, wheelchair- and bed-bound, in the summer of 2013, she took a few months' break from her classes so she could start learning how to manage his care. Ultimately, she went back and completed her studies but had to do a required internship—leaving early a few times to tend to Dale when he had troublingly high fevers. When it came time to graduate in 2014, Hinz looked around at the people getting ready to walk the stage with her, and she realized she was alone. The friends she'd entered school with had left years before.

As she celebrated her graduation, eating pizza and wings at a small party of family and friends her husband threw for her, Hinz felt proud of what she accomplished. "It was such a relief" to gradu- ate, she said.

But the life Hinz imagined when she started school—earning $16 to $18 an hour, working as a medical assistant—was no longer pos- sible. Dale required constant monitoring.

A Historical Blip Turns to a More Permanent Reality

Income-driven repayment was supposed to help in situations like Hinz's, essentially by providing insurance for when students' invest- ment in themselves didn't turn out as planned. The Obama adminis- tration's push to make income-based repayment more affordable and encourage its uptake came in the wake of the Great Recession, when many who attended college were finding out that once they left, their time and financial investment weren't paying off as they'd hoped.

Student loan borrowers had been forced to finance a larger share of the tuition than in the past due in part to disinvestment in pub- lic colleges and sluggish wage growth. Those forces also left their families with less money to use to pay for school, and then these graduates entered a labor market with high unemployment and where slow wage growth was making it difficult to find a job that paid decently. It felt like a historical blip that a certain cohort of students were unlucky enough to fall victim to. Expanding the student loan program's insurance option—which officials proposed as part of the White House Middle Class Task Force, headed by then vice president Joe Biden—seemed like a logical response.[27]

As the White House put it in materials discussing the expansion of income-based repayment, the option "protects borrowers by linking payments to their income and family size."[28]

And indeed, student loan and college-affordability advocacy groups praised the Obama administration's work on income-based repayment. The United States Students Association, a student-led advocacy group, called the administration's changes to the payment plan "a great step in making college more affordable." "College graduates are entering the worst job markets on record for young people," according to the association.[29] Campus Progress, a college-focused initiative housed at the Center for American Progress, a Democrat-affiliated think tank, said the changes "could not come at a better time for people struggling in this difficult economy."[30] Robert Shireman's organization, the Institute for College Access and Success, said the fixes would make income-based repayment "more effective for responsible borrowers, helping them stay afloat financially and stay out of default."[31]

By capping monthly payments at a maximum of 10% for eligible borrowers, the Obama administration did drastically reduce the amount of money that struggling Americans were expected to put toward their student loans. Still, a borrower who made $30,000 and owed $20,000 would be expected to pay $115 a month, the White House said, not necessarily an easy sum to come up with when every dollar is accounted for on a tight budget.[32]

"It became like the hot new thing in student debt," Mark Huelsman said of income-driven repayment in the early 2010s.

At the time, Huelsman was just starting to focus his research for think tanks and advocacy groups on higher education and college affordability.[33]

At events in conference rooms around Washington funded by various foundations, Huelsman sat through several panel discussions touting the promise of income-driven repayment. In the audience were other think-tank wonks, advocates, and higher education lobbyists who all seemed bullish on the role that expanding repayment options could have in mitigating the student loan problem, which by 2012 had surpassed $1 trillion.[34]

"If we expand income-based repayment, if we make more people eligible, if we do better outreach, if we automatically enroll people in [income-driven repayment], there should be no defaults on student loans because everyone will have an affordable monthly payment," he told me. "That was sort of the vibe."[35]

The faith in the ability of repayment plans to mitigate the nation's student loan problem was based in part on the notion that for most borrowers, student loans were a sound investment, and the government needed to provide protection only from the worst student loan outcomes for the relatively small share of borrowers for whom the system didn't work as planned. One Brookings Institution analysis argued that "the typical household with debt is no worse off today than a generation ago, with increases in lifetime earnings more than offsetting increases in debt, and monthly payment burdens kept manageable by longer repayment periods."[36] In a different Brookings publication, the same author, Matthew Chingos, wrote with Beth Akers, later a senior fellow at the right-leaning American Enterprise Institute, that the forgiveness provision of income-based repayment programs was in fact too generous to borrowers and too costly for taxpayers.[37]

In 2016, the two published a book called *Game of Loans: The Rhetoric and Reality of Student Debt.* It was one of two volumes published that year arguing that the way the media talked about student loans—as a crisis altering the lives of many Americans, particularly young people—didn't match the reality. Sandy Baum, author of the other book, *Student Debt: Rhetoric and Realities of Higher Education Financing*, for decades touted the notion that student debt generally pays off. A 1991 *Washington Post* story summarized (in part) the findings of a study she completed on student loan borrowers by saying that, for most, the "hardship seems more in the mind than in the lifestyle." "They say they don't like paying back, but would borrow the same or more if they had to do it all over again," Baum told the paper.[38] For nearly two decades, Baum had coauthored annual publications on trends in student debt and financial aid for the College Board, the organization that administers the SAT and Advanced Placement tests, and therefore has a vested interest in the notion that college is a good investment.[39]

Promoting her book in 2016, Baum held the line that there wasn't an issue with student debt overall, just in certain situations. "It's very difficult for people to distinguish among the different circumstances that borrowers actually face," she said, noting that, for many, student loans provided an opportunity to attend college that wouldn't otherwise be available. "We have to stop saying student debt in and of itself is always a problem," she said.[40] One of the ways to help borrowers in financial trouble and prevent them from sliding into delinquency and default, she said, was to automatically enroll them in repayment plans tied to income.

The Obama administration stopped short of doing that, but officials responded to the continuous growth in America's outstanding student loan balance and the increased number of borrowers contending with student debt after the Great Recession by expanding eligibility for income-based repayment programs and making them more generous.[41] Once again, the think-tank community cheered them on.

Kevin Carey, head of the education policy program at New America, asked in 2015 in the *New York Times* whether the student loan crisis had "already been solved." He repeated (and quoted others doing the same) the notion that income-based repayment provided insurance for historically unlucky borrowers. "The logic behind income-based repayment is that because students can't control whether they graduate in a recession, the student loan system is particularly vulnerable to the business cycle," Carey wrote. Carey quoted Rory O'Sullivan, then deputy director of Young Invincibles, a young adult advocacy group, saying that college degrees "pay off in the long run" and that income-based repayment could keep borrowers afloat during "early career struggles, layoffs, and tough economic times."[42]

Carey was so bullish on the expansion of income-based repayment that he argued it was "moving the federal government into the same role that state governments played for much of the 20th century: the foundational provider of broad, unqualified subsidies for higher learning."[43] Whereas in the past, states heavily subsidized public colleges, students attended for free or close to it and paid back those funds in the form of taxes, which fluctuate according to income, he argued that the federal government should essentially offer a similar system: loan the money up front to borrowers, who would pay it back based on their income.

But because at that point borrowers hadn't widely adopted income-driven repayment, the bullishness surrounding the plans was largely theoretical, Huelsman told me. For one, the proponents of the plan never really agreed on what was "affordable," he said. As wonks bandied about possible different versions of income-driven repayment, they used a think tank's calculator to see the implications of different terms of the plan—for example, what would happen if the government protected more or less income, or what would happen to borrowers if the repayment horizon was shorter or longer.

"We'd look at these monthly payments and people would say, 'That seems reasonable to me,'" Huelsman said. "That's a bunch of eggheads sitting in a room talking about what I think is affordable for low-income people, which is problematic on every level."

Once more widespread availability of income-driven repayment went from theory to reality, it became clear that borrowers were struggling to access the—albeit somewhat arbitrarily set—more affordable monthly payments. The Obama administration worked to publicize the programs to increase the number of people signing up and, in particular, to ensure that struggling borrowers were aware of their options.[44]

But the availability of the more generous payment plans wasn't enough to save borrowers from the struggle of repaying their debt; every time the government would introduce a new version of income-driven repayment, delinquency rates hardly budged. Part of that had to do with borrower confusion, and perhaps paralysis, surrounding so many options for repaying their student loans. That was a vestige of policymakers' and advocates' hesitancy to sunset available repayment plans, even as more generous ones were introduced, in response to fear from borrowers using—or advocates helping borrowers to use—the current plans that what came next wouldn't be as good, according to Shireman.

In addition, requiring borrowers to sign up themselves instead of automatically enrolling them, a design feature of the program that dates to the early 1990s, created a logistic burden that was difficult for many to overcome. "We all underestimated the administrative difficulty and the paperwork side of it," Shireman said. Borrowers who were struggling financially and would likely have most needed access to these kinds of options typically didn't have the time to call up their student loan company and enroll, Shireman said—they were juggling children, multiple jobs, and other responsibilities.[45]

The companies hired by the government to manage the student loan program likely exacerbated the issue. Over the course of my career reporting on student debt, I've heard from dozens of federal student loan borrowers who, struggling to make payments on their debt, called their student loan servicer looking for help. Instead of informing borrowers of their option to repay the loan as a percentage of their income, the companies pushed the borrowers toward forbearance, a status that pauses payments but during which interest still accrues on the debt, according to stories I heard from borrowers as well as in lawsuits and testimony by advocates.[46]

In the wake of the expansion of income-based repayment, regulators and advocates focused their attention on this behavior, arguing that student loan companies had an incentive to drive borrowers toward repayment plans that weren't the most beneficial to them. Enrolling borrowers in forbearance was a relatively quick process, but signing them up for income-based repayment would require at least several minutes of attention from customer service agents, who were encouraged to keep their calls quick to improve servicers' bottom line.[47]

Regulators paid particularly close attention to Navient, which, in 2014, spun off from Sallie Mae, the organization created by lawmakers during the Nixon administration to provide liquidity to the student loan market. In 2022, Navient agreed to settle a lawsuit brought by thirty-nine attorneys general in part over forbearance-steering allegations.[48] At the time, the company's chief legal officer called the claims in the suit "unfounded" and said the company agreed to the deal "to avoid the additional burden, expense, time and distraction to prevail in court."[49]

Scott Buchanan, the executive director of the Student Loan Servicing Alliance, a servicer trade group, said the companies were "part of the good and the bad of the student loan program." He acknowledges that borrowers have valid complaints about servicers, for example, that in some cases, they didn't listen to directions about where to apply payments. Still, he said that borrower advocates "misdirect" blame for the challenges borrowers face when dealing with programs like income-driven repayment onto servicers.

"When we say, 'Oh, the reason why [income-driven repayment] isn't working is because servicers suck,' that's just ridiculous," Buchanan said. "There are individual errors that are made along the way but if you don't like IDR, talk to the government."

And indeed, although borrowers and regulators reported that student loan servicers were throwing up obstacles for borrowers trying to access the repayment options to which they were entitled, it has also become clear over the past few years that the difficulty borrowers face paying down their student debt is about more than access to affordable repayment options.

The financial circumstances of student loan borrowers broadly and of those using income-driven repayment plans specifically were not what policymakers initially anticipated. In the early years of the program, close observers envisioned that those who would reap the most from the program would be a relatively small and particular group. "The biggest benefit of all would go to men and women who accumulated massive educational debt but then earned low incomes for many years," wrote Steven Waldman in *The Bill: How Legislation Really Becomes Law: A Case Study of the National Service Bill*, which chronicles the battle over the proposed national service bill and direct loan program in the early 1990s. "There aren't many such creatures, but the few that exist include doctors who work in low-income clinics or lawyers who become public defenders—in other words, those doing the public-service jobs Clinton admired," he said.[50]

By the mid-2010s, having an income too low to service student debt was almost the norm. Instead of a relatively small cohort of borrowers using the plans to manage repayment while pursuing public service or using them temporarily in the wake of challenging economic events like the Great Recession, a large share of borrowers were using the plans during a booming economy. By 2017, about 27% of student loan borrowers were enrolled in an income-driven plan, including nearly 40% of borrowers who attended graduate school.[51] By 2022, roughly 47% of student loan dollars were in repayment on an income-driven plan.[52]

When Department of Education officials initially attempted to estimate the cost of the repayment programs, they assumed the borrowers using them would eventually wind up better off financially than what happened in reality. That assumption—which presumed that many borrowers would make enough money to pay down their debt more aggressively—was part of what caused the agency to underestimate the overall cost of the student loan program by $311 billion, according to a 2022 report from the Government Accountability Office, a government watchdog.[53]

Instead of income-driven repayment plans functioning as a tool to protect borrowers during periods of bad luck, whether because of the business cycle or more personal events, they created a situation in which borrowers whose incomes were perpetually too low to service their debt were throwing money at the loans without making progress toward repaying them. The result was that many borrowers saw their balances actually grow in the period following the Great Recession despite technically being current on their debt.

In 2019, at least 25% of borrowers who had outstanding student debt in 2009 had a larger student loan balance than they did ten years earlier, according to research by Marshall Steinbaum, an economist at the University of Utah.[54] Ten percent of borrowers in that cohort had student loan balances in 2019 that were nearly four times the size of their balance in 2009. The challenge of non-repayment was particularly acute in majority-minority zip codes, where nearly 62% of borrowers aged eighteen to thirty-five, had a balance in 2019 that exceeded their original debt, compared to nearly 50% of borrowers in majority-white zip codes, Steinbaum found.[55]

And even as borrowers saw their balances grow, the promise of forgiveness in the income-driven repayment program was proving elusive. As of 2021, roughly two million Americans had been paying on their student loan debt for more than twenty years—a pattern that income-driven repayment should have theoretically eliminated.[56] Meanwhile, just thirty-two borrowers had actually had their debt canceled under an income-driven repayment plan.

The psychic and political cost of these seemingly never-ending debt balances was something that the architects of income-contingent repayment plans didn't totally anticipate, according to Shireman. He recalled what Joe Flader, the aide to Representative Tom Petri, said about the ballooning balances being theoretical. "He would say that, and I could see what he meant," Shireman said. "The reality is that for most people a growing balance is scary, and so having some kind of a cap on how much it can grow or something like that is important."[57]

The growing balance also served to undermine the student loan program in the eyes of its critics, Shireman said. Because balances appeared so large when borrowers were eligible for cancellation, it seemed as if they were getting a huge windfall, even though so much of the cancellation was just interest that had accrued over time.

"It creates a boogeyman that's convenient to say Democrats are wasting money or giving away money to people with graduate degrees," Shireman said of the ballooning balances.[58]

A Shift in Approach

By the time Hinz was writing to her congresspeople and student loan company about her debt, some policymakers' and wonks' views of the power of income-driven repayment to transform the student loan system had shifted. Julie Peller, who worked in Congress on student loan issues during the Bush and Obama administrations, pointed to a decision made in 2007 to illustrate the difference in approach.

In 2007, lawmakers created a new income-driven repayment plan, known as income-based repayment, and upped the cap students could borrow to pay for undergraduate college in the same bill. That was based on the notion that borrowers weren't as concerned with their overall balance as they were with managing their day-to-day payments, said Peller, who founded Higher Learning Advocates, a bipartisan advocacy group focused on students.[59]

"Today increasing loan limits on student loans would be an incredibly unpopular idea," Peller told me shortly after President Joe Biden announced a plan to cancel up to $20,000 in student debt for a wide swath of borrowers. "People would say, 'I don't care. How do you help me repay the debt? It's just too high.'"[60]

Part of that change in approach from some lawmakers and advocates was the result of seeing how the hope of income-driven repayment compared with the reality. Borrowers had to contend with obstacles to accessing the program thrown up by student loan companies. And although the repayment plans protected some income from being part of the monthly payment calculation, the payments were still too high for some borrowers to afford basic needs. Meanwhile, if they could access the repayment plans and stay on them, borrowers often faced the psychologically devastating experience of watching their balances grow even as they put money toward the debt.

Studying student debt with an eye toward how it disproportionately affects borrowers of color—a focus he started bringing to his work regularly in 2015—was one of the experiences that convinced Huelsman that "we're not going to repay our way out of this problem," he said. As a result of centuries of policies that blocked Black households' access to wealth building, Black students are more likely to borrow to pay for college, and when they do, they tend to borrow more and take longer to pay it off.[61] That made it clear that income-driven repayment wasn't enough to ameliorate the harm of America's debt-financed higher education system.

"Because it was always based on income and it doesn't factor in historical racial and other wealth disparities, it's never going to be perfect. It's never going to be the silver bullet that people were talking about," he said.[62]

For John King, a secretary of education in the Obama administration, income-driven repayment wasn't enough to solve all the problems he and his colleagues were hoping to address. Those included that the Pell Grant, which had once covered nearly 80% of college costs, was covering about 30%—a problem only Congress could solve. Other problems were that students were facing the risk of being preyed upon by for-profit colleges—an issue the administration made progress on but that was later undone during the Trump administration—and the fact that students of color had fewer sources of wealth to draw on to pay for college.[63]

"For the person who went to a quality institution from which they got a quality degree, they're in a position over time to earn the level where they can service their debt, income-driven repayment should make it more manageable for them," King told me in 2022. "I think that hypothesis still holds."

Nonetheless, he added, "IDR did not solve as much of the problem as we'd hoped; that's what draws me to a place of supporting debt cancellation."[64]

As part of the Biden administration's debt-relief plan, officials revamped income-driven repayment to address some of borrowers' and advocates' concerns. The new version of income-driven repayment protects more of a borrower's income, shortens the timeline to forgiveness to ten years for borrowers who have $12,000 or less of undergraduate debt, and covers unpaid monthly interest.[65] That gets rid of a challenge that so many borrowers faced under income-driven repayment: they watched their balances grow even as they threw money at the debt. The Biden-era Department of Education also did a review of borrowers' previous payments to determine whether servicers should have been counting them toward forgiveness under income-driven repayment.[66] They looked for situations where it appeared that borrowers might have been steered toward forbearance instead of income-driven repayment and counted those months spent in forbearance toward relief under IDR. The initiative has helped hundreds of thousands have their debt canceled and has brought many others closer to the finish line.[67]

In part as a result of these efforts, Carey is still bullish on the potential of income-driven repayment, he wrote to me in 2024, shortly after the Biden administration announced more student debt cancellation. He said it's taken longer than he originally expected when he championed income-driven repayment in 2015 for the program to provide major relief for borrowers. But he noted that, over the past several years, the Biden administration's actions, combined with more people learning how to navigate the system and accumulating the necessary time in repayment to qualify for debt relief have resulted in meaningful change. The Biden administration's revamped version of income-driven repayment will likely help a lot of borrowers, particularly those with smaller balances who struggle to pay them back, he said.

To Huelsman, the Biden plan improves on many of the provisions of income-driven repayment that so vexed borrowers and advocates. Still, it may be plagued by many of the same factors that have made income-driven repayment challenging for borrowers to access, including poor implementation by the government and its contractors. Even though the plan will likely change the experience of repaying student loans dramatically for some, with it, policymakers are still falling victim to the sunk-cost fallacy—investing more resources into tweaking a system that hasn't worked instead of completely revamping it.

"This is the best chance of making repayment humane, but making repayment humane is one piece of the puzzle," Huelsman said.[68]

An individual familiar with the Obama and Biden administrations' thinking on the White House's approach to income-driven repayment said in an interview that SAVE, or the Saving on a Valuable Education Plan, isn't enough to fundamentally revamp students' experiences paying for college and borrowers' experiences with student loans.

"It's a big deal," the individual said of SAVE. Still, they added dealing with America's student loan challenge requires "more than temporary debt forgiveness or a single repayment plan. It's about investing in our young people and the kind of opportunities we want to have in this country." Those investments require the support of Congress and state lawmakers.

The return to student loan payments following the pause of more than three years provided evidence of the limits of a more humane repayment plan to transform student loan borrowers' experiences. In the weeks leading up to getting their first bills, borrowers interested in enrolling in the government's new, more generous repayment plan spent hours on hold and received conflicting information from their servicers. Despite the fact that the government had taken steps to significantly cut down on their monthly payments, the sprawling student loan system and its reliance on third-party actors stymied borrowers' ability to access that promise. What's more, the plan has been a target of litigation from opponents, meaning that borrowers can't rely on having access to it to keep their bills manageable.

Years of Trying to Find Room for Student Loan Bills

For borrowers like Sandra Hinz, if the relief ever comes—through a more generous repayment program or cancellation—it will be after years of trying to find room for student loan payments amid other essential bills. Those included things like a van equipped with a lift to drive Dale around, changes to their home to make it easier for him to move through the space, and the constant crush of supplies that insurance won't cover.

If urinary bags or trach tubes were on back order, Hinz and her husband would buy those out of pocket on Amazon. They spend about $50 a month on medications prescribed by Dale's doctor but not covered by insurance. And then of course there are essentials like clothing and food, which can sometimes exceed the cost of the food stamps Dale receives.

The ability of Hinz's household to afford these things and other bills is dictated in large part by forces out of her control. Hinz and her husband, who turned sixty-nine in 2024, are Dale's main caregivers, with help from his older brother. At times, money is so tight that Hinz finds herself scrambling to find a job she could do from the house in between the moments when she isn't caring for Dale.

"It's really tedious," Hinz said of her job search. "Just looking, looking, looking . . . it's just really tiring along with everything else you have to do during the day."

She told me this a few months after the Biden administration announced its debt-relief plan in 2022—it was still mired in litigation, and few details were available. At the time, Hinz said she was hopeful she'd receive the relief, but she didn't have time to focus on things that may or may not happen in the future.

"I'm trying to deal with everything little by little, and there are things that I've got to do today or tomorrow—I'm not really planning on anything," she said. "I get stressed out easily with the finance part. I get really freaked out about the finances."

A few months earlier, before Hinz found out she'd be eligible for some debt forgiveness under Biden's proposed plan, she explained why it made sense for someone like her—a borrower who had taken on a modest sum in student loans to get the education and skills needed for a better-paying job, but for whom the debt wasn't worth it because of circumstances beyond her control—to get relief from the government. Both she and the government invested in her education on the assumption that it would provide her with a better financial life. That didn't pan out, and the government's safety net wasn't enough to protect her from debt payments that felt unsustainable to her.

"I'm not saying that I want this given to me for free," Hinz said of her education, but she added, "I'm never going to be able to work outside the house to use it."

"I miss it, but I'm not going to be able to do it now," she said. "That's my reasoning," for wanting some kind of debt cancellation, Hinz said. "Because I can't do anything."

7. Extraordinary Collection Powers

When a Loan Meant to Help Causes Harm

Patricia Gary was starting to get tired. For five years, Gary had taken the subway from her home in the Bronx to Manhattan in order to catch a tram that carried her over the East River to Roosevelt Island. There, she worked as a secretary in New York State's Division of Housing and Community Renewal for eight hours and then began the journey back home. The sometimes hours-long commute tacked on to her workday was beginning to wear on Gary's body, and she'd started to show up late to work. Gary and her employer tried to work out an arrangement so she could keep working, but eventually "it reached its limit, and I just didn't have that extra energy to keep pushing," Gary told me of the experience decades later.

Besides, she'd been thinking about starting her own business. Gary had never had much ownership over her secretarial work, and the idea of creating something she'd be responsible for appealed to her. Gary, a self-described "risk taker," left Guyana with her family when she was thirteen years old. Arriving to America's abundance from her impoverished home country was a "culture shock," but the United States also had the quality of a wonderland or fairy tale to Gary. "America shines a light that is so bright that it's delusional," she said.

That optimism and her entrepreneurial spirit are part of what motivated Gary to consider a career change. As she mused about going out on her own, she kept hearing about Wilfred Beauty Academy of Hair and Beauty Culture from neighborhood friends who'd taken courses there themselves and from stylists in training attending Wilfred who did her hair at a discounted price. In the 1980s, when Gary was considering Wilfred, the school ran television ads featuring women dressed in matching blue smocks in a brightly lit salon, using hairdryers as microphones to sing "it's a beautiful life when you love what you do."[1]

"You didn't have to go looking for it," Gary said. "It was an attractive school to be going to because it had that kind of popularity." The school's facility on Fordham Road in the Bronx had all the atmosphere of a salon and the facilities of a cosmetology school. There were sinks, hair-cutting stations, and mannequins to practice on. Gary decided to enroll.

There wasn't much discussion about how she was supposed to pay for it. Instead, school representatives made it seem as if the only way to become a Wilfred student was to take out a student loan. "It was just, 'You want to attend the class you want to attend the school, [then] this is the procedure,'" Gary said, so she borrowed the money and began attending classes.

At first, she enjoyed them. Every day Gary and her classmates brought their carrying cases filled with the comb, curlers, and other tools they'd purchased for the courses, and Gary threw herself enthusiastically into first learning how to put a single wave in a mannequin's hair and then more advanced lessons in styling. But about a year and a half into her coursework, Gary started to become frustrated.

She had an inkling that she wasn't getting the education and skills she'd signed up for. The administration was lumping classes together such that Gary, who was still learning to wash hair and then set it in a specific style to dry, was pushed into classes with students who were learning to color hair, a more advanced skill. Around the same time, Gary started to notice that teachers and staffers were leaving—she suspected that was why the school pushed the classes together. Gary had hoped to stay at the school long enough to take the state licensing exam, but she started to feel like the classes weren't preparing her to do so.

Although Gary had a sense that the school was disrupting her education, she didn't know that across the country Wilfred was using students like her—and their desire to gain skills to improve their economic circumstances—to get access to the federal student loan system. After the 1972 amendments to the Higher Education Act, which allowed for-profit colleges access to federal student aid, the small beauty school chain grew quickly, going from thirty-nine schools in the 1970s to fifty-eight schools by 1988, according to court documents. In the 1980s, when Gary attended Wilfred's Fordham campus, between 80% and 90% of the company's revenue came from federal student aid.[2]

The school targeted immigrants and low-income people as potential students and lured them into enrolling with promises of "free money," a lawsuit alleged. The hard sell came in part because admissions staff was motivated by a requirement to enroll a certain number of students within a given time to keep their jobs. In the mid-1980s, the Department of Education found that Wilfred signed students up who were ineligible to receive student loans because they didn't have a high school diploma or GED.[3]

Other former students' experience of Wilfred echoed Gary's. They attended the school in part because it seemed like "the thing to do," but they later realized the classes weren't going to result in employment or the ability to launch their own salon successfully.[4] As the sociologist Tressie McMillan Cottom documents in her book *Lower Ed: The Troubling Rise of For-Profit Colleges in the New Economy*, for-profit colleges often focus their recruitment efforts on women — particularly those without the safety net of a decent job with good benefits — who want the insurance that a degree theoretically provides but can't attend a more traditional school because of their work and caregiving responsibilities. In the end, those degrees are less likely to pay off than those from other types of schools.[5] In Wilfred's case, the Department of Justice eventually found that the company had embezzled millions of dollars from the Department of Education and that employees had lied on student loan applications, for example, by listing a student's family income as lower than it actually was so the student could access a larger student loan.[6]

Gary knew none of this, but her sense that the education wasn't going to give her what she signed up for pushed her to leave the school without her degree. Meanwhile, Wilfred continued to operate. The Department of Education tried to shut fifty-eight Wilfred locations out of the federal financial aid program, but the company was able to fight the move on procedural grounds.[7]

Ultimately, the company stopped operating in 1994.[8] Although Wilfred shuttered decades ago amid findings that it was lying to the government and its students, in 2022, Gary was still facing the consequences of the roughly $6,000 she originally borrowed to attend. Over the years she'd had her tax refund and her Social Security check garnished to repay the debt.

"That school has not been existing for over thirty years, so why you still trying to collect?" Gary asked.

That the money that Gary borrowed with the intention of bettering her life actually wound up haunting her for decades and threatening her livelihood in retirement is the result of a series of policy choices since the 1970s that turned federal student loans into a financial product, one that in some ways has fewer protections than other loans on the market. What fueled this shift? A combination of a media and political narrative that fostered skepticism of students' intentions, concerns about government waste and efficiency, and heavy reliance on commercial entities concerned with their bottom line to carry out a policy aimed at improving access to economic mobility.

A Policy Change Based on an Inflated Narrative

Perhaps one of the most widely known facts about student loans is that they're very difficult to discharge in bankruptcy—and some private student loans are collectible even after the borrower dies—but it wasn't always that way. In fact, in the mid-1970s, newspapers across the country chronicled how apparently easy it was for recent graduates to shed themselves of their student loans.

Pennsylvania's *Lancaster New Era* described a woman in Ohio who graduated with more than $4,100 in student debt but got rid of it through bankruptcy. In the meantime, she found a job that would pay her enough to repay the loan and made a down payment on a house.[9] The Associated Press cited a Wisconsin couple with $16,875 in student loans, which accounted for 98% of their debt, who filed for bankruptcy just months after finishing college.[10] The *New York Times* detailed the story of a student with a business degree and a master's in engineering who graduated from Stanford University Law School and filed for bankruptcy over $17,275 in student loans.[11] In a separate article, the *New York Times* News Service quoted a borrower who had discharged $12,000 in student debt through bankruptcy as feeling "no stigma whatsoever."[12]

Although some of the articles included caveats—for example, the premise of one piece was to say that graduates in a given town largely were not turning to bankruptcy to get rid of their student loans—many of the articles described a growing trend of recent students low on money in the present but with high earning potential getting rid of their student debt through bankruptcy while they

could.[13] The stories indicated that this apparent wave of bankruptcies could have implications for the student loan program, taxpayers, and the moral fiber of the country more broadly.

A quote in one of these stories from William J. Rubin, a federal
bankruptcy judge in Long Island, New York, exemplifies this tone.
"Sometimes when I see someone come before me with a job and no
other debt but a college loan—and not even a big one at that—I feel
like saying, 'Why you little stinker,'" he said, according to the *New
York Times* News Service. "Sometimes you know they're here to get
out of paying back a loan because they don't feel like having it any
more."[14]

The articles blamed many factors for what they saw as an uptick
in bankruptcies over student loans, including the country's changing
moral compass and a pamphlet published in 1975 that walked consumers through how to file for bankruptcy.[15] The reporters' sources
for many of these concerns: organizations that earned money by
making or collecting on (and in some cases both) federal student
loans as part of the bank-based loan program. In its discussion of
how student loan bankruptcies were "soaring," the *Lancaster New
Era* extensively quoted Kenneth Reeher, then the executive director
of the Pennsylvania Higher Education Assistance Agency. That state-
affiliated organization began in the 1960s and guaranteed federal
loans as part of the bank-based student loan program; it also eventually morphed into a lender and servicer.[16] Reeher told the paper
that in many cases, former students who file for bankruptcy are in
a position to pay the loan and are trying to "rip off" the system and
"avoid payment for as long as possible."[17]

He also complained of "pre-planned" bankruptcies, saying they
"really make you sick." "These are the persons who file for bankruptcy immediately upon completion of their education," the article
explained.[18] The article noted that Reeher worked with a local congressman to draft a bill that would ban student loan borrowers from
filing for bankruptcy within five years of graduating from school.[19]
The National Council of Higher Education Loan Programs, which

across the country represented organizations like the Pennsylvania Higher Education Assistance Agency, was also pushing for the change.[20]

In 1976, Congress did what these organizations urged and essentially banned borrowers from discharging federal student loans in bankruptcy for five years after a student left school, despite warnings from some about the potential consequences. (Later, lawmakers would make it nearly impossible for borrowers to discharge federal student debt through bankruptcy for the entire life of the loan.) Then congressman James G. O'Hara, a Michigan Democrat, wrote expressing his "deep disappointment" about the provision, describing it as "a discriminatory remedy for a 'scandal,' which exists primarily in the imagination."[21] He cited data indicating that concerns about an increase in student loan bankruptcies were overblown. For example, in Pennsylvania, a one-year 225% increase in bankruptcies related to student loans represented an uptick from four cases to only thirteen.[22]

"The proposal in this bill does not take away a special privilege from your children, and the growing number of adults, who have entered into educational indebtedness. On the contrary, it visits a special discrimination upon them," he wrote.[23] O'Hara also expressed skepticism of the stakeholders pushing for reforms, including "a number of those lenders who only make educational loans (and whose zeal to make ever more of them seems a little inconsistent with their apparent view that students can't be trusted)."[24] As O'Hara noted, the anecdotes of doctors and engineers discharging their student debt immediately after college were extremely rare— but the organizations that could benefit from banning borrowers from discharging their student debt used them as fuel to push for the change.

Banks that made other types of loans also opposed the provision because it would give institutions that loaned money to students privileges that were not available to other lenders. "This exception, in effect, gives the government agencies (which are the guarantors of many student loans) and educational institutions privileged treatment that is not warranted," the American Bankers Association told Congress. "This proposed change simply suggests that if sufficient political pressure can be generated, a special interest group can obtain special treatment under the bankruptcy law."[25]

About twenty years later, Congress quietly took another step that would take away an additional protection from student loan borrowers. Prior to that, there was a limit to how much time lenders and collectors participating in the student loan program had to bring a lawsuit. That statute of limitations was at least six years from when a borrower stopped paying on the loan.

In 1991, lawmakers changed that, apparently without much public discussion. They passed technical amendments—in theory, nonsubstantive changes to the law—to the Higher Education Act that, among other things, eliminated the statute of limitations on student loans. In other words, a lender could chase after students with loans for the rest of their life. In the one-paragraph explanation for the change provided in the *Congressional Record*, lawmakers expressed concerns similar to those they cited during the debate over exempting federal student loans from bankruptcy.

They called the statute of limitations on federal student loans "an arbitrary limitation of the Department of Education's ability to collect on older defaulted student loans." In addition, they wrote that getting rid of the statute of limitations was justified because student loans are a "unique type of debt" for which the ability to repay of someone who defaults on their student debt increases over time. "Moreover, student loans are made without regard to the credit worthiness of the borrower, and the benefits that the borrower receives through obtaining a student loan far outweigh any burden on the student resulting from the Federal Government's ability to collect on the loan over an indefinite period of time."[26]

That change opened the door for federal student loans to follow borrowers until they die. In a 2006 white paper, Deanne Loonin, a legal aid attorney who has been working in the student loan space for decades, noted how rare it is for a lender to be able to sue a borrower over a debt indefinitely. "This places student borrowers in unenviable, rarified company with murderers, traitors, and only a few violators of civil laws. Even rapists are not in this category since there is a statute of limitation for rape prosecutions, at least in federal law and in most state laws," she wrote.[27]

Congress Gives the Government Extraordinary Power to Collect Student Debt

In the 1990s, Congress expanded the government's collection powers once again, providing the feds with an extraordinary tool to claw money back from student loan borrowers who had defaulted on their debt. This time, the change was fueled by concerns from policymakers both in Congress and in the executive branch about the government failing to recoup taxpayer dollars.

Shortly after President Clinton entered office, his administration launched its "reinventing government" initiative.[28] The idea was to bring private-sector efficiency to the federal bureaucracy. As part of the initiative, the administration convened a group of federal employees to review all government agencies for areas in which they could streamline their processes and cut costs. In reviewing the Department of Education, the group recommended that the agency develop a strategy to maximize student loan collections.[29] "There is little doubt the average citizen expects the department to maximize its net revenues from debt collection," they wrote.[30]

A few years later, a bipartisan pair of lawmakers looked to make it easier to collect government debt of all kinds, in part to align with the reinventing government goals and, as the articles discussing it noted, to "ease pressure on the federal budget."[31] One of the representatives, Carolyn Maloney, a New York Democrat, hoped to approach the problem similarly to how she'd addressed New York City's debt collection woes as a member of the city council. At the time, she surveyed city agencies about the money they were owed.

"Later she summoned embarrassed agency officials before a city council committee to explain why they were not doing a better job of making deadbeats pay," the *Washington Post* wrote.[32]

In the survey of federal agencies that Maloney and Representative Steve Horn, a California Republican, conducted, they found that the government was owed between $50 billion and $55 billion. Maloney touted the idea of the government becoming increasingly aggressive in collecting funds owed to it as a liberal one, saying, "If you run your government better, you have more money for AmeriCorps, for school lunches."[33]

Although policymakers cited the need to recoup taxpayer funds and alleviate budget pressure as the main reasons they wanted to make it easier for the government to collect on its debts, there was another undercurrent to the discussion: that those who owed the money were choosing to shirk their loans. Maloney said the reason the government wasn't getting its money was because it was lax about collection, not because borrowers couldn't afford to pay. "Many delinquent debtors are able to pay," she wrote in a letter to the *New York Times*.[34] Although that may have been true of some, Maloney offered little evidence to back her assertion. In news stories, the parties that owed the money were described as "deadbeats," whether they were former college students, military veterans, or foreign governments.[35]

The result of this concern about the government's coffers and the assumption that those who owed the feds were choosing to walk away was the Debt Collection Improvement Act. The law, enacted in 1996, allowed, among other things, the federal government to garnish a borrower's Social Security benefits and federal tax refund to pay for a defaulted student loan.

In 2005, a decision by the Supreme Court officially combined the government's ability to collect a student loan indefinitely with its extraordinary collection powers, creating a scenario in which borrowers faced the feds slashing their Social Security benefits to repay a decades-old loan. The case was brought by sixty-seven-year-old

James Lockhart, a former postal worker who filed a lawsuit to try to stop the government from garnishing part of the $874 he received in Social Security.[36] As part of Lockhart's case, his attorneys argued that the 1991 change to the Higher Education Act removing the statute of limitations on federal student debt collection didn't apply to Social Security benefits—which at the time the case was brought, couldn't be garnished more than ten years after a borrower had stopped paying a loan—because when the law was passed in 1991, the government couldn't offset Social Security to repay student loans. Between 1984 and 1990, Lockhart took out student loans to attend a series of colleges.[37] By the time he filed his lawsuit, he had roughly $80,000 in student debt.[38]

The Court unanimously decided that the ten-year limit on offsetting Social Security benefits didn't apply to student loan collection.[39] Lockhart still had to pay, even with his only income coming from his Social Security check.

"I'm Still Not Financially Where I Need to Be"

Over the past several decades, the slow march of the student loan program to give the government extraordinary power to pursue debtors who default on their student loans has had consequences for borrowers like Patricia Gary.

After she left Wilfred Beauty Academy, Gary needed to figure out what she was going to do next. She'd ended up on public assistance, and as part of that program, she'd been matched with a volunteer opportunity working at a high school in the Bronx for pregnant teens. While Gary was volunteering, a position at the school became open and she took it. She then earned enough money to get off public assistance and to pay her student loan bills. But in 1995, Gary stopped receiving the bills. "They weren't being consistent, so when they stopped sending me statements for payment, I just assumed they just put it to the side or they moved on," Gary said. She didn't question why they had stopped or why she hadn't received any notification that her case was closed. Instead, she hoped that maybe the government had taken another look at her situation given that she owed money she borrowed to attend a school that shut down. But her wishful thinking didn't prove true; she defaulted in 1996 on the student loans she had borrowed to attend Wilfred.

A few years later, the government took her tax refund. It was only once Gary called the debt collector hired by the government to recoup her debt to inquire about the refund that she learned that she'd lapsed in repaying her beauty school loans and they'd gone into default. Gary and the debt collector came to an arrangement in which she would pay $100 a month.

Gary's experience with the fraudulent beauty school didn't deter her from pursuing higher education in the hope that it would improve her circumstances. While she was still paying that $100 a month toward her defaulted beauty school loan, Gary decided to try college again, this time paid for by her employer. "I knew I wanted to take advantage of the opportunity," Gary said, so when work ended in the afternoon, she'd take the subway to her evening classes. Throughout the five years of studying, Gary balanced her responsibilities to her work, her daughter, her husband, and keeping up her home with her course load. By the time she graduated with her degree in psychology and social work, Gary wasn't exactly proud, but she felt she'd overcome those distractions and challenges to achieve a goal she'd wanted to complete.

Gary enrolled in graduate school right away, which she and her then husband paid for out of pocket, to study human services. "I knew in order for me to make a life comfortable for myself, I needed to advance," Gary said, "so that's why I went right after to make sure that I was preparing myself for some better protection and security."

"I was able to achieve a lot of good things in my life because of those opportunities that were available," Gary added, "but I'm still not financially where I need to be."

And indeed, that financial precarity made it difficult for Gary to keep up with the payment plan she'd arranged with the debt collector. After sixteen years of making those $100 monthly payments, Gary was no longer in a position to pay down the loan. She was retired, divorced, and living on her Social Security and a small pension, which she put toward necessities.[40] Gary had just $700 a month to pay for food and medicine, so once again she fell behind on the debt she had borrowed to attend Wilfred.

In 2019, she received a letter indicating that the government was going to take part of her Social Security check to repay the loan. "That I could not allow them to do because I would have been in a terrible position," Gary said. She called an attorney, and during a meeting with him, Gary learned how much she had already put toward the debt. In the more than thirty years since Gary had left Wilfred out of frustration, she'd paid $23,000, although she originally borrowed $6,000 and still owed $3,882—$3,337 of which was principal, meaning that the decades of loan payments didn't even cover half of the original amount Gary borrowed. She remained plagued by the debt when we spoke in 2022. The only thing keeping it manageable was the federal government's pause on student loan payments and collections.

"Having this longevity of this student loan is very annoying to me," she said. "I'm seventy-four years old—why am I still paying this loan? It makes no sense to me. Why would I continue paying you for something that has been overpaid three times?"

Gary is one of the dozens of people her attorney, Johnson Tyler, encounters who are facing the harshest consequences of the student loan system. Typically, they come to him because their defaulted student loan has them caught in a financial bind—they can't borrow to go back to school; their wages, Social Security benefits, or tax refund have been taken. Witnessing this experience is a large part of what motivated Tyler to focus his legal aid practice on student loan issues.

"I spent a lot of time helping people get benefits," Tyler said of Social Security checks. "That's what I started doing when I got out of law school. I could see how crucial those benefits were for people to get by. I spent a lot of time trying to protect those benefits from creditors. To have the federal government doing the same thing just seemed really outrageous." The government's approach to this population is particularly egregious, Tyler told me, given that borrowers are typically in default because they can't afford to pay the loans that were supposed to help them improve their economic circumstances. To Tyler, that dynamic made the system seem "out of whack." "It's not doing what it was supposed to do."[41]

Despite that the reason these borrowers defaulted is often tied to a failure of the student loan system—whether by leaving them vulnerable to being taken advantage of by an unscrupulous college or making it more difficult than necessary to enroll in an affordable repayment plan—Tyler is often struck by how the system treats the borrowers.

Of Gary, for example, he said, "I think she's devalued." After Wilfred, Gary spent her career contributing to her community by working with foster youth; she made payments on her loan when she could afford to—and yet it ballooned. "Too many borrowers in default are thought of as, 'Oh, you're just irresponsible,'" Tyler said. "It really doesn't paint the picture of who they are."[42]

Gary is just one of millions of borrowers who are at risk of losing out on their Social Security checks, tax refunds, or wages over a student loan. Roughly 6.8 million borrowers had loans in default as of September 2023, out of a total of forty-three million student loan borrowers.[43] That's despite programs like income-driven repayment that are meant to protect borrowers from falling behind on their student loan payments even when they're facing financial strain.

Once these borrowers default, the government can take their tax refunds and Social Security checks, just like it took Gary's. The number of borrowers entering retirement with this concern lingering is only likely to grow. Between 2003 and 2019, borrowers aged sixty to sixty-nine years old saw their student loan balances grow the fastest.[44] And because there's no statute of limitations on the debt, and it's extremely difficult to get rid of it in bankruptcy, the government can take these borrowers' Social Security—as long as they leave the borrower with at least $750 in Social Security benefits, a floor that hasn't been adjusted since the Debt Collection Improvement Act was signed into law in 1996—until they die.

Younger borrowers trying to achieve economic security for their families can also get ensnared by the government's powerful collection tools. The government can take defaulted borrowers' Earned Income Tax Credit, or EITC, to repay their student loans. That's even though the tax credit is an antipoverty program geared toward helping working families and policymakers from both parties agree it works. I've spoken with home health aides, bus drivers, stroke survivors, and others who were relying on their EITC to catch up on bills and buy shoes for their children.[45] Often, losing the EITC money can be counterproductive, advocates say, because without the necessary funds to fix a car or pay for childcare, people struggle to find work that would ultimately help them repay their student loan.

The government does offer borrowers pathways out of default so they can protect future Social Security checks or tax refunds from being offset. But the sprawling student loan system, which over the years has involved a variety of private actors, can make it difficult for borrowers to complete the process—or even know about it.

For decades, the government has worked with private collection agencies to recoup defaulted student loans, despite consumer advocates' concerns about how debt collectors treat borrowers. Historically, these companies' financial incentives have largely driven borrowers' experiences. And it's no wonder given the companies' dual and conflicting mandates to collect defaulted student debt and advise borrowers on how to exit default. For example, at least since the early 1990s, borrowers have had the right to negotiate a payment plan that would lead them toward a pathway out of default that was in line with their economic circumstances. But for years, in practice, debt collectors would rarely allow borrowers to make a monthly payment that was less than a certain percentage of the loan. At the time, the Department of Education paid a debt collector its full commission only if it collected that percentage. Once the agency changed its policy in 2012 to pay a full commission even when debt collectors made payment arrangements that were in line with a borrower's income, the number of borrowers taking advantage of this route to get out of default increased tremendously.[46]

In the years since, the design of the student debt collection system made it challenging in other ways for borrowers in default to become current on their loans. To exit default, borrowers can either rehabilitate or consolidate their loans. Rehabilitation requires borrowers to make nine on-time monthly payments within ten months. Once that period ends, the borrower's account is transferred to a student loan servicer where, theoretically, they have access to income-driven repayment to keep monthly payments manageable and avoid defaulting again.

But the Consumer Financial Protection Bureau has repeatedly found that debt collectors and student loan servicers throw up obstacles on this months-long journey that can make it difficult for borrowers to cure their default and avoid defaulting once again. But because of the payment structure for debt collectors and the fact that borrowers in default often aren't adequately counseled on their options and what's needed to stay current, a large share of defaulted borrowers have, at least historically, used rehabilitation to get out of default, even if it's a risky path to keeping their loans manageable, according to Persis Yu, the deputy executive director of the Student Borrower Protection Center who has worked on student loan issues, and default in particular, for years.[47] For example, the process of transferring a borrower's account from the debt collection agency to a student loan servicer where they can access income-driven repayment can take several months, the Consumer Financial Protection Bureau found. And once a borrower's loan reaches a servicer, enrolling in income-driven repayment can be time-consuming as well as paperwork heavy for both the borrower and the student loan company, which can put the borrower at risk of not enrolling in the plan.[48] The agency also noted that in some cases, borrowers pay a certain amount to a debt collector that is based on a verbal agreement, but later the company invalidates those payments once it has received the borrower's income documentation.[49]

Despite these challenges, roughly 70% of defaulted borrowers who became current did so through rehabilitation, the Consumer Financial Protection Bureau estimated in 2016.[50] That's even though consolidation is often a simpler process. When a borrower consolidates a loan out of default, it's immediately placed with a student loan servicer, and the borrower can start making payments under an income-driven plan. In 2023, the government settled a lawsuit with defaulted borrowers, who alleged they didn't receive information about getting out of default quickly through consolidation. Instead, they lost out on their tax refunds during the several-month period when the rehabilitation process was being completed. As part of the deal, the government agreed to overhaul the notices to inform borrowers that they can stop collections through consolidation.[51]

That rehabilitation even exists as an option is a vestige of the bank-based student loan program originally created in the 1960s and the interests of the commercial entities that participated in it. In that system, when a borrower defaulted on student debt, the loan would transfer to a guaranty agency, which would facilitate the government's payment to the lender, and then the guaranty agency would work to collect on the debt. It would also need to sell the loan to another lender, and a history of on-time monthly payments would make the loan look like a more attractive investment.[52]

Although the government stopped making loans through the bank-based lending program in 2010, the student debt collection system remains so sprawling, with so many actors involved, that even when the government has wanted to cut it off, it has struggled to do so. During the COVID-19-era payment freeze, the government paused collection activity on most defaulted student loans, and yet thousands of borrowers still had their wages garnished to repay the debt months into the pause.[53] As part of a lawsuit filed on behalf of some of these borrowers, the government revealed that it tried to communicate to employers that they should stop garnishing wages, and yet hundreds of employers continued to do so. Instead of continuing to attempt to contact the employers or work to stop them from garnishing borrowers' wages in other ways, the government closed the post office box where the firms were sending their employees' funds. That way, the feds could say that, technically, during the pandemic, they'd stopped collecting on defaulted student debt through wage garnishment, even though some borrowers were still seeing a portion of their paychecks disappear.[54]

Policymakers' Choices Steadily Increase the Government's Power

It is possible for a decades-old student loan to continue to haunt Patricia Gary, threatening her livelihood in old age, only because of a series of choices by policymakers over the years that steadily increased the government's power to collect on a student loan. Some decisions were based more explicitly than others on a narrative that borrowers who defaulted on their loans were deadbeats, deserving of aggressive collection activity because they were shirking their responsibility to the government and to taxpayers.

More recently, at least, the narrative has shifted among some to acknowledge that aspects of our debt-financed higher education system may be trapping defaulted borrowers unfairly in financial purgatory. For example, policymakers have learned that students who attended for-profit colleges like Gary account for 10% of enrolled students but make up about half of borrowers who default on their student loans.[55] This reality has pushed policymakers in the direction of increasing accountability and more readily canceling the debt held by former for-profit college students in cases where the schools have collapsed amid allegations of fraud.

At the time of this writing, the government is in the midst of a years-long overhaul of the student loan servicing and collections system, which has included terminating the contracts of the private collection agencies collecting defaulted student loans (although some were rehired into the new system).[56] In addition, the government has indicated that it will be less aggressive when challenging federal student loan borrowers' efforts to discharge their debt in bankruptcy.[57] Although the law making it very challenging to get rid of federal student debt in bankruptcy remains on the books, because the government is typically the lender, the feds' decision to change the government's posture toward borrowers who try to discharge these debts should make it easier for them to get rid of the loans. Finally, the Biden administration brought defaulted borrowers current on their loans during the COVID-19-era pause on federal student loans and gave them a year from when the freeze ended to take steps to remain current on their loans.

Still, these changes don't address "the fundamental problems" with the government's system for collecting on defaulted student loans, said Persis Yu, who has focused on the student debt collection system as an attorney representing low-income borrowers and as an advocate. That's because the proposals don't end the "punitive nature" of student loan debt collection, she told me. These practices are one of many examples of the ways a system originally envisioned to better the lives of individuals and the country has fallen short of those goals due to its design. And yet we continue to sink more time and money into it. "There's a better fundamental way to think about people who are in financial distress and what services should we be providing to get them into a better place," she said.[58]

Indeed, the reality remains that borrowers like Patricia Gary can be haunted for decades by their decision to try to improve their economic circumstances through education—a choice that for many, because of the government's extraordinary power to collect on student loans, ended up exacerbating their financial precarity instead of improving it.

"Does it ever stop?" Gary asked of the efforts to collect her debt, "or they just want to keep taking money because they can do it?"

8. Forgiveness

A Radical Solution Goes Mainstream

On a sunny morning in September 2022, dozens of student loan advocates gathered in an office building in downtown Washington, DC, to discuss "what happens next ~~if~~ now that student debt is canceled," as the agenda and other materials advertised. The scratched-out word signaled how the conversation surrounding student debt forgiveness had changed in the weeks leading up to the meeting. Some milled about a registration table and cardboard carafes of coffee, making small talk and reliving the best moments from the reception the night before. Others, including some wearing masks with the phrase #CancelStudentDebt, sat in a room closed off from the lobby with glass doors as they waited for the program to start.

Amid the din, a hush came over the several rows of chairs in the meeting room, and those outside the glass doors rushed to take their seats. Heads swiveled to the aisle as Senator Elizabeth Warren walked to the podium at the front of the room to deliver remarks.

"We have to celebrate how far we've come because this is a big damn deal," she told the crowd. Just weeks earlier, President Joe Biden had announced a plan to cancel up to $10,000 in student debt for most borrowers and up to $20,000 in student debt for borrowers who had received a Pell Grant in college.[1] It wasn't as much as many in the room, including Warren, had hoped for. "Is there anyone who doesn't know how much student loan debt cancellation I wanted?" she quipped.

But Biden's announcement represented a mainstreaming of student loan forgiveness, an idea that only ten years earlier was often dismissed as radical by the media and student loan experts. "Many millions of people across the country thought we could never get there," Warren said to the crowd.

And indeed, for years, advocates and activists had been pushing the idea forward in the face of skepticism. One of them was Nathan Hornes II, whose experience with the student loan system had moved him to agitate.

A Commercial That Signaled Opportunity

While growing up in Missouri, Hornes was sure he'd become a pop star. When he was a little kid, Hornes's aunt, who worked in the music industry, noticed he could sing and that his sister could write and perform. Ever since, his aunt had taken a keen interest in establishing their careers. Hornes's mom was in on the mission; she signed Hornes up for piano lessons, and the siblings participated in studio recording sessions as teenagers. Eventually, a few independent labels started taking an interest in Hornes, and the family moved to Southern California to bring them closer to the industry.

Once they arrived, Hornes, who packed more energy than it seemed his compact stature could hold, wrote songs for other artists, worked on a web series, helped a celebrity with an activism-related side project, and scored a record deal but then had it fall through. Now he was coming up against a deadline. "My mom was like, 'If you can't financially support yourself in two years, you're going to school,'" Hornes recalled. "Those two years came up." The money and connections Hornes and his sister had cobbled together still weren't enough to financially sustain them. They started thinking about school.

When a commercial for Everest College came on the television during a talk show, the ad piqued Hornes's interest. The school seemed to be offering the opportunity to pursue a degree while working, and Hornes and his sister were hoping to fit in their classes around practices and recording sessions. Hornes called the number in the commercial. "After that phone call, for weeks and weeks on end, they would call me seven to ten times a day," Hornes said of Everest's recruiters.

Everest was part of Corinthian Colleges, a chain of for-profit schools that had been in operation since 1995 and listed on the stock market since 1999.[2] In the years before Hornes saw that Everest commercial, Corinthian officials and staffers worked aggressively to lure students and the student loan dollars that came with them, according to a Senate investigation. Training documents instructed admissions officers to deflect any time a prospective student would ask questions about the cost of classes.[3] Recruiters allegedly signed up homeless students with no ability to repay their debts, and admission staff bragged to potential enrollees about job placement rates that they inflated by as much as 37%.[4]

The strategy worked. Between 2006 and 2010, the year Hornes enrolled, Corinthian's enrollment grew from 67,143 to 113,818.[5] That increase in enrollment substantially boosted Corinthian's revenue, which climbed from $909 million in 2006 to $1.67 billion in 2010.[6] Although in the years leading up to Hornes's encounter with Everest, Corinthian had faced some regulatory pushback—attorneys general had periodically investigated, sometimes sued, and even settled with the company—its schools continued to operate.[7] The two accrediting bodies that oversaw most of Corinthian's campuses, organizations that serve as gatekeepers to federal financial aid for colleges, hadn't pulled their seal of approval. Corinthian executives flitted in and out of accreditors' leadership ranks.[8]

Eventually, after the barrage of phone calls, Hornes and his sister decided to visit the school. They took the bus to Everest's Ontario-Metro campus, about forty miles east of Los Angeles, to take a tour. When they arrived, an admissions representative told them it was the end of her day and there wouldn't be time for the tour. The siblings would have to sign up for classes that day or else spots would run out. The two should enroll, she urged, so they could set a good example for their younger sister by starting college. She told the pair not to worry about the cost; they qualified for financial aid and scholarships. Suddenly the siblings found themselves on the phone with their mom, asking her for financial information so they could enroll. "The financial aid situation happened extremely fast," Hornes said.

To Hornes, the school looked and felt like a community college. That's what he and his sister assumed they'd signed up for. Most students at the school commuted, and there weren't any dorms. But the hurried enrollment process made their mom skeptical.

"We were like, 'This is great, we'll still be able to go to school and do our music and live our dream,'" Hornes remembered.

As Hornes worked toward his associate's degree in business, there were moments that made him suspicious about the value of his education at Everest. Adjunct professors with experience in their fields would warn Hornes and his fellow students about continuing on at Everest; a student who had completed a class a few weeks before was suddenly teaching it; some students could get by with passing grades even while playing Monopoly in class.

Then there was the school's aggressive approach to financial aid. Every six months or so, Hornes would be called into an office with several cubicles. By the time Hornes sat down, a financial aid staffer had already filled out paperwork with Hornes's name and personal details. They would ask him to type in his unique ID from the federal financial aid system, flip to the last page of the documents, and tell him to sign. All he had to do was agree, and they would "repack"— shorthand for *repackage*—his financial aid. "All of this stuff is literally going over my head," Hornes recalled of those meetings. The staffers sold Hornes on the new financial aid package, telling him he'd receive a full benefit. "You're thinking you don't have to pay," Hornes said.

But it wasn't until he'd spent two years at Everest and earned his associate's degree that Hornes started to suspect that his school wasn't like most others. He and a friend shopped their transcript around to different California public colleges, hoping they could transfer for the remaining two years of their bachelor's degrees. The colleges all told Hornes they wouldn't accept the credits he'd already earned. "Excuse me?" Hornes thought. The colleges told him he'd have to start all over. "There was no way that I was doing that," Hornes recalled.

Those conversations were the first time Hornes heard Everest described as a for-profit college. "We actually are stuck," he realized. "There is no way out—once you're in, you're in until you're done." Every job application Hornes reviewed required a bachelor's degree, but if he wanted to earn the credential without beginning his college education from scratch in his early twenties, he'd have to stay at Everest despite his growing suspicions.

A Movement Begins in Zuccotti Park

In 2011, around the same time Hornes was studying at Everest and becoming increasingly skeptical of its offerings, on the other side of the country, activists gathered at New York City's Zuccotti Park to publicly question everything about America's financial system, including the value of higher education and the student debt often required to earn a degree.

One of them was Ann Larson, the daughter of public school teachers. She'd attended college and graduate school in the hopes that the degrees would help her attain a middle-class life. But instead, she found herself in debt and struggling to get a foothold in the academic job market. While she was in graduate school and borrowing to attend, she worked as a part-time instructor at the City University of New York and watched her students borrow to be in her class.[9] "It was depressing," she said.

Larson had always thought of herself as a leftist, and she was looking for a way to engage when she first started to hear on Facebook about what would become Occupy Wall Street.[10] "I was searching. I was looking for something—when that happened I recognized immediately those are my people," she said of Occupy. So Larson went to the park and became connected with other activists who were interested in tackling the issue of student debt and higher education. They came up with an idea to ask borrowers to pledge not to repay their student debt once one million others had agreed to do the same. The activists hoped it would pressure stakeholders to address their demands, including free public college and writing off existing student debt.

Shortly after the police evicted protesters from Zuccotti Park, the group launched its campaign with a mock graduation ceremony. Larson and others stood in graduation gowns and mortarboards made of trash bags, holding signs that read No More Student Debt and Education for the 99%. "We have been thrilled to have you, you and you, and all of your money at this institution," the fictional college president said.[11] Larson found herself standing next to Thomas Gokey, another activist who'd been drawn to Occupy in part by his experience with higher education.[12]

A few years earlier, as a graduate student earning a master's degree in fine arts, Gokey had conceived of a project aimed at interrogating the value of his degree. He used roughly $49,983—the amount of his student debt at the time—in shredded currency he'd received from the Federal Reserve to create four large sheets of paper on which he planned to draw his diploma, but he never did. A few years later, Gokey started to sell that work piecemeal, often in $5 increments, at ArtPrize, an annual festival in Grand Rapids, Michigan, where artists display and sell their work. At the time, Gokey saw his debt as an individual problem, so he was trying to solve it by doing something "just clever enough to get people to send you a little bit of money," he said. But at the same time, he started to learn about the history and philosophy underpinning his debt and others through texts like David Graeber's *Debt: The First 5,000 Years*.

Eventually, Gokey ended up on an email thread with several Occupy activists, including Graeber, who explained in an email how credit card debt was worth much less on the secondary market. If an original creditor, like a credit card company, decides it is unlikely to collect on a debt, it will sell it to a debt buyer, often for much less than what the borrower owes. The debt buyers make money by collecting whatever they can on the loan, and because they often got it for pennies on the dollar, almost anything they collect is profit. The combination of that revelation and the relative success to that point of the Occupy protests persuaded Gokey that he needed to be in Zuccotti Park fighting that lopsided balance of power. "Forty-eight hours after being in Zuccotti, my brain flipped," Gokey said of his arrival at Occupy Wall Street in the fall of 2011. "I couldn't see debt the same way anymore." Once there, he started attending meetings with Larson and others and doing more research on the idea of buying up consumer debt on the secondary market and canceling it.

By the time Astra Taylor started attending Occupy-adjacent meetings focused on student debt, Gokey was already deep in his research about how to contact debt brokers to buy up the loans. Taylor's experience with student loans also had her questioning the higher education finance system. Lured by prestige, she'd taken out the maximum amount in student debt to attend Brown University for a year as an undergraduate. Taylor ultimately ended up finishing her degree for free by transferring to the University of Georgia and paying for school through the HOPE Scholarship, the merit-based state grant program on which Bill Clinton had based his mid-1990s tax credit proposal. Taylor transferred in part because she was nervous about how borrowing for Brown would affect her future, but she went on to earn a master's degree and again found herself borrowing to pay for it. When the economy crashed a few years after Taylor graduated, she defaulted on her debt.

That experience, plus some reading she'd been doing on the topic, gave Taylor a "growing political sense that student debt was a systemic issue," she said. "I was like, 'Yeah, this is really different, the baby boomer generation didn't take on this much debt,'" she said. But she was mostly thinking those thoughts on her own. "What was really pivotal was going to Occupy and suddenly finding myself in a community of people also talking about this issue."

After Occupy ended, some of the people involved in student debt work during the protests, along with a new group of activists, decided to see whether they could signal how worthless medical debt was to its owners and how liberating it would be for borrowers to be free of it by buying up and canceling some debt. Larson began building a website where donors could pitch in to buy up the loans. Even relatively small donations could have a big impact—$5,000 was enough to purchase more than $100,000 in debt that borrowers owed. For several months, she obsessed over the project, neglecting other parts of her life while fearing that the idea wouldn't take off, especially because the initial debt refusal pledge had flopped. Taylor used her media and entertainment industry connections—her partner was part of the popular indie rock band Neutral Milk Hotel—to organize a kickoff event.

At Le Poisson Rouge, a concert venue and bar in Manhattan's Greenwich Village, the comedians Janeane Garofalo and Hari Kondabolu performed, and musical acts took the stage. By the end of the night, they'd raised more than $300,000 for the project, which they were calling the Rolling Jubilee, inspired by the biblical tradition of regularly freeing slaves and debtors from their obligations.[13] The campaign's success, while exciting, also made organizers wary.

Ever since the group working on the project, then known as Strike Debt, had an online presence, debtors would email the organization, sharing stories of how their loans had affected their lives. "You really felt an obligation to those people who you didn't know, but who saw in what they were seeing in Strike Debt and Rolling Jubilee, some hope," Larson said. Taylor called the event's success "literally overwhelming." "We've committed to spending this money ethically," she remembers thinking.

Gokey was anxious too. The group needed to find the right kind of loan portfolios—the file still held by the original lender or, at a minimum, sold only once or twice—and the debts had to be recent enough that an address in a borrower's file was current. In addition, before the group bought a portfolio, Rolling Jubilee had to be sure that a debt buyer hadn't also sold the file to someone else. The caution was important, according to Gokey, because "it's really, really easy if you don't know what you're doing to be taken advantage of and to be sold junk."

Gokey took on the responsibility of vetting the portfolios before Rolling Jubilee made a purchase. Donors would often send notes with their PayPal transfers to the group, explaining how little money they had or how much debt they were in but how important it was to them to send the group one or five dollars anyway. "Being responsible for all of that money was terrifying," Gokey said, so he would spend months in his Syracuse apartment researching a portfolio before the group bought it. In some cases, even after Gokey spent several forty-hour weeks vetting a file, he would deem the transaction too risky, and he'd have to go looking for a new one.

Shocked by Draconian Tactics

In the years leading up to and following the Occupy protests, Eileen Connor was starting to see the impact that for-profit colleges, like the one Hornes attended, were having on low-income New Yorkers. Connor was looking for ways to fight the systems making and keeping people poor through litigation as part of her work at the New York Legal Assistance Group, a nonprofit law firm. Through that work, it became clear that for-profit colleges were luring low-income New Yorkers to an education that didn't provide the economic advancement they were promised—and a lot of debt.

Connor was not only shocked by the "scummy stuff that the schools would do"; she was also struck by the way the Department of Education was approaching the issue. On the one hand, the department continued to let the schools operate in the federal student loan program. On the other hand, the department was "just being draconian in their insistence on collecting debt even in the face of very strong evidence that the debt should probably be discharged," Connor said.

At a meeting in the early 2010s, during which the Department of Education convened stakeholders to discuss a potential rule to hold for-profit colleges accountable for providing students with decent labor market outcomes, Connor began to understand a bit more the dynamics behind the mismatch in policy.

"I saw just how much pressure was being put on the department from the side of industry," she said. "There were think tanks and policy organizations who thought, 'There's a smarter way for us to be doing our investment in higher education—we really should be making sure that people complete.' Their interests were aligned with borrowers, but it wasn't borrowers—people who had the most skin in the game were not being represented," she said.

In the early 2010s, other legal aid attorneys started sharing the devastation on borrowers' lives they were witnessing with staffers at the newly formed Consumer Financial Protection Bureau, including Mike Pierce, one of the first hires in the bureau's student loan division. Pierce came to the work with a sense that the system was rigged against households trying to pay for college. As a law student, he'd interned at the Department of Education, but as Pierce neared graduation, then New York attorney general Andrew Cuomo exposed a scheme whereby college financial aid offices were taking money from student loan companies to push them toward certain lenders, including by creating preferred lender lists.[14] "My financial aid office where I went to college was taking kickbacks," Pierce learned.

He decided that working in Congress would provide him with a better opportunity to address the issues than returning to the Department of Education. Pierce begged his way into a fellowship on the staff of Maryland congressman John Sarbanes, who was both his hometown representative and had a seat on the House of Representatives committee overseeing education. One day, then professor Elizabeth Warren came to the office to meet with Sarbanes about the new consumer bureau she was charged with launching, Pierce remembers. But Sarbanes was out on a vote, so Pierce spoke with Warren about the bureau, and she connected him with Rohit Chopra, who would become the agency's first student loan ombudsman.

Warren "was the first public official I had heard talking about student debt in household terms rather than a symptom of college costs," Pierce said. "I just wanted them to just sign me up," Pierce said of Warren and Chopra, who became the Consumer Financial Protection Bureau's director during the Biden administration. "It was a very exciting moment. I had been struggling to grab a toe hold on this thing that I had perceived to be a big public policy problem."

The student loan office started out by focusing on the private student loan market, where a story similar to what had happened in the mortgage crisis was playing out. Investor interest in assets backed by the loans, as well as the decision by lenders to loosen underwriting criteria, fueled growth in the private student loan market in the mid-2000s.[15] As the economy turned and borrowers struggled to pay their student loan bills, lenders started to retreat from the private student loan market.[16]

In complaints the bureau received about private student loans and in discussions with legal aid attorneys, Pierce and other staffers began to hear about students at for-profit colleges who were pushed into predatory loan products. What they learned from the advocates is that in the absence of traditional private lenders, these schools launched their own affiliated loan programs. The schools needed their students to have access to private loans in order to stay in compliance with the federal student loan program. The schools would inflate tuition prices above federal student loan limits, pushing students toward the private loan product and ensuring that at least 10% of their revenue came from a source other than federal financial aid—in line with the 90/10 rule, or the requirement that for-profit colleges get at least 10% of their revenue from sources other than federal financial aid. The regulation so carefully considered in the early 1990s was once again easily undone by unscrupulous for-profit colleges.[17]

Graduation Followed by Protest

After learning he couldn't transfer his credits, Hornes continued at Everest, determined to earn his bachelor's degree. Despite the fog of suspicion that hung over his classes and interactions with staff, Hornes was determined to get what he could out of his education. He absorbed all he could from the accounting and human resources courses taught by decent teachers. And so by the time he was ready to graduate in 2014 with a 3.9 grade point average and a bachelor's degree in business administration, Hornes was excited to celebrate his accomplishments by walking across the stage in a cap and gown.

But as he and his fellow students were gathered in a room, putting on their regalia and taking pictures with one another, school officials walked in and asked to make an announcement. The officials told Hornes and his fellow graduates that they would need to sign a form to walk across the stage. By signing the paperwork, the graduates agreed not to sue Everest if they couldn't find a job. "That was a major red flag for me," Hornes said. But like most of the other graduates gathered in the room, he'd already invested so much in his education. Hornes signed the paper.

About a week later, Hornes was walking around campus and saw a fellow student who also worked in the school's library standing outside his now-former employer, holding up a sign saying he'd been fired. The student was protesting because he believed the school's plan was to hire him temporarily all along to boost its job placement numbers and then lay him off once his employment had been counted for the statistics. "At that point I was like, 'We're making a change right now,'" Hornes said. He decided that he needed to understand how his school truly worked and what it was hiding from its students. Hornes and a handful of his friends began meeting and contacting students at other California Everest campuses to see what they could learn and what recourse they might have against the school.

Debt Organizers Have a Breakthrough

In the couple of years following the success of the Rolling Jubilee, momentum around Strike Debt started to fizzle, but a core group of organizers, including Larson, Taylor, and Gokey, stayed in touch. Then, as Larson would write later on her Substack blog, called *Leverage*," "a breakthrough occurred" that the group "could not have scripted in advance."[18] They read about a group of former students from an Everest College campus who were starting to question the amount of debt they took on to attend the school and the education it was providing them—and to protest about it.[19]

Around that time, the organizers bought up and canceled some student loans held by Corinthian Colleges. But even when the students had the debt their school held canceled, they were still often plagued by tens of thousands of dollars in federal student loans. Another member of the group, Luke Herrine, began researching whether there was a way for the former students to get rid of their federal loans.

Herrine had become involved with the group through post-Occupy meetings in New York City's Judson Memorial Church, a house of worship that had long been a home for activism, ranging from pre-*Roe v. Wade* abortion counseling to funerals for AIDS victims as they were turned away from other churches. Herrine, then a law student, walked the block from his school to the brown-brick building with arched windows at the edge of Washington Square Park to the first open Rolling Jubilee meeting. "It was still broadly run in an anarchist way," Herrine recalled of the first meetings. "It was easy to just show up and figure out what was going on and contribute."

By the summer of 2014, Herrine was working as a legal intern at the Consumer Financial Protection Bureau, but outside of work, he would spend time poring over the Higher Education Act, the statute governing the federal student loan system, looking for any hook the group could latch onto with its cause. Eventually, buried in its hundreds of pages, he found a reference to a borrower's ability to assert a defense against repayment of their federal student loans in cases when school representatives misled students in the process of enrolling them. Essentially, the Higher Education Act allowed students who had borrowed money from the government to attend schools that officials shouldn't have sanctioned in the first place to argue their debts should be canceled.

"This seems a little too easy," Herrine thought. He wondered why, if there was a legal mechanism borrowers could use to get rid of their federal student loans, no one had done it. Soon, he learned it wasn't for lack of trying.

Searching for Ways to Hold Corinthian Accountable

While borrowers and activists were searching for ways to get rid of student loans from Corinthian, staffers at the Department of Education were looking for strategies to hold the school accountable. The office of the California attorney general, then Kamala Harris, was actively investigating claims that Corinthian misled students about job placement rates. Attorneys there had secured Corinthian's

placement data as well as student records and were using a foren-
sic accounting firm to calculate how the real placement rates compared to the company's advertising. The Department of Education
and Harris's office came to an agreement that essentially depu-
tized Harris as an agent of the department, according to Aaron
Ament, who served as chief of staff in the Department of Education's Office of General Counsel during the later years of the Obama
administration.

As part of the joint investigation, the Department of Education
requested more student records from Corinthian. When the company failed to produce the records, the agency said it would delay
access to its federal financial aid funds. That put such a squeeze on
Corinthian's bottom line that the company began winding down its
operations. Still, the school continued to enroll new students.[20]

The Consumer Financial Protection Bureau also started taking
action against Corinthian to try to stop the practice it had initially
heard about from legal advocates and borrowers. In 2014, it sued
the company over its private lending program, which the bureau
called an "illegal predatory lending scheme." The bureau alleged
that Corinthian used false job placement rates to lure students into
taking on private loans and illegally strong-armed students into repaying those loans, including by pulling them out of class to shame
them into paying the debt and withholding diplomas.[21]

Less publicly, bureau staffers were also monitoring the companies that the government hired to manage the federal student loan
program. The first prominent result of its efforts was a $60 million deal
between Sallie Mae and the Department of Justice to settle claims
that Sallie Mae failed to provide servicemembers with student loan
benefits to which they were entitled. The Justice Department's investigation spun out of complaints from servicemembers received by
the Consumer Financial Protection Bureau. Although the conduct
and settlement applied to a discrete group of borrowers, it hinted
at broader challenges that borrowers might face in getting access
to the student loan benefits they're entitled to. "Every student who

has taken out a federal student loan should have the peace of mind that the department's servicers are following the law and treating all borrowers fairly," then secretary of education Arne Duncan said in announcing the settlement.[22]

Preparing to Strike

Larson and other activists flew out to Los Angeles to meet Hornes and other students who had attended Corinthian-owned campuses and were looking for ways to fight back against the school. Strike Debt was by then Called the Debt Collective, a nod to the idea that had fueled the organization since its early days—a union of debtors could wrest power from creditors. "They were the ones who knew what happened to them, they were the ones who had compelling personal stories," Larson said. But the Debt Collective organizers brought some knowledge with them, including that the students couldn't fight the company through a class-action lawsuit because they'd signed away their rights to sue. They worked to redirect the former students' energy.

"We told them, 'Your main target is not the school. Your main target is the Department of Education in Washington, DC. That's your enemy. They're responsible for this,'" Larson said.

For Hornes, meeting members of the Debt Collective at a coffee shop legitimized the conversations he'd been having over the past few months. Hornes had never heard of the idea of organizing—or bringing together a group of people to exert their unified power—until the Debt Collective arrived, but he realized that's what he'd been doing all along. Hornes also learned that his experience transcended Everest and California—there were victims of high-pressure sales tactics, misleading financial aid conversations, and shoddy classes at other schools across the country.

Hornes was also beginning to understand the extent of the harm he suffered by attending Everest. A few months after graduating, Hornes received a letter from a student loan company telling him that he owed roughly $68,000. Hornes didn't remember signing up for any federal student loans. Every time he was called into the financial aid office at Everest and asked to put his information into the federal financial aid website, he thought he was signing up for grants—an experience shared by other former Corinthian students, at least according to litigation. At one point, financial aid officers told him the grant aid wouldn't cover the cost of his classes, but they had signed him up for a private loan he could repay while in school. (That private loan was part of a school-affiliated loan program that drew the ire of the Consumer Financial Protection Bureau; Corinthian officials allegedly lured students into taking on these debts so that the school could stay compliant with the 90/10 rule).[23]

Hornes always knew he'd taken on a private loan to pay for Corinthian, but when he saw the bill for his federal debt, he called the company to see if there was a mistake. The representative asked him if his name was Nathan Hornes and whether he attended Everest College from 2010 to 2014. Hornes couldn't deny that was the case. He realized he owed the money but had no idea how he would repay it—the sum was untenable on the salary he was earning at a local airport.

The borrowers, with help from the Debt Collective activists, took their plight to Department of Education staffers. They testified to Ted Mitchell, undersecretary of education at the time, at an agency field hearing in Anaheim, California, about how they'd been lured into taking on debt with promises of career help and advancement but found themselves taking near-minimum-wage jobs as fast-food workers and housekeepers.[24] A few months later, the borrowers and activists decided to turn up the pressure. Larson and others began recruiting former Corinthian students to participate in a debt strike. Although they warned them of the consequences—borrowers who don't pay their loans for long enough can wind up defaulting, ruining their credit score and putting their Social Security, wages, and tax refunds at risk of garnishment—many already were not paying.[25] It was "politicizing what was already happening," Larson said.

More than a dozen former Corinthian students agreed to strike, and the Debt Collective brought together many of them in a house in San Francisco to prepare for what that might mean. They showed them how to log in to the Department of Education's borrower portal to figure out exactly how much they owed and who their servicer was. The former students practiced answering questions from the media like "Why do you think your debt should be forgiven?" and "Aren't you worried about your credit score?"[26]

Lawyers also explained to Hornes and his fellow for-profit college alumni the consequences of striking. Hornes and the other borrowers already couldn't get car loans or afford to buy the items their kids requested. Because the debt was wreaking havoc on their finances anyway, Hornes and the others decided they might as well use the experience to draw attention to the scam they'd experienced.

"We've already risked this much," Hornes and his fellow strikers thought. "What harm could it do to take it to this step?" he wondered.

Around the same time, Eileen Connor filed her first borrower defense application on behalf of a former for-profit college student. The woman had attended a New York City campus of Sanford-Brown, a for-profit college chain, to learn to become a sonogram technician. She borrowed more than $14,000 in federal student loans on the basis of promises from the school that, after completing her coursework, she'd be able to sit for the licensing exam. After graduating, she learned that she wasn't eligible to take the exam because Sanford-Brown's program wasn't accredited.[27]

Connor also started working with Herrine to build an online web form that would make it easier for former for-profit college students to file borrower defense applications without legal representation. Because of her experience representing students like the one who attended Sanford-Brown, Connor had a sense of the types of misrepresentations these students were often subject to and how those mapped onto various state laws. If a school was found to have violated state law in recruiting students, the students would be eligible to have their debt discharged. "We just wanted to make something that would have the right prompts and would kind of spit out a form," she said.

On the last night of the San Francisco trip, Herrine stayed up in a hotel room until 2 a.m. working with tech-savvy former Occupiers on the online defense-to-repayment form. Over the following few weeks, he found time in between his law school classes to tweak and test the page to make sure it would be ready for what the group hoped would be an influx of applications.

After that meeting in San Francisco, the Debt Collective announced that fifteen former Corinthian College students would be taking a strike from their debts. Applications using the form Herrine and Connor created started flooding in. But it wasn't just former for-profit college students paying attention to the strike announcement—the strike generated headlines and convinced officials from the Consumer Financial Protection Bureau and the Department of Education to meet with the group.

The invitation to Washington marked a hint of recognition of their budding movement. "This weird thing I'm doing on the side might get to be real," Herrine thought. "We're not just a bunch of random people on the internet saying, 'Fill out this form and the Department of Education will cancel your debt.'"

But Herrine and the other Debt Collective cofounders knew that they'd need to use a stunt more reminiscent of their grassroots work if they hoped to pressure those in the room to do more than just meet with borrowers. So Herrine found a box, the kind used to hold files in bank office towers and white-shoe law firms, and in the days leading up to their meeting, he took it to his apartment in Brooklyn, spray-painted it red, and filled it with the printouts of the applications for debt relief the group had received.

As soon as the government officials called the Debt Collective asking to meet, Hornes knew that the group's strategy—criticizing the feds for allowing fraudulent schools to participate in the student loan program and then doing little to help the students who had been duped into enrolling—had worked. He was excited to get into a room with some of America's top student loan policy officials and force them to listen to his story. The group traveled together to the Consumer Financial Protection Bureau's temporary headquarters in Washington's NoMa (for "north of Massachusetts Avenue") neighborhood, an area full of food halls, coffee shops, and upscale grocery stores in the shadow of Union Station. The borrowers wore black with a pop of red to symbolize that they were in the red on their debts.

The borrowers shared their stories with the officials, to polite nods and follow-up questions.[28] At the end of the meeting, Herrine presented Mitchell, the official who had first heard some of the strikers' stories at the field hearing in Anaheim, with the red box full of hundreds of borrower defense applications and challenged the officials to do something about it.

A few months after that meeting, Corinthian filed for bankruptcy.[29] Faced with thousands of students and former students in the lurch following the company's shutdown and continued pressure from the Debt Collective and the strikers, Department of Education officials said they would look to consider canceling the debt of certain groups of former Corinthian students at once instead of requiring individual borrowers to prove on their own they'd been defrauded. Initially, the former students who would be eligible were limited to certain borrowers who attended only one Corinthian-owned chain and only during a five-year period. "If you've been defrauded by a school, we'll make sure that you get every penny of the debt relief you're entitled," then secretary of education Arne Duncan promised. Still, officials were wary of canceling debt en masse without requiring borrowers to raise their hands and prove they'd been defrauded—as the Debt Collective was proposing—even when evidence from state attorneys general and elsewhere indicated the borrowers had been scammed. "We're going to make that as simple as we legally can, while also safeguarding the interests of taxpayers," Duncan said.[30]

The department also appointed a special master, Joseph Smith, who had overseen the implementation of an agreement between the government and the largest mortgage lenders in the wake of the housing collapse, to review claims and develop a set of procedures for adjudicating claims in the future. Smith warned that the department would need to take "baby steps" as it evaluated the claims.[31]

The borrowers and activists were pushing officials to move more quickly. "Why should they have to reprove something that one arm of the government has already shown is true?" Taylor asked of the borrowers. "They wanted to drown people in this bureaucratic paperwork."

Some lawmakers and state law enforcement officials also called for the Department of Education to move more swiftly to discharge borrowers' debts in groups.[32]

John King, who took over as secretary of education in the months following some of the initial announcements, said at the time the department was focused on standing up a system for debt relief that, until that point, hadn't existed. Indeed, the few borrower defense claims filed by Connor in the years before the Corinthian collapse had largely been ignored. "We were building a process that hadn't existed before, so there was on the part of activists a tremendous sense of urgency about addressing the pending claims," King said in a 2022 interview. "They were doing the right thing to push us, and we were trying to move as quickly as we could."[33]

After King took over in 2016, the department also directed its attention to beefing up its ability to investigate and address potential violations of law, largely with respect to the federal financial aid program.[34] In addition, the department also took action against ITT Technical Institute, a for-profit college chain that had been accused of using inflated job placement and graduation rates to lure students into taking on debt and was facing scrutiny from its accreditor.[35] The Department of Education asked the company to increase its letter of credit, or the amount of money the Department of Education could draw on in case of a shutdown. Officials also said the school would have to abide by more strict rules when drawing down federal financial aid funds on behalf of students. Those actions, as well as a ban on enrolling new students receiving federal financial aid, pushed the company to shut down.[36]

Suddenly, thousands more students and former students were facing an uncertain future, left with a suspect education and debt. After meeting with stakeholders, the Department of Education created what it called "consistent, clear, fair, and transparent processes" for students seeking to have their debt discharged through borrower defense.[37] The regulations were announced on November 1, 2016, a week before the presidential election. The new rules were scheduled to take effect on July 1, 2017.

In the wake of the election of Donald Trump, King told reporters that the agency would "work as quickly as possible to move through the borrower defense claims—and that was true before the election and it's true post-election."[38] Hornes had his borrower defense application approved and his debt wiped away in January 2017.

Also shortly before Obama left office, the Consumer Financial Protection Bureau and two state attorneys general announced lawsuits alleging that Navient, at the time a major student loan servicer, was, among other things, pushing struggling borrowers toward forbearance, a status that pauses payments but in which interest still accrues. The company's representatives steered borrowers in that direction, regulators alleged, because it was less time-consuming—and therefore more beneficial to the company's bottom line—to enroll them in forbearance than income-driven repayment, which would allow borrowers to stay current on their debt while making payments tied to their income that also counted toward debt forgiveness after twenty or twenty-five years.[39] In the years following the suit, the company described the bureau's allegations as "false" and "baseless."[40]

As discrete groups of borrowers, like those scammed by for-profit colleges, were arguing that their debts should be canceled, the Navient litigation built on the notion raised by the settlement between the government and Sallie Mae over how the company treated military borrowers—that the student loan system wasn't functioning how it was supposed to for much broader swaths of borrowers.

What the Consumer Financial Protection Bureau and the attorneys general were finding is that Navient had "been effectively vetoing this piece of the student loan safety net that its boosters said was preventing student debt from being a policy failure," Pierce said. "The kinds of policy changes you need to fix a system that doesn't work are very different from the kinds of policies you need to deal with a series of one-offs."

Scott Buchanan, the head of the servicer trade group, said the narrative that student loan servicers are at the center of the student loan system's problems is "utterly distracting." He's worked for student loan companies for decades, beginning at Sallie Mae right out of college, when he accompanied members of Congress to local communities for free financial aid workshops. To Buchanan, it's misguided to point to private-sector involvement in the student loan system over the past several decades as a major source of trouble for borrowers. Before the government completely took over the federal student loan program, "the boogeyman of the day" was the private lenders who made loans with a government guarantee, he said.

"Then it's got to be Navient, then they leave," he said, referring to the company's decision to exit the student loan system in 2021. "Everyone that has been purported to be the problem when they've left and the problem persists. At some point you can keep trying to pick bogeymen here, but the real problem is people are borrowing levels that they shouldn't be borrowing and then they are upset," he said.

The Betsy DeVos Era

When Betsy DeVos started her job as secretary of education during the Trump administration, she took a different approach to dealing with student loan issues than the one the findings of the Consumer Financial Protection Bureau, the Debt Collective, and others would imply. DeVos tried to stymie efforts by states to crack down on the kinds of alleged servicing abuses outlined in the CFPB's lawsuit.[41]

Under her watch, the Department of Education also denied a wide swath of borrower defense claims, stalled on adjudicating them, and in some cases offered only minimal relief for claims they approved.[42]

That borrowers who were scammed by their schools were suddenly facing officials who were hostile to providing them with relief was a plight that Debt Collective activists and others blamed on the Obama administration's relatively slow and individualized approach to the borrower defense process. "The Obama administration passed these applications to Betsy DeVos," Taylor said, which "did an incredible amount of damage."

Still, DeVos and the Trump administration proved a useful foil to galvanize organizing around student debt. Pierce and Seth Frotman, the CFPB's second student loan ombudsman, launched a student borrower advocacy organization. Former Department of Education lawyers started a group focused on representing student loan borrowers in court. Connor and her colleagues filed headline-grabbing lawsuits challenging DeVos's tactics, which they alleged illegally stalled or denied relief to scammed students. The Student Debt Crisis Center, a longtime student debt advocacy group, educated and organized borrowers about the future of Public Service Loan Forgiveness and other student loan benefits and protections.

Toward the end of the Obama administration and in the early years of the Trump era, researchers started to raise questions about whether the promises of economic mobility assumed by boosters of higher education and the student loan system were coming true. Many of these scholars specialized in studying wealth inequality, not higher education, so they brought a frame to the data that focused less on the wage premium a college degree provided over a high school diploma and more on how investing in higher education affected families' balance sheets—and whose asset picture it harmed the most.

One of these scholars was Louise Seamster. She came to student debt "kind of by accident" as a PhD student when she became interested in investigating a troubling statistic—that the Great Recession wiped out half of Black Americans' wealth.[43] "It seemed really important for me to understand why," Seamster said. "I was bothered by it especially because we tend to focus more on the historical factors for the racial wealth gap and talk about it as this intractable issue. We were less focused at the time on contemporary dynamics that could be extending the gap or making it worse."

The best way to investigate this question, Seamster thought, was to focus on how debt broadly was affecting Black households, given that much of the Recession-era wealth loss had been explained by subprime mortgages, which lenders pushed disproportionately on homeowners of color in the lead-up to the housing crash.[44] When Seamster started looking more closely at debt among Black households, she saw that student debt, like mortgages, climbed steeply during that period. But what she realized is that, unlike housing debt, which at least disappears if the bank takes your home, it's extremely difficult to get rid of student debt even if it proves worthless to you. "The difference between the housing crisis and the student debt crisis is that the student debt crisis can't pop," she said.

Around the same time, other researchers, including Fenaba Addo and Jason Houle, were finding that not only were Black borrowers taking on more student debt than their white counterparts; they also struggled more to repay it. Even parents' high net worth wasn't enough to protect Black students from having to put themselves at financial risk—by borrowing—to attend college.[45] What's more, they found in later research that the gap in student debt held by Black and white borrowers grows over time, suggesting that Black borrowers struggle more to pay off their already-higher debt loads.[46]

These and other studies started to build the case that student debt, a tool conceived to create economic mobility, actually ended up fueling inequality—thanks in large part to policy choices. One study made this argument explicitly. The research, published by the Roosevelt Institute, a progressive think tank, highlighted how much of the so-called college wage premium was driven by the declining value of a high school diploma. The institute also noted that, just because borrowers were avoiding the harshest consequences of the student loan system, which come through defaulting, they weren't necessarily making progress paying down their debt.

At the time, Julie Margetta-Morgan, one of the authors of the study, said she hoped the findings would help shift the way the public and policymakers thought about the student debt crisis. "We are making several policy decisions right now based on the idea that student debt is essentially a benign mechanism for funding higher education," Margetta-Morgan told me in 2018. "Our research suggests that is not, in fact, that case." "We've essentially engaged in a failed social experiment where the government thought that it would be fine to give people student debt because that would pay off in the long run, and we're seeing that's not the case," she added. "Individuals shouldn't bear all the burden for paying for that mistake."[47]

A little more than a year later, Senator Elizabeth Warren became the first presidential candidate to announce a proposal to cancel student debt. She called for canceling up to $50,000 in student loan relief for borrowers earning $100,000 or less. Borrowers earning between $100,000 and $250,000 would qualify for some debt relief—but less than the $50,000 offered to less well-off borrowers—on a sliding scale based on income.[48]

As soon as Warren made the announcement, Gokey, who was on a trip to Albany, watched as his phone started blowing up with text messages. Gokey was excited that a presidential candidate was pushing for the idea he and the other Debt Collective activists had been advocating for so long. The year 2020 was the third presidential election cycle since the group first met at Occupy Wall Street, but in the two campaigns before, Democratic candidates hadn't touched student debt cancellation. During the 2012 election, Obama focused on student loan interest rates.[49] In 2016, the leading Democratic candidates, Bernie Sanders and Hillary Clinton, had called for making public college free.[50] Still, Gokey was disappointed at the limits placed on the debt-relief proposal.

Several weeks before the announcement, Seamster was asked by a colleague to be part of a meeting with Warren's staff on debt and racial equity. "It turned out that they were asking us to assess various levels of student debt cancellation parameters through the lens of the racial wealth gap," she said. The colleague who invited Seamster had heard her respond at a panel to a question on her student debt research about possible policy solutions by quipping that the government could just cancel student debt. "I was really grateful to have the opportunity to put the money where my mouth was" by working with Warren's team, she said.

As scholars were pointing to data to make the case for a more comprehensive overhaul of the student loan system, activists and lawyers were drawing attention to the notion that the government had legal authority to cancel student debt that was broader than just getting rid of loans for scammed students. Not only that, they said, the president could take the action without Congress. Urged by the Debt Collective, Herrine, who by then was pursuing his PhD, wrote an article arguing that Congress had already given the agency the authority to "compromise, waive, or release" student debt.[51] The idea grew out of earlier work by legal aid attorneys who had tried to push the Department of Education to use the authority to get rid of debt held by their low-income clients who had attended for-profit colleges. Margetta-Morgan, who at the Roosevelt Institute had called on lawmakers and officials to rethink student loan policy, messaged Herrine asking him to write a white paper on the idea for the think tank.

Margetta-Morgan ultimately ended up working for the Warren campaign. In early 2020, Warren announced that, if elected, she would cancel up to $50,000 in federal student debt for many borrowers on the first day of her administration.[52]

A Pandemic Pushes a Radical Idea toward Reality

A few months after the announcement, the COVID-19 pandemic hit, ushering in an unprecedented economic and health-care crisis. To help borrowers mitigate the economic fallout, the Trump administration used its authority to pause payments and collections on federal student loans and set their interest rate to 0%.[53]

Many who had worked with borrowers for years—including Persis Yu, then an attorney at the National Consumer Law Center who had represented hundreds of low-income clients—believed that canceling student debt had the potential to solve many borrowers' problems and challenges with the system. But there wasn't a sense that policymakers would take the idea seriously.

"There was a general agreement by a lot of people that that would be great," Yu told me of cancellation, but the reality at the time was "I can't get the government to get my borrower into income-driven repayment." She'd worked with borrowers to get them into programs that would lift them out of default or make their payments more manageable, but she wasn't sure how many faced challenges once again after they lost touch because of the paperwork burden required to stay current in the system and keep student loans manageable. "This is the thing that keeps me up at night. I'm here helping people, but am I really?" Yu said of how she thought at the time.[54]

The COVID-19 payment pause created space for policymakers to think more ambitiously about student debt. At the time of the announcement, "I didn't necessarily think through all of the implications," Herrine said, but he remembers thinking that "it was clear that this now changes the baseline." For one, the pause proved that the government could stop collecting student loan payments without much impact on the budget or other spending priorities. In addition, the Trump administration used its executive authority to freeze student loan payments, interest, and collections for almost all federal student loan borrowers, indicating that there was a legal justification for the executive branch to use its power for some cancellation—putting interest on the loans at 0% essentially amounted to a write-down of some of the debt for borrowers.

As the pause dragged on and officials from both administrations faced pressure to renew it each time it was scheduled to expire, "it became obvious that the politics had shifted," Herrine said. The idea of turning the system back on without some kind of cancellation looked increasingly untenable—both because of the politics and because previous, smaller pauses indicated that once payments resumed, economically distressed borrowers would be at risk of slipping into delinquency and default.

Even before Joe Biden was elected president, Democratic lawmakers were urging any incoming president to use executive authority to cancel up to $50,000 in student loans.[55] Although it was Congress that had the power to fundamentally transform the college finance system, including by using a federal partnership to encourage states to make their public colleges more affordable, the focus of advocates and lawmakers was for the executive branch to make change. That was in large part because there was little hope of Congress taking action given the years-long partisan stalemate.

Once Biden was elected, the pressure on him to cancel debt continued to mount.[56] On the campaign trail, Biden had vowed to cancel up to $10,000 in student debt as a COVID-19 relief measure. Once elected, he voiced skepticism about doing more and about doing it without Congress. "I'm going to get in trouble for saying this, [but] it's arguable that the president may have the executive power to forgive up to $50,000 in student debt," Biden said in December 2020. "Well, I think that's pretty questionable. I'm unsure of that. I'd be unlikely to do that."[57] In addition to Biden's skepticism around legal authority, he also seemed hesitant to give a benefit to a group perceived by many to be well-off. "The idea that you go to Penn and you're paying a total of 70,000 bucks a year and the public should pay for that? I don't agree," he told *New York Times* columnist David Brooks in May 2021.[58]

Months dragged on as administration officials said they were considering the president's legal authority to cancel debt and promising a memo on the topic that was slow to materialize.[59] Meanwhile, the administration focused on providing what it called "targeted relief" to student loan borrowers—essentially, where the law was already clear that borrowers were entitled to forgiveness, officials tried to remove process and paperwork barriers to discharge debt en masse. They announced a waiver that would help public servants take better advantage of the Public Service Loan Forgiveness program.[60] They made it easier for borrowers who are severely disabled to have their debt wiped away.[61] And in June 2022, the Biden administration canceled all the remaining federal student loan debt held by former Corinthian College students.[62]

Seven years earlier, Obama administration officials were taking self-described "baby steps" toward setting up an individualized cancellation process for Corinthian College borrowers, but the Biden announcement signaled that "they came around to our point of view," Taylor said. John King, who oversaw some of the setup of this process as secretary of education, announced that he favored canceling debt for all student loan borrowers.[63] That safety-net programs like income-driven repayment weren't working as well as officials had hoped was part of "what draws me to a place of supporting debt cancellation," King told me later.[64]

Advocates and activists continued to pressure the Biden administration to do more and cancel student debt for a wide swath of borrowers. They got on planning phone calls and drafted coalition letters. A breakthrough of sorts came when the most prominent labor unions agreed to push Biden toward cancellation, indicating that it wasn't graduates from Penn clamoring for forgiveness as Biden had told David Brooks. "Please note that the vast majority of borrowers—nearly 90 percent—are not attending Ivy League or other elite colleges; almost half of borrowers come from public colleges such as your alma mater," the AFL-CIO wrote on a petition.[65]

Thanks to years of research and activism, it had also become increasingly clear that efforts to ameliorate student debt would have a disproportionate impact on Black borrowers. By the time the discussion reached the question of whether the president would actually cancel some student debt, the NAACP had been advocating around the issue for roughly a decade, said Wisdom Cole, the national director for the organization's Youth and College Division.

As advocates and lawmakers pushed Biden toward a debt-relief proposal, "we needed to make sure that folks understood that student debt cancellation was a racial justice issue," Cole told me. "There are generations of oppression in our community that cripples our ability to pay for college and we have to take out loans."[66]

Indeed, the government's earliest investment in Americans' higher education, the GI Bill, provided disproportionate benefits to white borrowers. More recently, as colleges across the country have become less white, states have pulled back their investments in public colleges, leaving less opportunity for an affordable public option just as schools have become more diverse. In addition, decades of racist policies locked Black Americans out of wealth-building opportunities, leaving them with fewer resources to tap to pay for college.

The COVID-19 pandemic and the activism following the killing of George Floyd in 2020 helped to bring issues of racial justice, including the disproportionate impact of student debt on Black borrowers, to the forefront of Americans' and policymakers' consciousness, Cole said. When Biden announced his student debt-relief plan in August 2022, racial justice was part of the rationale. "The burden is especially heavy on Black and Hispanic borrowers, who on average have less family wealth to pay for it," Biden said of student debt.[67]

Biden announced he would cancel $10,000 in student debt for borrowers earning up to $125,000 and $20,000 in debt for borrowers who had received a Pell Grant. It wasn't as much as advocates and activists had been calling for, and the plan included a means test, which they worried could bury in paperwork those borrowers most in need of relief. Still, the addition of the extra $10,000 for Pell Grant recipients—who were low-income when they attended college and majority Black and Hispanic—which went beyond Biden's campaign promise, signaled that perhaps he and his staff had absorbed the data that borrowers of color and low-income borrowers are disproportionately struggling with student debt.[68]

But almost immediately after Biden announced the plan, opponents began strategizing for how to challenge it through the courts.[69]

The Biden administration was forced to defend the legality of the policy publicly in court. After a couple of years when Herrine was one of a few outside voices making the argument for using executive authority to cancel student debt, "it felt sort of fun" to watch government lawyers have to do it, he said.

In roughly ten years, activists, legal advocates, researchers, and borrowers pushed a relatively fringe notion emanating from Occupy Wall Street into the White House. They highlighted how choices by policymakers over the previous several decades had turned a system originally imagined as a way to provide some with a leg up into one that often widened persistent gaps in American society. President Biden's embrace of mass student loan cancellation signaled a recognition that tweaks to the student debt system likely wouldn't be enough to stop the crisis. Still, it was less than proponents had been pushing for and too much for critics, who were ultimately able to stop Biden's first try at mass student debt relief.

Conclusion

Going Forward

On a cloudy winter morning in late February, hundreds of protesters gathered near the steps of the Supreme Court. The mood was festive. "OK, it's lit," one demonstrator remarked upon exiting a car and hearing the New Orleans-style live music coming from the five-piece band. Protesters milled about in yellow beanies emblazoned with the NAACP's logo and light-blue sweatshirts in the style of college apparel that featured their student debt load in the spot where a school's name would normally be. They carried signs reading 40 Million Families Need Student Loan Relief and Student Loan Debt Relief Is Legal. The idea behind the rally was to remind the nine Supreme Court justices, the media, and the groups challenging the Biden administration's debt-relief plan what was at stake for borrowers.

But just a few hours later, in a room with marble columns where security guards stalked the aisles, Supreme Court Justice Sonia Sotomayor highlighted how little control the borrowers had over their financial fate.[1]

"There's 50 million students who . . . will benefit from this who today will struggle. Many of them don't have assets sufficient to bail them out after the pandemic. They don't have friends or families or others who can help them make these payments. The evidence is clear that many of them will have to default. Their financial situation will be even worse because, once you default, the hardship on you is exponentially greater. You can't get credit. You're going to pay higher prices for things. They are going to continue to suffer from this pandemic in a way that the general population doesn't," Sotomayor told the hushed room, which included James Campbell, the attorney representing six Republican-led states suing the Biden administration over the debt-forgiveness initiative. "And what you're saying is now we're going to give judges the right to decide how much aid to give them."

What Sotomayor described is ultimately what happened. The Supreme Court's conservative majority struck down the Biden administration's debt-relief plan.[2] One of the main questions in the cases that brought the student debt issue to the court was whether any party would have standing, or the right to sue over the policy, because it had been directly harmed by it. For the justices to rule on the legality of the Biden administration's plan, they had to first find that the parties bringing the suits had standing.

The Court found that the relationship between Missouri—one of the six Republican-led states that sued—and the Missouri Higher Education Loan Authority, or MOHELA, was enough to confer standing.[3] MOHELA said its executives were not involved in the states' decision to sue.[4] MOHELA is a student loan servicer that first entered the student loan system as a secondary market organization, or a firm that raised capital through tax-exempt bonds to buy up or make student loans. It was one of the many third-party entities that policymakers invited into the system and continued to placate in order to keep capital flowing to student loan borrowers.[5]

Decades after Missouri created MOHELA, the court's conservative majority found that a possible cost to its revenue was enough to knock down what is arguably the most dramatic change to the student loan system since its inception—mass debt forgiveness. The episode offers another example of how obstacles to broader reform keep pushing policymakers to iterate at the margins and sink more into the system that's already cost borrowers and taxpayers so much.

Shortly after the court struck down his plan, President Joe Biden vowed to take another stab at debt forgiveness using a different legal authority. In the lead-up to the 2024 presidential election, Biden provided more detail on the proposal. It focused on some of the most acute challenges pockets of student loan borrowers face, including some of the borrowers profiled in this book. In addition, it aimed to mitigate the burden of student debt for those who experience financial hardship repaying it. The Biden administration also proposed canceling up to $20,000 in unpaid interest for a wide swath of borrowers. But many, ranging from ordinary voters to those who have the power to challenge the plan legally, opposed it.[6]

Going forward, the battle over debt-forgiveness initiatives will likely continue to elide an important fact: a large share of student loans are unlikely to ever be completely repaid. In 2020, roughly 60% of student loan balances were higher than when borrowers initially took the debt out, according to research from the Jain Family Institute.[7] In other words, instead of investing in programs to make higher education more affordable on the front end, such as by making public college broadly free or debt-free, the government is issuing loans to finance more expensive degrees and canceling a large portion of the balance on the back end. In this way, policymakers continue to fall victim to the sunk-cost fallacy, favoring adjustments to the current system that has already cost borrowers and taxpayers so much instead of pushing toward a more radical solution.

An Aggressive Approach That May Not Be Enough

In the nearly sixty years between when President Lyndon Johnson signed the Higher Education Act and Justice Sotomayor chided James Campbell, student loans have traveled from a tool intended to help students who couldn't afford college achieve economic mobility to a burden that often hinders it. Sotomayor's statement offers an extreme version of what many student loan borrowers face every day. Whether their debt will be manageable rests on how well policymakers implement government programs that promise to keep them afloat and the level of customer service they receive from private actors who have fought to stay part of the student loan system for decades.

Or as James Kvaal, undersecretary of education when the Biden administration designed and pushed forward its forgiveness efforts, told me, "There are many aspirations we have for our higher education system around upward mobility, equity and public service that are not compatible with a model that uses student loans as the primary means of financing higher education."

During the first few years of the Biden administration, lawmakers and the Department of Education took several steps to make the experience of repaying a student loan more humane. Officials discharged all the remaining outstanding federal student debt held by former Corinthian College students.[8] They revamped income-driven repayment to allow borrowers to put a much smaller share of their income toward their loans each month and to stop the balance on the debt from growing even when borrowers' payments don't cover the interest.[9] They temporarily expanded the Public Service Loan Forgiveness Program so more public servants would qualify for the relief they'd been promised by Congress and made the forgiveness easier to access going forward. Lawmakers closed the 90/10 loophole that turned veterans like Murray Hastie into "uniforms with dollar signs."[10] Officials vowed to give borrowers in default an extra year of protection from collections after the COVID-19-era payment pause ended in order to give them more time to become current on their loans.[11] They made it easier for borrowers who were at risk of defaulting on their loans to be automatically enrolled in an affordable repayment plan, which could help more borrowers avoid the harshest consequences of the student loan system. And of course the White House proposed to cancel some student debt.

The Biden administration has taken the most expansive approach of any administration to deal with the student debt problem; in the first three and a half years of Biden's presidency, officials approved $167 billion in debt cancellation for 4.75 million borrowers.[12] Roughly one in ten federal student loan borrowers have seen some debt canceled through these initiatives. But the administration's efforts don't fundamentally change the dynamic that Sotomayor highlighted in her remarks. Borrowers are still relying on policymakers to implement programs successfully and for opponents not to challenge them so that their student loans can become a manageable part of their financial lives. That's true of many of the borrowers featured in this book.

Patricia Gary ultimately had her debt wiped away and received a refund for some of the money she paid. But getting to that outcome required the work of attorneys like Eileen Connor and Johnson Tyler to push the government to treat Gary and other borrowers who were scammed by their schools differently. Gary said she's grateful for the relief, but it's no salve for the decades she spent living with the student loan. The government has "given me back what was rightfully mine because you kept taking it and taking it and taking it without any kind of consideration," Gary said shortly after receiving the relief. "It doesn't match up with the years that I had to go through the harassment, I had to go through the garnish years, I had to go through the phone calls, threatening calls—I went through a lot with these people," she said. Gary was seventy-five by the time she was free of the debt.

Despite the launch of a new repayment plan that has the potential to make monthly payments more affordable, ahead of the end of the COVID-19 payment pause, Sandra Hinz was anxious about how she'd manage the loans. She didn't have time in between caretaking for her son Dale and searching for a part-time job to research and fill out the paperwork necessary to access the plan.

For Kathleen White, the Biden administration's efforts helped. After decades of paying student loans both for herself and on behalf of her children, she ultimately had her debt canceled. The relief came through the Public Service Loan Forgiveness program, which White first began trying to access in 2017. The idea behind the program is that teachers, social workers, firefighters, and other public servants could have their debt canceled after at least ten years of payments. White was rejected twice, despite working as a community college educator for three decades. Her approval came as part of efforts by the Biden administration to make it easier for borrowers to access Public Service Loan Forgiveness without getting thrown off by technicalities. Ultimately, the program wiped away nearly $30,000—a hefty sum, but far less than the $305,000 she had paid on loans for herself and her children.

Shortly after having her debt discharged, White told me she was grateful to Biden for making the bureaucracy of the student loan system easier to navigate. Still, she said it took "a long frickin' time" for her to receive relief. White said she also worries that other borrowers who are entitled to student debt forgiveness won't have the stamina that she did to push for what they're owed. Before her debt was canceled, White had spoken with servicers and student loan borrower advocates and filed a complaint with the Consumer Financial Protection Bureau about her situation. "I'm still frustrated because you shouldn't have to be this tenacious. It shouldn't take this much out of anybody. I've got friends and young people I know who are in public service who just don't want to deal with it."

MaNesha Stiff's relationship to the Biden administration's initiatives was more complicated. About two months before the freeze on student loan payments, interest, and collections was supposed to end, Stiff said she was "scared" about how she would afford her bill when payments resumed. Her language hadn't changed much since 2021, when she first told me she was "scared shitless" about the government turning payments back on.

The debt made Stiff so anxious that she was hesitant to log in to her student loan account, where her full balance would be on display. Ultimately, she signed in because she wanted to see if she could get credit toward Public Service Loan Forgiveness, a program that allows those working for the government or certain nonprofits to have their debt canceled after at least ten years of payments. Stiff saw that she owed roughly $200,000 in debt.

Stiff worked for nonprofit organizations for about seventeen years after she graduated from college in 2003. Although the Public Service Loan Forgiveness program had been on the books since 2007, Stiff didn't learn about it until 2023. At that point, "it was just coming through on my Google," she said, referring to the alerts and news she monitors regarding student loans. Her situation was not uncommon. For years, advocates complained that servicers didn't provide qualifying borrowers with enough or the right information about Public Service Loan Forgiveness, putting them at risk of continuing to pay on their debt even when they had the right to have it canceled.[13] In part to deal with these errors, the Biden-era Department of Education reviewed borrowers' accounts to see if the time they spent in repayment should have counted toward debt forgiveness. Hundreds of thousands of borrowers had their debt canceled thanks to these adjustments.[14]

When Stiff logged into her student loan servicer's account to prepare for the end of the payment freeze, she discovered that her debt had been discharged. She'd logged on to enroll in a new payment plan that she was told would save her money. Once Stiff saw the $0 balance, she was hesitant to double-check it with her servicer, anxious it was a mistake that would disappear if she drew attention to it. Ultimately, Stiff got through to her servicer after two tries and learned her debt had indeed been canceled. She asked the representative on the phone to send her the letter confirming the debt forgiveness. Stiff screamed when she saw it in her message portal.

"I was practically in tears, just saying thank you," Stiff told me in August 2023. "I printed the letter out. I'm framing it," she said at the time. Stiff started thinking about doing all of the things the debt had held her back from, like making repairs to her home and adopting a child. But about six months later, she had to put a halt to those plans.

In early 2024, she received a letter from her servicer, MOHELA, saying that the initial letter declaring her debt forgiven was sent in error. She began researching the problem and learned that other borrowers were having a similar experience. Stiff started looking for lawyers. "I don't even know what this case would be, but I'm not going down without a fight," she said. "I'm not going to allow them to send me an official letter saying that my student loan debt has been forgiven and then turn around and say 'oops.'" She hadn't just received a letter. The government and MOHELA had taken other steps to clear her debt. For example, the loans were wiped off her online dashboard with the Department of Education.

MOHELA's press team told me in an email that an estimated five hundred borrowers or fewer received notices reversing their PSLF cancellation. "These notices were sent to the affected borrowers by MOHELA under the direction of the US Department of Education's Office of Federal Student Aid," the press team wrote. "All borrowers entitled to PSLF are expected to receive forgiveness once they meet the requirements, including many who received reversal notices."

A Biden-era Department of Education official told me that the blame for Stiff's challenges rests with servicers. "The Department will not stand for egregious servicer errors that have harmed borrowers and perpetuated problems in the broken student loan system," the official wrote in an email. They highlighted actions the agency took during the Biden administration with the aim of holding servicers accountable.

Stiff received the letter from MOHELA retracting her debt relief shortly before her birthday. It upset her so much that she wasn't sure she wanted to go through with her plans to celebrate with her mother. "I was so sick," she said. The experience had her feeling just like she had the entire COVID-19 pause as she waited with trepidation for payments to resume. "I'm reverting back to the old days when I didn't know what I was going to do about my student loans, and it was stressful," she said. "I'm livid and I am so upset."

For White and the nearly five million borrowers the Biden administration's efforts have helped as of this writing, debt cancellation can be life changing. But for many, it comes after years and even decades of struggling to access student loan benefits they were eligible for under the law. The time spent needlessly paying on the debt may have deferred other dreams and economic activity, like owning a home or starting a family. Some, like Stiff, who appear to meet the spirit of these programs, are still fighting to access the cancellation.

What's more, the future of debt-relief measures is precarious because they rely, at least, for now, on executive authority. Ensuring that borrowers have access to the help they're entitled to under the law or that more borrowers receive debt cancellation to correct past failures of the student loan system requires White House officials who are committed to those policies and courts that look favorably on them.

Fixes Are Helpful, but Structural Issues Remain

Decoupling borrowers' financial fate from the decisions of policymakers and student loan company officials will require addressing the large, structural issues that underpin the student debt crisis. Those stem from a shift in the way we think about the country's role in investing in college students in the decades since Lyndon Johnson first signed the Higher Education Act into law. Where once higher education finance policy indicated some tension between the benefit that college provides to the individual and to society, today the way the United States funds higher education sends the message that it's an individual good for which individuals should incur the financial risk. The federal government's main scholarship program for low-income students covers a much smaller fraction of college costs than it used to, and many of the cheapest public colleges are unaffordable for low-income students thanks in part to state disinvestment.[15]

Investing in public colleges or the Pell Grant will require political will from policymakers at many levels—and a philosophical shift—to change our higher education system to one in which individuals take on less of the risk and taxpayers take on more. "The problem of college finance is not just one of Department of Education regulations, but one that's going to require colleges and states and congress to also contribute to the solution," Kvaal said.

In recent years, some states and localities have tried to make public college free for certain students, but because these programs often require students to raise their hand, fill out paperwork, and in some cases tap their other financial aid, like Pell Grants, before using state funds, they can be difficult to access and in some cases still require students to take on debt for living expenses. Many also exclude returning adults.[16] Kendra Brooks's household illustrates the challenge students face in actually attending college for free through these programs. Although Brooks fought "very hard" as a Philadelphia city council member to create a scholarship that would make the Community College of Philadelphia free for thousands of students, her daughter didn't apply for it.[17]

"I've met several other folks who didn't know it existed," Brooks said. "We had an event with public high schools this summer and we were talking to seniors, and they didn't even know they could apply for this scholarship," she told me in 2022.

During high school and college, Justice Passe hustled to gather as many resources as he could to pay for school without loans. But the nation's complicated higher education finance system, with no clear free option, forced him to consider some tough choices. In the fall of 2023, as Passe was preparing to start his second semester at Temple, he was considering leaving the school. He'd enjoyed his classes and professors during his first semester, but he'd gotten caught up in the challenges of paying for college.

The delay in receiving some of his scholarships and a mix-up over Passe's state grant created a gap in the cost of tuition and the money he had to pay it quickly. Because he owed Temple money, the school wouldn't let him register for classes, he said. He ultimately paid the funds, but by the time the hold was lifted, courses that would go toward his requirements for graduation were full. Passe's full-time internship schedule also made balancing in-person schooling at a place like Temple difficult. "If I had the chance to just do school, I would love that," he said. "In my time in college, I've prioritized work. I never had the luxury of doing one or the other."

Passe managed to turn his extensive career experience into a full-time corporate job that doesn't require a college degree. His employer also offers tuition reimbursement. Passe has decided to leave Temple and take advantage of his employer's offer, but at a more affordable, online-only school, where he can fit his classes in with his job.

"Back in high school, I jokingly said I would like college to pay for itself, and hopefully I could have a company pay for me," he said. "I didn't really think that would become a reality until now. I just thought I would have to survive through scholarships. Now I have another avenue to pursue my degree without taking out debt. I'm very proud of myself."

Passe is on his way to a successful career and a degree that he likely won't have to pay much for, but his path is not without risks. Some research indicates that outcomes for students who attend college exclusively online are worse than for those who attend in person.[18] In addition, tuition reimbursement programs like the one at Passe's employer typically require the employee to commit to staying at the company for a certain amount of time or risk repaying the tuition. Passe is confident he will meet this commitment. Still, the agreements can pose challenges for some workers.[19]

In addition, Passe's experience highlights the success of someone who took exceptional steps to pursue college without taking on loans. Unfortunately, it's unlikely to provide a map for a policy prescription for a wide swath of students. Despite announcements from a slew of companies to drop degree requirements, their hiring practices are still focused on candidates with a bachelor's degree.[20]

Students like Passe are still regularly confronted with the reality that they need a college degree to succeed economically with no clear path to earning the credential without some debt. Universal and truly free public college would go a long way in addressing some of the reasons America's outstanding student debt continues to climb, but ameliorating the issue will also require lawmakers to go beyond higher education policy and address some of the fundamental inequities in our economy. As Louise Seamster, a University of Iowa sociologist, notes, part of the reason attending college has become so important is that it's difficult to get a decent, stable job without some kind of degree.[21]

In American society, higher education is thought of as "the opportunity to get ahead," Seamster said, "which is explicitly to get ahead of other people. It's not trying to establish a floor of protections for everybody." That framing can make the debt seem like a good or even necessary investment, even if the degree doesn't pay off as we would expect, she said. "It allows us to always be looking ahead at the potential of moving up rather than at the reality of a lot of people treading water or even sinking—and blame them if that's the case."

In my years reporting on student debt, I've spoken with dozens of borrowers who told me that, at eighteen years old, they didn't feel ready or knowledgeable enough to take on loans that would ultimately haunt them for years. Or perhaps they were older, but they believed they needed the degree to be successful, so they took on whatever debt was necessary to get it. In many cases, a better understanding of interest rates or how a monthly payment fit into their budget wouldn't have protected them from the consequences of student debt. They needed the loan to follow what their parents, teachers, and society broadly told them was the surest path to a decent financial life. Mitigating the student loan crisis will require returning that path to the much less risky one it was decades ago when states and the federal government subsidized college at higher rates.

Whether helping students afford college is a value Americans share is something that voters and policymakers will have to hash out. But lawmakers launched the government's student loan program in part with the idea that an investment in boosting college attendance was an investment in the country more broadly. As long as American society pushes people toward higher education but subsidizes that education as if it only conferred an individual benefit, the stories of borrowers struggling to buy homes, pay for childcare, or simply stay current on their student loans will never disappear.

Acknowledgments

Over the past decade of reporting on student debt, I've spoken with hundreds of students and borrowers whose stories and perseverance have shaped my understanding of the student loan problem. I'm so appreciative of the time they spent speaking with me and their willingness to be so frank in discussing their financial lives.

I'm particularly grateful to the students and borrowers whose experiences are featured in this book: MaNesha Stiff, Murray Hastie, Jennifer Esparza, Justice Passe, Kathleen and Sean White, Kendra Brooks, Sandra Hinz, Patricia Gary, and Nathan Hornes II. They allowed me into their lives on and off for years, kept me updated on any changes to their situation, and were so generous with their time and insights.

Sources in the advocacy, policy, activist, and industry community have spent countless hours explaining to me the minutiae of student loan policy, walking me through the history of a particular provision, and connecting me with borrowers. Some of them are featured by name in this book; in other cases, their influence is present even when their name is not. This book and my reporting over the past decade would not have been possible without them.

MarketWatch has been such a supportive professional home for me both in my day-to-day reporting and in allowing me the opportunity to delve into this project. I'm particularly grateful to Jeremy Olshan, who hired me to cover student loans in 2015 and who has championed this book and my career more broadly. In addition, Nathan Vardi helped improve my reporting and writing and has served as an invaluable sounding board as I navigate a professional journalism career and the book-writing process.

I began working on this project in Samuel Freedman's book-writing class at Columbia Journalism School. Sam's guidance and his faith in my ability to execute it are what transformed this book from idea to reality. Sam also connected me with my wonderful agent, John Rudolph, at Dystel, Goderich & Bourret. John has been a vital guide throughout this process, providing expertise and patience through multiple proposal rewrites, a pregnancy-related delay, and more.

I'm so grateful that Elizabeth Branch Dyson at the University of Chicago Press saw potential even in a very early version of this project and ultimately acquired it. Her insight has been crucial in structuring this book, defining its scope, and helping me clarify what it is I'm trying to say.

Three anonymous readers provided feedback that improved the manuscript tremendously. I'm thankful they took the time to read it and respond. Andy Kroll, Hannah Levintova, and Zack Wainer also reviewed parts of the manuscript and proposal. Their suggestions helped to shape both individual chapters and my approach to the book more broadly. In addition, Joanna Arcieri made sure I was accurately portraying information gleaned from sources published decades ago. I feel lucky to have such a wonderful fact-checker as a friend.

Finally, I could not have completed this project without the backing of my family: My mother, Marsha Gentner, who has always struck a balance between believing I could accomplish almost anything and never pressuring me academically or professionally. My father, Joe Berman, who isn't alive to see this day but knew it would come. My in-laws, Janet, Larry, Andrew and Russell Hoffer, and Sophia Rutkin, who have taken an interest and pride in all of my efforts. Cookie "Mema" Hoffer, who didn't go more than a few weeks without asking whether I'd come up with a title for this book. Judah Hoffer, whose pleasant demeanor, both in utero and on the outside, gave me the time and space to complete this project while still getting enough sleep. And finally, Steven Hoffer, my forever editor and partner whose support has made all of this possible.

Notes

Introduction

1. Johnson, "Remarks at Southwest Texas State College."
2. National Association of Realtors, "Student Loan Debt Holding Back Majority of Millennials from Homeownership."
3. Steinbaum, "Student Debt Crisis Is a Crisis of Non-Repayment."
4. Beamer, "America's Student Loans Were Never Going to Be Repaid."
5. Hillman and Weichman, "Education Deserts," 2.
6. US Department of Education, "FAFSA Data by Demographic Characteristics."
7. DC Office of the State Superintendent of Education, "DC Tuition Assistance Grant."
8. Burd, "Crisis Point."
9. Cahalan et al., "Indicators of Higher Education Equity in the United States," 112.

10. Penn, "Hello, Cruel World."
11. Dunleavey, "Paying for College without the Home Equity Option."
12. Fulford et al., "Making Ends Meet in 2022," 42.
13. Baum and Looney, "Who Owes the Most in Student Loans."
14. Miller, "Continued Student Loan Crisis for Black Borrowers."
15. Huelsman, "Debt Divide," 17.
16. Gallagher and Rendon, "CFI in Focus."
17. Monarrez and Matsudaira, "Trends in Federal Student Loans for Graduate School," 2.
18. Monarrez and Matsudaira, 8.
19. Lumina Foundation, "Today's Student."
20. Lumina Foundation.
21. Brooks, "Has Biden Changed?."
22. White House, "Remarks by President Biden Announcing Student Loan Debt Relief Plan."
23. Mark Huelsman (@markhuelsman), "Lots of (important!) chatter this week about the number of people with student loans and no degree or credential. Among those who take out student loans, about 4-in-10 students overall, including 54% of Black students, do not finish college within six years," November 20, 2020, 11:21 a.m., https://x.com/MarkHuelsman/status/1329822197406453762?s=20.
24. Carnevale, Cheah, and Hanson, "Economic Value of College Majors," 5.
25. Berman, "America's Educational System Is an 'Aristocracy Posing as a Meritocracy.'"
26. Korn, Fuller, and Forsyth, "Colleges Spend Like There's No Tomorrow.'"
27. Burd, "Crisis Point."

Chapter 1

1. "Fulton County, Then and Now."
2. Roosevelt, "Message to Congress on the Education of War Veterans."
3. *The Servicemen's Education and Training Act of 1944: Hearings before the Committee on Education and Labor, United States Senate*, 78th Congress (1943), 83 https://babel.hathitrust.org/cgi/pt?id=uc1.31822006683395&view=1up&seq=5&skin=2021.
4. Special to the New York Times, "George Zook Dies; Education Leader."
5. 78th Congress, "Servicemen's Education and Training Act of 1944," 120.
6. "Young Men Declared Dodging Military Duty."
7. "Atherton, Legion Leader, Blasts Those Retarding War Effort."
8. "Harry Walter Colmery on the Oberlin College Baseball Team."
9. Colmery, "Testimony Concerning the GI Bill of Rights Presented by Harry W. Colmery," 10.
10. Frydl, *GI Bill*, 120.
11. Frydl, 104.
12. Frydl, 121.
13. Author's personal interview with Kathleen Frydl.
14. Frydl, *GI Bill*, 134.

15. Katznelson, "When Affirmative Action Was White," 114.
16. Frydl, *GI Bill*, 139.
17. Frydl, 131–32.
18. Frydl, 132.
19. Frydl, 132.
20. Frydl, 139.
21. Frydl, 141.
22. Frydl, 193.
23. "Care Urged on GI's in Picking Schools."
24. Gray, "Report on Education and Training under the Servicemen's Readjustment Act," 66.
25. Gray, 66.
26. Gray, 66, 74.
27. Gray, 74.
28. Gray, 49.
29. Gray, 9.
30. Ellis, "General Accounting Office Report of Survey," 81.
31. Ellis, 86.
32. Author's personal interview with Kathleen Frydl.
33. Frydl, *GI Bill*, 246.
34. Frydl, 250.
35. Frydl, 240.
36. Harris, *State Must Provide*, 4–5.
37. Frydl, *GI Bill*, 241.
38. Brookings Institution, "For-Profit College System Is Broken and the Biden administration Needs to Fix It."
39. Berman, "All the Ways Student Debt Exacerbates Racial Inequality."
40. Carnevale, "Separate & Unequal," 7.
41. US Senate Health, Education, Labor, and Pensions Committee, "For Profit Higher Education," 308.
42. Clark, "How I Did It."
43. US Senate Health, Education, Labor, and Pensions Committee, "For Profit Higher Education," 311.
44. US Senate Health, Education, Labor, and Pensions Committee, 320.
45. "Veteran's Whirl."
46. "Tiger Teague to Give Congress Plenty Color."
47. *Veterans Readjustment Assistance Act of 1952: Hearings before the Special Subcommittee on Veterans' Education and Rehabilitation Benefits of the Committee on Labor and Public Welfare, United States Senate*, 82nd Cong. (1952), 37, https://babel.hathitrust.org/cgi/pt?id=uiug.30112119745252 &view=1up&seq=4&skin=2021%0A.
48. *Veterans Readjustment Assistance Act of 1952*, 36.
49. *Veterans Readjustment Assistance Act of 1952*, 32.
50. Kokalis, "Proprietary Schools," 148.
51. Kokalis, 150.
52. Author's personal interview with Bernard Ehrlich.
53. Ehrlich interview.

54. Whitman, *Profits of Failure*, 164.
55. *Veterans Readjustment Assistance Act of 1952*, 144.
56. Author's personal interview with Bernard Ehrlich.
57. Frydl, *GI Bill*, 216, 218.
58. Frydl, 216.
59. Berman, "Elizabeth Warren Accuses College Watchdog of Not Biting."
60. "GI Bill History."
61. Frydl, *GI Bill*, 316, 318.
62. Frydl, 308.
63. Frydl, 243.
64. Winerip, "Billions for School Are Lost in Fraud, Waste and Abuse."
65. Winerip, "Overhauling School Grants."
66. Shebanow, *Fail State.*
67. Author's personal interview with Elena Ackel.
68. Ackel interview.
69. Winerip, "Overhauling School Grants."
70. Winerip.
71. Winerip, "House Panel Is Facing Vote on School Aid."
72. Babcock, "Loan Abuses by Some Trade Schools Leave Taxpayers with Big Bill."
73. Hegji, "90/10 Rule under HEA Title IV," 5.
74. Author's personal interview with Elena Ackel.
75. Petraeus, "For-Profit Colleges, Vulnerable GI's."
76. US Senate Health, Education, Labor, and Pensions Committee, "For Profit Higher Education," 500.
77. US Senate Health, Education, Labor, and Pensions Committee, 501.
78. Aronson et al., "Educating Sergeant Pantzke."
79. Glantz, "Legislation to Close A Loophole in GI Bill Fails."
80. Kirkham and Zarembo, "Recruiting Vets for Cash."
81. Berman, "These Colleges Use a Loophole to Make Billions Off the GI Bill."
82. Berman, "Nearly 200 For-Profit Colleges Get Over 90% of Their Funding from the Government."
83. US Senate Health, Education, Labor, and Pensions Committee, "For Profit Higher Education," 436.
84. US Senate Health, Education, Labor, and Pensions Committee, 446.
85. US Senate Health, Education, Labor, and Pensions Committee, 437.
86. US Senate Health, Education, Labor, and Pensions Committee, 443.

Chapter 2

1. Potempa, "Indiana Locations a Real World Reminder of Jean Shepherd's 'A Christmas Story.'"
2. Bigott, "Hammond, IN."
3. US Census Bureau, "QuickFacts Hammond City, Indiana."
4. National Defense Education Act, Pub. L. No. 70, 72 Stat. 1580 (1958), https://www.govinfo.gov/content/pkg/STATUTE-72/pdf/STATUTE -72-Pg1580.pdf.

5. Eisenhower, "Our Future Security."
6. Folsom, "Folsom's Memorandum on School Aid."
7. Furman, "President Backs House School Bill."
8. Associated Press, "House Votes 900 Million in School Aid."
9. Furman, "Senate Approves Science Aid Plan."
10. Furman, "Conferences Back 900 Million Fund to Aid in Education."
11. National Defense Education Act (1958).
12. "Business-Guaranteed Student Loans Spread in Massachusetts."
13. "Business-Guaranteed Student Loans Spread in Massachusetts."
14. "A Conversation with Richard Cornuelle," YouTube video, posted by Online Library of Liberty (Liberty Fund), 1:04:14, https://www.youtube .com/watch?v=FdQGnD4PI84
15. "Conversation with Richard Cornuelle."
16. "Conversation with Richard Cornuelle."
17. Cornuelle, *Reclaiming the American Dream*, 80.
18. Cornuelle, 81.
19. Cornuelle, 82.
20. Cornuelle, 83.
21. Cornuelle, 83; Barger, *College on Credit*, 7.
22. Cornuelle, *Reclaiming the American Dream*, 84; "Nationwide Loan Fund For College Students Gets $2 Million Grant."
23. "Nationwide Loan Fund for College Students Gets $2 Million Grant."
24. Barger, *College on Credit*, 8.
25. Barger, 11.
26. "Nationwide Loan Fund for College Students Gets $2 Million Grant."
27. Klein, "Alice Rivlin, Queen of Washington's Budget Wonks."
28. Rivlin, *The Role of the Federal Government in Financing Higher Education*, 2.
29. Rivlin, 118.
30. Rivlin, 140.
31. Rivlin, 140.
32. Rivlin, 158.
33. Rivlin, 152.
34. Rivlin, 128.
35. "Johnson Offers 100-Million Bill on Student Loans."
36. Johnson, "Remarks upon Signing the Higher Education Facilities Act."
37. Johnson, "Special Message to the Congress."
38. Johnson.
39. *Higher Education Act of 1965: Hearings before the Subcommittee on Education of the Committee on Education and Labor, House of Representatives* (1965), 40, https://babel.hathitrust.org/cgi/pt?id=umn.31951d02113104z &seq=9.
40. *Higher Education Act of 1965*, 26.
41. *Higher Education Act of 1965*, 213.
42. Zimmerman, "Student Loan Program Troubled Increasingly by Lagging Repayment."
43. *Higher Education Act of 1965*, 437.
44. *Higher Education Act of 1965*, 445.

45. *Higher Education Act of 1965*, 284.
46. Evans and Novak, "LBJ Out to Ax Loan Sharks."
47. Evans and Novak, "Student Loans Are Big Business."
48. Johnson, "Remarks at Southwest Texas State College Upon Signing the Higher Education Act of 1965."
49. Johnson.
50. *Higher Education Act of 1965*, 644.
51. Snyder, "120 Years of American Education," 18–19.
52. National Center for Education Statistics, "College Enrollment Rates."
53. US Commission on Civil Rights, "Equal Protection of the Laws in Higher Education," 180.
54. Brooks and Levitin, "Redesigning Education Finance," 24.
55. Pomfret, "Bankers Promote Student Aid Loan."
56. Pomfret.
57. Hillman and Weichman, "Education Deserts."
58. *Education Amendments of 1971: Hearings before the Subcommittee on Education of the Committee on Labor and Public Welfare, United States Senate,*" 92nd Cong. (1971), 435, https://babel.hathitrust.org/cgi /pt?id=uc1.b3603377&view=1up&seq=9&skin=2021.
59. *Education Amendments of 1971*, 58.
60. *Higher Education Amendments of 1971: Hearings before the Special Subcommittee of the Committee on Education and Labor, House of Representatives,*" 92nd Cong. (1971), 619, https://babel.hathitrust.org/cgi /pt?id=mdp.39015033366934&view=1up&seq=7&skin=2021.
61. *Guaranteed Student Loan Program: Hearings before the Permanent Subcommittee on Investigations of the Committee on Government Operations, United States Senate*, 94th Cong. (1975), 23, https://babel.hathitrust.org /cgi/pt?id=uc1.b5142224&view=1up&seq=11&skin=2021.
62. *Guaranteed Student Loan Program*, 247.
63. *Guaranteed Student Loan Program*, 14.
64. Guaranteed Student Loan Amendments of 1976, H.R. Rep. 94-1232, at 78, https://babel.hathitrust.org/cgi/pt?id=uc1.31210024844647&view=1up &seq=1&skin=2021&q1=bankruptcy.
65. Guaranteed Student Loan Amendments of 1976, at 8.
66. Wurtz, "Guaranteed Student Loan Program's Internal Controls and Structure Need Improvement," 12.
67. Waldman, *The Bill*, 75.
68. Waldman, 56–57.
69. Waldman, 134.
70. Gose, "Bush Administration Decides to Fight Lawsuit Brought by Lenders against the Education Dept."
71. Author's personal interview with Thomas Butts.
72. Higher Education Amendments of 1992, Pub. L. No. 102-325, 106 Stat. 448 (1992), https://www.govinfo.gov/content/pkg/STATUTE-106/pdf /STATUTE-106-Pg448.pdf.
73. Eaton, *Bankers in the Ivory Tower*, 39.

74. Eaton, 37–38.
75. *Reauthorization of the Higher Education Act of 1965: Hearings before the Subcommittee on Education, Arts and Humanities, United States Senate,* 102nd Cong. (1991), 751, https://babel.hathitrust.org/cgi/pt?id=purl.327 54076781495&seq=761.
76. Ma and Pender, "Trends in College Pricing," 32.
77. Babcock, "Rising Tuitions Fill Loan Firm Coffers."
78. Miller, "From the Ground Up, an Early History of Lumina Foundation for Education," 4–5.
79. Miller, 4.
80. Author's personal interview with Jon Oberg.
81. Dillon, "Whistle-Blower on Student Aid Is Vindicated."
82. Berman, "Little-Known Student Loan Middlemen Who Are Threatening Debt Forgiveness."
83. Berman, "One Company."
84. Dillon, "Whistle-Blower on Student Aid Is Vindicated."
85. Sampson, "Dear Colleague Letter."
86. Drawbaugh, "US Rep Miller Defends Student Loan Bill."
87. Berman, "Little-Known Student Loan Middlemen Who Are Threatening Debt Forgiveness."
88. Berman, "All the Ways Student Debt Exacerbates Racial Inequality."
89. Berman, "'I Can't Imagine the Day When I'm Not Paying.'"

Chapter 3

1. Miller, *Uncommon Man,* 35.
2. Honan, "Claiborne Pell, Patrician Senator Behind College Grant Program, Dies at 90"; Miller, *Uncommon Man,* 54–56, 63.
3. "Funeral Service for Claiborne Pell."
4. "Funeral Service for Claiborne Pell"; Honan, "Claiborne Pell, Patrician Senator Behind College Grant Program, Dies at 90."
5. Honan.
6. Miller, *Uncommon Man,* 152.
7. Miller, 159.
8. Gladieux and Wolanin, *Congress and the Colleges,* 85.
9. National Center for Education Statistics, "Average Undergraduate Tuition, Fees, Room and Board Rates Charged for Full-Time Students in Degree-Granting Postsecondary Institutions, by Level and Control of Institution."
10. Gladieux and Wolanin, *Congress and the Colleges,* 90–91.
11. Gladieux and Wolanin, 90–91.
12. Gladieux and Wolanin, 51.
13. Gladieux and Wolanin, 172.
14. *Education Amendments of 1971: Hearings before the Subcommittee on Education of the Committee on Labor and Public Welfare, United States Senate,"* 92nd Cong. (1971), 433, https://babel.hathitrust.org/cgi /pt?id=ucl.b3603377&view=1up&seq=9&skin=2021..

15. Gladieux and Wolanin, *Congress and the Colleges*, 70.
16. Education Amendments of 1972, Pub. L. No. 92-318, 86 Stat. 235 at 248 (1972), https://www.govinfo.gov/content/pkg/STATUTE-86/pdf/STATUTE-86-Pg235.pdf.
17. Education Amendments of 1972, 250.
18. Education Amendments of 1972, 265.
19. "College Saving Plan Can Avoid Tax Bite."
20. National Center for Education Statistics, "Average Undergraduate Tuition, Fees, Room and Board Rates Charged for Full-Time Students in Degree-Granting Postsecondary Institutions, by Level and Control of Institution."
21. Chisolm, "Black Caucus Reports."
22. Pine, "Carter Aid Plan Seeks to Head Off a Tuition Credit."
23. Pine.
24. *College Opportunity Act of 1978: Joint Hearing before the Committee on Human Resources, United States Senate and the Committee on Education and Labor, House of Representatives*, 95th Cong. (1978), 16, https://babel.hathitrust.org/cgi/pt?id=purl.32754076293343&view=1up&seq=1&skin=2021.
25. *College Opportunity Act of 1978*, 8.
26. *Middle Income Student Assistance Act: Hearings before the Subcommittee on Postsecondary Education of the Committee on Education and Labor, House of Representatives*, 95th Cong. (1978), 44, https://babel.hathitrust.org/cgi/pt?id=purl.32754076286859&view=1up&seq=3&skin=2021.
27. Pine, "Tuition Tax Credit Gets Boost in the House."
28. Meislin, "Tax Relief Plan for College Costs Enacted by Albany."
29. Cook and King, "2007 Status Report on the Pell Grant Program," vii.
30. Fiske, "Student Debt Reshaping Colleges and Careers."
31. Fiske, "Quotation of the Day"; Hechinger, "Reagan Effect."
32. Rankin, "Your Money."
33. Rankin.
34. Hunter, "Study Finds Large Overpayments in Aid for Needy College Students."
35. Bell, "Thirteenth Man," 75.
36. Author's personal interview with David Bergeron.
37. Bergeron interview.
38. Bergeron interview.
39. Douglas-Gabriel and Harden, "To Protect Taxpayer Dollars, the Education Dept. Is Disproportionately Auditing Black and Latino College Students."
40. DeBaun, "New FSA Data Revise Verification Melt Estimate Downward & Other Tidbits."
41. Special to the New York Times, "Bell Assails Criticism of Plans to Cut Student Aid as Unjust."
42. Broder, "Bennett Replaces Watt . . ."
43. Fiske, "Cuts in College Aid Placing Students in a Vise."

44. Vobejda, "Educators Score Reagan's Spending Proposals."
45. Taylor, "Reagan Sends Congress Plan to Limit Student Aid Programs."
46. Fiske, "Student Debt Reshaping Colleges and Careers."
47. Green, "Statement Prepared for Public Hearings on College Costs Held by the Subcommittee on Postsecondary Education," 3.
48. Fiske, "Minority Enrollment in Colleges Is Declining."
49. Fiske, "Student Debt Reshaping Colleges and Careers."
50. US Department of Education, College Scorecard, "Albright College."
51. "Drexel University Tuition & Financial Aid."
52. Temple University Undergraduate Admissions, "Tuition & Costs."
53. Pine, "Senate Votes to Expand Student Loan Programs."
54. McPherson and Shapiro, "New Higher Education Act Worth Little to College Students."
55. Adam, "In Quest to Help the Middle Class, House Passes a College Loan Bill."
56. Henry, "Pell Grants Face Further Cutbacks."
57. Clinton, "Address to the Nation on the Middle Class Bill of Rights."
58. Folkenflik, "A Boon or a Shuffle of Benefits?"
59. Kelly, "Gingrich Spells Out 'Revolution' to College Heads."
60. Roache, "College Plans Get Some Low Grades."
61. Nagourney, "Dole to Advocate 15% Cut in Taxes, His Campaign Says."
62. Author's personal interview with Robert Shireman.
63. Shireman interview.
64. Shireman interview.
65. Shireman interview.
66. Burd and Lederman, "Clinton Proposes 25% Increase in Spending on Pell Grants."
67. Crenshaw, "If It's for College Taxes Are Deferred."
68. McCullers and Stefanescu, "Introducing Section 529 Plans into the US Financial Accounts and Enhanced Financial Accounts."
69. College Savings Plan Network, "History of 529 Plans."
70. "If It's for College Taxes Are Deferred."
71. McCullers and Stefanescu, "Introducing Section 529 Plans into the US Financial Accounts and Enhanced Financial Accounts"; Arenson, "College Savings Plans Are a Growing Draw."
72. O'Neill, "With Less Aid, College Dreams Slip Away."
73. Morgan, "Change Means Fewer Students Will Be Eligible for Pell Grants."
74. Winter and Schemo, "Bill Clears Way for Government to Cut Back College Loans."
75. Sanger, "Bush's Budget Will Seek Modest Rise in Pell Grants."
76. Author's personal interview with David Bergeron.
77. CNN Wire Staff, "CNN Fact Check."
78. White House Office of the Press Secretary, "Fact Sheet: A Simpler, Fairer Tax Code."
79. US Government Accountability Office, "Higher Education."

80. Weisman, "Obama Relents on Proposal to End '529' College Savings Plan."
81. Author's personal interview with Stephen Burd.
82. Author's personal interview with Jon Oberg.
83. Oberg interview.
84. Riley, "Letter to College Presidents."
85. Turner, "Economic Incidence of Federal Student Grant Aid," 2.
86. Author's personal interview with Stephen Burd.
87. Burd, "Undermining Pell: How Colleges Compete," 7.
88. Author's personal interview with Stephen Burd.
89. Burd, "Undermining Pell: Volume IV," introduction.
90. Burd, "Crisis Point," introduction.
91. Author's personal interview with Stephen Burd.
92. Ngo, "After Dropping Free Community College Plan, Democrats Explore Options."
93. Bykowicz, "Why Biden's Plan for Free Community College Will Likely Be Cut from Budget Package."
94. Levine and Ritter, "Racial Wealth Gap, Financial Aid, and College Access."
95. Board of Governors of the Federal Reserve System, "Dealing with Unexpected Expenses."

Chapter 4

1. Ellis, "How to Pay for College without Student Loans"; Ward, "6 Alternatives to an Expensive Undergrad Degree."
2. Berman, "'It's Not Just about Tuition, It's about How I'm Going to Eat.'"
3. Chambers, "Appropriations of State Tax Funds for Operating Expenses of Higher Education 1964–1965"; National Center for Education Statistics, "Digest of Education Statistics."
4. Marginson, *The Dream Is Over*, 14.
5. Master Plan Survey Team, "A Master Plan for Higher Education in California," 174.
6. Master Plan Survey Team, xi.
7. Douglass and Bleemer, "Approaching a Tipping Point?," 11.
8. Marginson, *The Dream Is Over*, 12.
9. Marginson, 15.
10. Master Plan Survey Team, "A Master Plan for Higher Education in California," 146.
11. Master Plan Survey Team, 152.
12. Master Plan Survey Team, 183–86.
13. Master Plan Survey Team, 173.
14. "Had Advance On UC Report, Reagan Says."
15. Greenberg, "Reagan Hits Choice of Regents for UC Inquiry."
16. Korman, "Brown and Reagan Clash over S.N.C.C."
17. "Diversity in Higher Education Series Part I."
18. Bates and Meraji, "Student Strike That Changed Higher Ed Forever."

19. "A Bill for Minority Education.
20. Trombley, "Changing University."
21. US Department of Education, College Scorecard, "Eureka College."
22. Trombley, "Changing University."
23. Zeman, "Reagan Favors Tuition Fee but No Budget Cuts."
24. Zeman.
25. "Reagan Ax Falls."
26. Korman, "Reagan Loses Tuition Fight with Regents, However He Gains Special Funds."
27. Hechinger, "Reagan vs. Kerr."
28. "Gov. Reagan Proposes Cut Back in U. of California Appropriation."
29. Zeman, "Reagan Drops Tuition Plans, Raises Budgets $38 Million."
30. United Press International, "Governor Renews Tuition Plan Campaign."
31. Trombley, "UC Regent Group Backs Rise in Fees."
32. Davies, "Regents Battle Reagan's Vetoes."
33. Davies, "Reagan Promises to Rid Campuses of 'Anarchists.'"
34. Trombley, "Education Budget Fight Looming for Governor."
35. Korman, "Tuition Imposed at U. of Cal."
36. New York Times News Service, "Reagan Cuts State Budget by $503 Million."
37. Trombley, "Changing University."
38. Krop, Carroll, and Rivera, "Trends in the California Higher Education Sector and Its Environment," 1.
39. Author's email exchange with the California State University Public Affairs Department.
40. Public Policy Institute of California Higher Education Center, "Investing in Public Higher Education."
41. Public Policy Institute of California Higher Education Center.
42. US Census Bureau, "Historical Census of Housing Tables."
43. Author's personal interview with Manuel Pastor.
44. Pastor, "After Tax Cuts Derailed the 'California Dream,' Is the State Getting Back on Track?"
45. Brinkley, "Reagan's Revenge as Invented by Howard Jarvis."
46. Pastor, "After Tax Cuts Derailed the 'California Dream,' Is the State Getting Back on Track?"
47. Author's personal interview with Manuel Pastor.
48. Pastor interview.
49. Pastor interview.
50. Pastor interview.
51. California Budget Project, "Proposition 13: Its Impact on California and Implications," 3.
52. King, "School Still Feels Bakke Aftermath."
53. My calculations, based on data from the Department of Education (https://nces.ed.gov/programs/digest/d22/tables/dt22_306.20.asp) and State Higher Education Executive Officers Association (https://shef.sheeo.org/data-downloads/) data, accessed March 20, 2024.

54. Ma and Pender, "Trends in College Pricing."
55. My calculations, based on data from the Department of Education (https://nces.ed.gov/programs/digest/d22/tables/dt22_306.20.asp) and State Higher Education Executive Officers Association (https://shef.sheeo.org/data-downloads/) data, accessed March 20, 2024.
56. Ma and Pender, "Trends in College Pricing."
57. My calculations, based on data from the Department of Education (https://nces.ed.gov/programs/digest/d22/tables/dt22_306.20.asp) and State Higher Education Executive Officers Association (https://shef.sheeo.org/data-downloads/) data, accessed March 20, 2024.
58. Ma and Pender, "Trends in College Pricing."
59. Douglass and Bleemer, "Approaching a Tipping Point?," 12.
60. Douglass and Bleemer, 12.
61. Chavez, *Color Bind*, 34–35.
62. Chavez, 40.
63. Trombley, "Spending Dip Called Threat to Education."
64. Trombley.
65. Chandler, "Enrollment in Community Colleges Drops."
66. Chandler.
67. State Higher Education Finance, "State Profile: California."
68. State Higher Education Finance.
69. California State University, "Historical Tuition Rates."
70. Berkeley Office of the Registrar, "Fee Schedule Archive."
71. University of California, "Fall Enrollment at a Glance."
72. Eaton et al., "Affording the Dream," 1.
73. US Department of Education, College Scorecard, "University of California-Merced."
74. Hamilton and Nielsen, *Broke*, 86, 14.
75. Hamilton and Nielsen, 104, 124.
76. Hamilton and Nielsen, 174.
77. National Center for Education Statistics, "Fast Facts."
78. Demos, "When Congress Went to College," 23.
79. Baum, Blagg, and Fishman, "Reshaping Parent PLUS Loans," 3.
80. Baum, Blagg, and Fishman, 4.
81. Baum, Blagg, and Fishman, 4.
82. Baum, Blagg, and Fishman, 4.
83. *Reauthorization of the Higher Education Act of 1965: Hearings before the Subcommittee on Education, Arts and Humanities, United States Senate*, 102nd Cong. (1991), 74–75, https://babel.hathitrust.org/cgi/pt?id=purl.32754076781495&seq=761.
84. *Reauthorization of the Higher Education Act of 1965*, 58.
85. Higher Education Act Amendments of 1992, H.R. 4471, 102nd Cong. (1991–1992), https://www.congress.gov/bill/102nd-congress/house-bill/4471/text.
86. *Hearings on the Reauthorization of the Higher Education Act of 1965: Stafford Loans: Hearings before the Subcommittee on Postsecondary Education of the*

Committee on Education and Labor, 102nd Cong. (1991), 52, https://babel
.hathitrust.org/cgi/pt?id=pst.000018280036&seq=3.

87. *Hearings on the Reauthorization of the Higher Education Act of 1965*, 272.
88. *Hearings on the Reauthorization of the Higher Education Act of 1965*, 242.
89. Author's personal interview with Tom Butts.
90. Jackson, Williams, and Mustaffa, "Parent PLUS Loans Are a Double-
    Edged Sword for Black Borrowers."
91. Author's personal interview Tom Butts.
92. *Hearings on the Reauthorization of the Higher Education Act of 1965*, 242.
93. Berman, "Little-Known Student Loan Middlemen Who Are Threatening
    Debt Forgiveness."
94. Author's personal interview with Tom Butts.
95. Granville, "Parent PLUS Borrowers."
96. Granville.
97. Granville.
98. Granville.
99. Fishman, "Wealth Gap PLUS Debt," 2.
100. Burd et al., "Decoding the Cost of College," 1.
101. Hobbs and Fuller, "How Baylor Steered Lower-Income Parents to Debt
    They Couldn't Afford."
102. Anderson, "Tighter Federal Lending Standards Yield Turmoil for
    Historically Black Colleges."
103. Grunwald, "US Government's Predatory-Lending Program."
104. Grunwald.
105. Baum, Blagg, and Fishman, "Reshaping Parent PLUS Loans."
106. Congressional Budget Office, "Federal Student Loan Programs," 7.
107. Ma and Pender, "Trends in College Pricing," 12.
108. AARP Policy Institute, "AARP Analysis Shows Student Loan Debt
    Growing at Alarming Rates for Americans 50-Plus."
109. Department of Education, "How the New SAVE Plan Will Transform
    Loan Repayment and Protect Borrowers."
110. Berman, "This Government Loan Forgiveness Program Has Rejected 99%
    of Borrowers So Far."
111. Goldrick-Rab et al., "College and University Basic Needs Insecurity," 2.
112. Zumper, "San Francisco, CA Rent Prices"; Zillow, "San Francisco Home
    Values."
113. Berman, "Online Courses Could Help Make College Affordable, but This
    $1 Billion Industry Is Standing in the Way."
114. Hamilton et al., "Private Side of Public Universities," 1.
115. US Government Accountability Office, "Education Needs to Strengthen
    Its Approach to Monitoring Colleges' Arrangements with Online
    Program Managers," 15.

Chapter 5

1. Lawrence Summers (@LHSummers), "I hope the Administration does
   not contribute to inflation macro economically by offering unreasonably

generous student loan relief or micro economically by encouraging college tuition increases," X, August 22, 2022, 9:07 a.m., https://twitter.com/lhsummers/status/1561701542591356931.

2. Jason Furman (@jasonfurman), "Student loan relief is not free. It would be paid for. Part of it would be paid for by the 87% of Americans who do not benefit but lose out from inflation. Part of it would be paid for by future spending cuts & tax increases—with uncertainty about who will bear those costs," X, August 19, 2022, 10:02 a.m., https://x.com/jasonfurman/status/1560632892476325889.

3. Jason Furman (@jasonfurman), "Pouring roughly half trillion dollars of gasoline on the inflationary fire that is already burning is reckless. Doing it while going well beyond one campaign promise ($10K of student loan relief) and breaking another (all proposals paid for) is even worse," X, August 24, 2022, 1:15 p.m., https://x.com/jasonfurman/status/1562503985529233410?lang=en.

4. Goldstein, "Goldman Sachs Has Run the Numbers on Student-Loan Forgiveness."

5. Krugman, "Two Big Questions about Student Debt Relief."

6. Biden, "Remarks by President Biden Announcing Student Loan Debt Relief Plan."

7. Tressie McMillan Cottom @tressiemcphd, "It has absolutely always been about an ideological battle through policy. If you forgive some student loan debt, you admit that a key assumption of economic policy failed. These are priests arguing for their god," August 25, 2022, 1:41 p.m., https://twitter.com/tressiemcphd/status/1562857719257649153?s=21&t=zBlM9aJUH5Fnor-dvMDynw.

8. Brooks, "Calling on the Federal Government to Enact a Plan by the End of President Biden's First 100 Days."

9. Economic Policy Institute, "State of Working America Data Library, Wages by Education."

10. Collins, *Credential Society*, 135–36.

11. Collins, 135–36.

12. Collins, 146.

13. Groeger, *Education Trap*, 140.

14. Groeger, 142.

15. Groeger, 141.

16. Collins, *Credential Society*, 160–61.

17. Collins, 165.

18. Collins, 166.

19. Collins, 170.

20. Collins, 171.

21. Groeger, *Education Trap*, 51.

22. Groeger, 191, 209.

23. Groeger, 184.

24. Rothwell, "Using Earnings Data to Rank Colleges."

25. Groeger, *Education Trap*, 220–21.

26. Groeger, 233–34.

27. Groeger, 235–36.
28. Groeger, 234.
29. Groeger, 234.
30. Groeger, 244.
31. Collins, *Credential Society*, 265–66.
32. Groeger, *Education Trap*, 244.
33. Groeger, 250–51.
34. Eide, Hilmer, and Showalter, "Is It Where You Go or What You Study?";
    Klein, "How Wall Street Recruits So Many Insecure Ivy League Grads."
35. Rivera, "Pedigree," 15–16.
36. Rivera, 17.
37. Author's personal interview with Anthony Carnevale.
38. Carnevale interview.
39. US Bureau of Labor Statistics, "Union Membership Rate Fell by 0.2
    Percentage Point to 10.1 Percent in 2022."
40. Modestino, Shoag, and Ballance, "Upskilling," 1.
41. Modestino, Shoag, and Ballance, 2.
42. Pinto and Steinbaum. "Long-Run Impact of the Great Recession on
    Student Debt," 3.
43. Pinto and Steinbaum, 1.
44. Pinto and Steinbaum, 3.
45. Blagg, "Rise of Master's Degrees," 3.
46. Blagg, 1.
47. Monarrez and Matsudaira, "Trends in Federal Student Loans for
    Graduate School," 2.
48. Miller, "Graduate School Debt."
49. Monarrez and Matsudaira, "Trends in Federal Student Loans for
    Graduate School," 1.
50. Monarrez and Matsudaira, 7.
51. Asch, Grischkan, and Nicholson, "Lower the Cost of Producing Doctors,
    Not Just the Price of Going to Medical School."
52. Monarrez and Matsudaira, "Trends in Federal Student Loans for
    Graduate School," 9.
53. Carey, "Creeping Capitalist Takeover of Higher Education."
54. Monarrez and Matsudaira, "Trends in Federal Student Loans for
    Graduate School," 8.
55. Berg et al., "Current Term Enrollment Estimates, Spring 2023," 1.
56. Korn and Fuller, "'Financially Hobbled for Life.'"
57. Marcus, "Graduate Programs Have Become a Cash Cow for Struggling
    Colleges."
58. Krivacsy and Usher, "Requirements of the Job"; Meyer, "Causes and
    Consequences of Graduate School Debt."
59. Author's personal interview with Jason Delisle.
60. "Deficit Reduction Act of 2005 Conference Report," 151 Cong. Rec.
    30635, https://www.govinfo.gov/content/pkg/CRECB-2005-pt22/pdf
    /CRECB-2005-pt22-Pg30556-3.pdf.
61. Ma and Pender, "Trends in College Pricing and Student Aid 2022."

62. Deficit Reduction Act of 2005, S. 1932, 109th Cong. (2005–2006), https://www.congress.gov/bill/109th-congress/senate-bill/1932/text.
63. Mitchell, "Is the US Student Loan Program Facing a $500 Billion Hole?"
64. Author's personal interview with Jason Delisle.
65. Delisle interview.
66. Author's personal interview with Barmak Nassirian.
67. Nassirian interview.
68. Lee and Looney, "Headwinds for Graduate Student Borrowers."
69. Author's personal interview with Jason Delisle.
70. Kelchen, "An Empirical Examination of the Bennett Hypothesis in Law School Prices."
71. Author's personal interview with Robert Kelchen.
72. Black, Turner, and Denning, "PLUS or Minus?," 1.
73. Whitman, "GOP Reversal on For-Profit Colleges in the George W. Bush Era."
74. Author's personal interview with Barmak Nassirian.
75. Nassirian interview.
76. National Center for Education Statistics, "Graduate Degree Fields."
77. Bennett, "Labor Market Returns to MBAs from Less-Selective Universities: Evidence from a Field Experiment during COVID-19," 2.
78. Monarrez and Matsudaira, "Trends in Federal Student Loans for Graduate School," 12.
79. Monarrez and Matsudaira, 5.
80. Scott-Clayton and Li, "Black-White Disparity in Student Loan Debt More Than Triples after Graduation."
81. Green, "Lawsuit Charges For-Profit University Preyed on Black and Female Students."
82. Berman, "They Thought a Degree."
83. Jaquette, "In Pursuit of Revenue and Prestige."
84. Ochoa, "Dear Colleague Letter on Program Integrity Regulations," 12.
85. Hill, "OPM Market Landscape and Dynamics."
86. Carey, "Creeping Capitalist Takeover of Higher Education."
87. Carey.
88. US Government Accountability Office, "Education Needs to Strengthen Its Approach to Monitoring Colleges' Arrangements with Online Program Managers," 11–12.
89. Knott, "Congressional Democrats Want Legal Review of OPMs."
90. Berman, "Online Courses Could Help Make College Affordable, but This $1 Billion Industry Is Standing in the Way."
91. Brown and Warren, "Senators' Letter to OPM Providers," 2.
92. US Department of Education, "US Department of Education Launches Review of Prohibition on Incentive Compensation for College Recruiters."
93. Mitchell, "Letter from Ted Mitchell on Bundled Services."
94. Berman, "Educational Stock That Went from $98 to $1."
95. Bennett, "Labor Market Returns to MBAs from Less-Selective Universities," 1.
96. Korn and Fuller, "'Financially Hobbled for Life.'"

97. Petersen, "Master's Trap."
98. Author's personal interview with Ozan Jaquette.
99. Jaquette interview.
100. See my analysis of HEA Group Data, file "8.1.2023+PRGM+LEVEL _DATA+HEA+NSLDN," at https://t.co/YCHrosktsv.
101. Author's personal interview Ozan Jaquette.
102. Jaquette interview.
103. Perry and Weingarten, "Gov. Tom Corbett Has Slashed Funding for Pennsylvania's Neediest Students."
104. Berman, "A High-School Diploma Is Pretty Much Useless These Days."
105. Berman, "This Government Loan Forgiveness Program Has Rejected 99% of Borrowers So Far."
106. Author's personal interview with Anthony Carnevale.

Chapter 6

1. Friedman, "Role of Government in Education."
2. Friedman.
3. Friedman.
4. Berman, "Would It Work in America?"
5. Shireman, "Learn Now, Pay Later," 191.
6. Shireman, 188.
7. Author's personal interview with Robert Shireman.
8. 137 Cong. Rec. 21954 (daily ed. August 2, 1991), https://www.congress .gov/bound-congressional-record/1991/08/02/senate-section.
9. Author's personal interview with Robert Shireman.
10. Shireman interview.
11. Shireman interview.
12. Shireman interview.
13. Reardon, "Dukakis' College Tuition Loan Plan Has Some Merit, Experts Say' "; Shireman, "Learn Now, Pay Later," 196.
14. Shireman, 195.
15. Ifill, "1992 Campaign."
16. Waldman, *The Bill*, 53.
17. Waldman, 156–57.
18. Kelly, "Gingrich Spells Out 'Revolution' to College Heads."
19. Shireman, "Learn Now, Pay Later," 196.
20. Shireman interview with Robert Shireman.
21. Shireman interview.
22. Shireman interview.
23. American Council on Education Government and Public Affairs, "College Cost Reduction and Access Act of 2007."
24. Shireman, "Learn Now, Pay Later," 197.
25. Slack, "Income Based Repayment."
26. Author's personal interview with Robert Shireman.
27. White House. "Annual Report of the White House Task Force on the Middle Class."

28. White House, 38.
29. Cendana, "United Students Association Letter to Vice President Joe Biden."
30. Halperin, "Campus Progress Letter to Vice President Joe Biden."
31. Asher, "Institute for College Access & Success letter to Vice President Joe Biden."
32. White House, "Annual Report of the White House Task Force on the Middle Class," 38.
33. Author's personal interview with Mark Huelsman.
34. Huelsman interview.
35. Huelsman interview.
36. Chingos, "Why Student Loan Rhetoric Doesn't Match the Facts."
37. Akers and Chingos, "Student Loan Safety Nets."
38. Quinn, "Student Loans."
39. Urban Institute, "Sandy Baum Author Bio."
40. Berman, "Why This Author Is Skeptical of the Student Loan Crisis."
41. Douglas-Gabriel, "Obama Administration's Plan to Lower the Student Debt Payments of Millions More Americans."
42. Carey, "A Quiet Revolution in Helping Lift the Burden of Student Debt."
43. Carey.
44. Douglas-Gabriel, "Obama Administration's Plan to Lower the Student Debt Payments of Millions More Americans."
45. Author's personal interview with Robert Shireman.
46. Berman, "Student Loan Borrowers Share Tales of Woe with Regulators."
47. Berman, "Feds Sue Student Loan Giant Navient."
48. Pennsylvania Attorney General's Press Office, "Attorney General Josh Shapiro Announces $1.85 Billion Landmark Settlement with Student Loan Servicer Navient."
49. Navient, "Navient Announces Successful Resolution of Legal Matters with State Attorneys General."
50. Waldman, *The Bill*: 236.
51. Gunn, Haltom, and Neelakantan, "Should More Student Loan Borrowers Use Income-Driven Repayment Plans?"
52. US Government Accountability Office, "Student Loans," 5.
53. US Government Accountability Office, 10.
54. Steinbaum, "Student Debt Crisis Is a Crisis of Non-Repayment."
55. Steinbaum.
56. Berman, "2 Million Americans Have Been Repaying Their Student Loans for 20 Years."
57. Author's personal interview with Robert Shireman.
58. Shireman interview.
59. Author's personal interview with Julie Peller.
60. Peller interview.
61. Berman, "12 Years after Starting College, White Men Have Paid Off 44% of Their Student Loans While Black Women Owe 13% More."
62. Author's personal interview with Mark Huelsman.

63. Institute for College Access & Success, "How to Secure and Strengthen Pell Grants to Increase College Access and Success."
64. Author's personal interview with John King.
65. White House, "Biden-Harris Administration Launches the SAVE Plan."
66. US Department of Education, "Department of Education Announces Actions to Fix Longstanding Failures in the Student Loan Program."
67. White House, "Statement from President Joe Biden on Student Loan Debt Cancellation for More Than 800,000 Borrowers."
68. Author's personal interview with Mark Huelsman.

Chapter 7

1. "Wilfred Beauty Academy Commercial," 1988, YouTube video, 0:29, posted by VaultMasterDBT, November 29, 2007, https://www.youtube.com/watch?v=RwAEgzevSQQ.
2. New York Legal Assistance Group, "Ana Salazar, Marilyn Mercado, Ana Bernardez, Jeannette Poole, Edna Villatoro, Lisa Bryant and Cherryline Stevens," 11.
3. New York Legal Assistance Group, 14.
4. New York Legal Assistance Group, 37.
5. Berman, "Broken Promises and Persuasive Charms of For-Profit Colleges, by a Former Employee."
6. Gallagher, "Beauty School Employees Charged with Loan Fraud."
7. New York Legal Assistance Group, "Ana Salazar, Marilyn Mercado, Ana Bernardez, Jeannette Poole, Edna Villatoro, Lisa Bryant and Cherryline Stevens," 15.
8. New York Legal Assistance Group, 17.
9. Huber, "Student Loan Bankruptcies Soaring."
10. Associated Press, "Local Students Pass Up Bankruptcy."
11. Vidal, "Students Default on College Loans."
12. New York Times News Service, "Bankruptcy Being Used to Lapse Student Loans."
13. Associated Press, "Local Students Pass Up Bankruptcy."
14. New York Times News Service, "Bankruptcy Being Used to Lapse Student Loans."
15. Huber, "Student Loan Bankruptcies Soaring."
16. Klaus, "Remembering."
17. Huber, "Student Loan Bankruptcies Soaring."
18. Huber.
19. Huber.
20. Associated Press, "Local Students Pass Up Bankruptcy."
21. Guaranteed Student Loan Amendments of 1976, H.R. Rep. 94-1232, at 73, https://babel.hathitrust.org/cgi/pt?id=uc1.31210024844647&view=1up&seq=1&skin=2021&q1=bankruptcy.
22. Guaranteed Student Loan Amendments of 1976, at 74.
23. Guaranteed Student Loan Amendments of 1976, at 75.

24. Guaranteed Student Loan Amendments of 1976, at 75.
25. *Hearings before the Subcommittee on Postsecondary Education of the Committee on Education and Labor House of Representatives First Session on H.R. 3471 and Related Legislation*, 94th Cong. (1975), 628, https://babel.hathitrust.org/cgi/pt?id=purl.32754076275621&view=1up&seq=3&skin=2021&q1=bankruptcy.
26. 137 Cong. Rec. 13764 (1991), https://www.govinfo.gov/app/details/GPO-CRECB-1991-pt10/.
27. Loonin, "No Way Out:," 40.
28. White House. "Clinton Presidency."
29. Staff of the National Performance Review, "Department of Education: Accompanying Report of the National Performance Review," 37.
30. Staff of the National Performance Review, 36.
31. Cooper, "Lawmakers Pursue Money Owed to US."
32. Cooper.
33. Cooper.
34. Maloney, "Debt Collection Bill Could Reduce Deficit."
35. Cooper, "Lawmakers Pursue Money Owed to US."
36. Leland, "Cheers and Boos after Ruling"; Stuart Rossman, "Amicus Curiae Brief in Support of the Petitioner on Behalf of the National Consumer Law Center, AARP, National Senior Citizens Law Center, and the National Organization of Social Security Claimants' Representatives (NOSSCR)," 5 (in author's possession).
37. Lockhart v. United States, 546 U.S. 142 (2005), https://supreme.justia.com/cases/federal/us/546/142/#tab-opinion-1962006.
38. Leland, "Cheers and Boos after Ruling."
39. Lockhart, 546 U.S. 142 (2005).
40. Patricia Gary's testimony to James Kvaal was provided to me by her lawyer and is not publicly available.
41. Author's personal interview with Johnson Tyler.
42. Tyler interview.
43. Federal Student Aid, "Federal Student Aid Posts New Quarterly Reports to FSA Data Center."
44. Gallagher and Rendon, "CFI in Focus."
45. Berman, "'Morally Suspect' Way the Government Collects Student Loans during Tax Season."
46. Loonin, "Pounding Student Loan Borrowers," 17-18.
47. Author's personal interview with Persis Yu.
48. Consumer Financial Protection Bureau, "Annual Report of the CFPB Student Loan Ombudsman," 4.
49. Consumer Financial Protection Bureau, 26.
50. Consumer Financial Protection Bureau, 19.
51. Berman, "They Lost Their Tax Refund over Defaulted Student Debt."
52. Consumer Financial Protection Bureau, "Annual Report of the CFPB Student Loan Ombudsman," 35.
53. Berman, "Borrowers Are Still Having Their Paychecks Seized over Defaulted Student Loans."

54. Berman, "Elizabeth Warren Calls for New Leadership to Oversee Student Loans."
55. Shiro and Reeves, "For-Profit College System Is Broken and the Biden Administration Needs to Fix It."
56. US Department of Education, "Department's Decision to Terminate Private Collection Agency Contracts," 5.
57. Department of Justice, "Justice Department and Department of Education Announce a Fairer and More Accessible Bankruptcy Discharge Process for Student Loan Borrowers."
58. Author's personal interview with Persis Yu.

Chapter 8

1. White House, "President Biden Announces Student Loan Relief for Borrowers Who Need It Most."
2. US Senate Committee on Health, Education, Labor, and Pensions, "For-Profit Higher Education," 379.
3. US Senate Committee on Health, Education, Labor, and Pensions, 387.
4. Waldman, "How a For-Profit College Targeted the Homeless and Kids with Low Self-Esteem"; US Senate Committee on Health, Education, Labor, and Pensions, "For-Profit Higher Education," 399.
5. US Senate Committee on Health, Education, Labor, and Pensions, 379.
6. US Senate Committee on Health, Education, Labor, and Pensions, 379.
7. US Senate Committee on Health, Education, Labor, and Pensions, 399.
8. Waldman, "Who's Regulating For-Profit Schools?"
9. Larson, "Chapter One, Occupy Wall Street."
10. Larson.
11. "Occupy Student Debt Campaign Launch," posted by StudentDebtCampaign, YouTube video, 2:26, December 15, 2011, https://www.youtube.com/watch?v=sCxLQMDBy-0&t=1s.
12. "Occupy Student Debt Campaign Launch."
13. Larson, "Chapter Five, The Rolling Jubilee."
14. Associated Press, "College Loan Scandal 'Like Peeling an Onion.'"
15. Consumer Financial Protection Bureau, "Private Student Loans," 3.
16. Consumer Financial Protection Bureau, 3.
17. Consumer Financial Protection Bureau, "CFPB Sues For-Profit Corinthian Colleges for Predatory Lending Scheme."
18. Larson, "Chapter Nine, A Meeting with Corinthian College Protestors."
19. Larson.
20. Consumer Financial Protection Bureau, "CFPB Sues For-Profit Corinthian Colleges for Predatory Lending Scheme."
21. Consumer Financial Protection Bureau.
22. US Department of Justice, "Justice Department Reaches $60 Million Settlement with Sallie Mae to Resolve Allegations of Charging Military Servicemembers Excessive Rates on Student Loans."
23. Consumer Financial Protection Bureau, "CFPB Sues For-Profit Corinthian Colleges for Predatory Lending Scheme."

24. Larson, "Chapter Eleven, A Movement Is Born."
25. Larson.
26. Larson, "Chapter Fourteen, Student Debtors on Strike."
27. Project on Predatory Student Lending, "Tina Carr and Yvette Colon v. Elisabeth DeVos."
28. Larson, "Chapter Fifteen, An Historic Meeting in Washington."
29. Berman, "Corinthian Colleges Files for Bankruptcy Protection; Students Scramble for Restitution."
30. Berman, "Students Duped by For-Profit Colleges Might Get Some Relief."
31. Berman, "Man Who Oversaw Mortgage Crisis Settlement to Guide Corinthian Debt Relief."
32. Senator Dick Durbin Press Office, "Durbin Meets with Department of Education Special Master"; Office of the Attorney General Maura Healey, "AG Healey Submits Application to US Department of Education to Cancel Thousands of Loans for Former Corinthian Students."
33. Author's personal interview with John King.
34. Bidwell, "ED Launches Student Aid Enforcement Unit, Asks for $13.6 Million in Funding."
35. Fain, "Education Department Slaps Serious Sanctions on ITT."
36. Berman, "ITT Is the Second Major For-Profit College to Declare Bankruptcy since Last Year."
37. Office of Postsecondary Education, "A Rule by the Education Department."
38. Berman, "Obama Administration Prepares to Hand Student Debt Challenge to Trump."
39. Consumer Financial Protection Bureau, "CFPB Sues Nation's Largest Student Loan Company Navient for Failing Borrowers at Every Stage of Repayment."
40. Navient, "Legal Action Facts."
41. Berman, "States to DeVos."
42. Berman, "90% of Borrowers Who Claim They Were Scammed by Their Schools Were Denied Relief"; Berman, "Scammed Student-Loan Borrowers Accuse Betsy DeVos of Illegally Stalling on Debt-Cancellation Claims."
43. Carr, Anacker, and Hernandez, "State of Housing in Black America," 4.
44. Badger, "Dramatic Racial Bias of Subprime Lending during the Housing Boom."
45. Addo, Houle, and Simon, "Young, Black and (Still) in the Red."
46. Berman, "Black-White Wealth Gap Is Fueled by Student Debt."
47. Berman, "America's $1.5 Trillion Student-Loan Industry Is a 'Failed Social Experiment.'"
48. Warren, "My Plan to Cancel Student Debt on Day One of My Presidency."
49. Mui and Sonmez, "Obama, Romney Focus on Student Debt as Campaign Issue."
50. Berman, "Hillary Says Bernie Will Play Robin to Her Batman in Crusade to Fix Student-Loan Mess."

51. Herrine, "Future of the Education Department's Power to Cancel Student Loan Debt."
52. Stratford, "Warren Promises to Cancel Student Loan Debt Using Executive Powers."
53. US Department of Education, "Delivering on President Trump's Promise."
54. Author's personal interview with Persis Yu.
55. Elizabeth Warren Newsroom, "Schumer, Warren."
56. Berman, "Should the Biden Administration Cancel Student Debt?"
57. Brooks, "Has Biden Changed?"
58. Brooks.
59. Egan, "White House Promised a Memo on Biden's Authority to Cancel Student Debt."
60. Berman, "New Student-Loan Forgiveness Guidelines Explained."
61. US Department of Education, "Over 323,000 Federal Student Loan Borrowers to Receive $5.8 Billion in Automatic Total and Permanent Disability Discharges."
62. US Department of Education, "Education Department Approves $5.8 Billion Group Discharge to Cancel All Remaining Loans for 560,000 Borrowers who Attended Corinthian."
63. Barnes, "Former Education Secretary Calls for Cancellation of Debt for All Student Loan Holders."
64. Author's personal interview with John King.
65. AFL-CIO Staff, "Take Action."
66. Author's personal interview with Wisdom Cole.
67. White House, "Remarks by President Biden Announcing Student Loan Debt Relief Plan."
68. National Center for Education Statistics, "Status and Trends in the Education of Racial and Ethnic Groups, Indicator 22."
69. Berman, "Fate of Student-Loan Forgiveness May Rest with the Courts."

Conclusion

1. Biden v. Nebraska, No. 22-506, slip op. at 111–12, https://www.supreme court.gov/opinions/22pdf/22-506_nmip.pdf.
2. Biden v. Nebraska.
3. Biden v. Nebraska, slip op. at 2.
4. MOHELA to Missouri Rep. Cori Bush, October 28, 2022, https://bush .house.gov/imo/media/doc/letter_to_hon_cori_bush.pdf.
5. Berman, "Little-Known Student Loan Middlemen Who Are Threatening Debt Forgiveness."
6. Berman, "Biden Vows to Cancel Student Debt for Millions."
7. Beamer and Steinbaum, "Opinion."
8. US Department of Education, "Education Approves $5.8 Billion Group Discharge to Cancel All Remaining Loans for 560,000 Borrowers who Attended Corinthian."

9. US Department of Education, "The Biden-Harris Administration Launches the SAVE Plan."

10. Shane, "Feds Close 90/10 Loophole Involving Veterans Education Benefits."

11. US Department of Education, "A Fresh Start for Federal Student Loan Borrowers in Default."

12. US Department of Education, "Biden-Harris Administration Announces Additional $7.7 Billion in Approved Student Debt Relief for 160,000 Borrowers."

13. Berman, "Why Teachers and Social Workers May Not Get the Student Debt Forgiveness They're Counting On."

14. Berman, "More Than 800,000 Student-Loan Borrowers to Start Seeing Their Debt Canceled, Biden Administration Says."

15. Anthony, Nguyen, and Hillman, "Introducing the 2022 Pell Access and Completion Series"; Berman, "More Than Half of Community Colleges Are Too Expensive for Low-Income Students."

16. Jones, Ramirez-Mendoza, and Jackson, "A Promise Worth Keeping."

17. Community College of Philadelphia, "Community College of Philadelphia Now Accepting Applications for Octavius Catto Scholarship."

18. Smith et al., "Promising or Predatory?," 4.

19. Berman, "Companies Have a New Weapon in the Hunt for Talent."

20. Sigelman, Fuller, and Martin, "Skills-Based Hiring."

21. Carnevale, Jayasundera, and Gulish, "Good Jobs Are Back, College Graduates Are First in Line."

Bibliography

AARP Policy Institute. "AARP Analysis Shows Student Loan Debt Growing at Alarming Rates for Americans 50-Plus." March 31, 2021. https://press.aarp.org/2021-3-31-AARP-Analysis-Shows-Student-Loan-Debt-Growing-at-Alarming-Rates-for-Americans-50-plus.

Adam, Clymer. "In Quest to Help the Middle Class, House Passes a College Loan Bill." *New York Times*, July 9, 1992.

Addo, Fenaba R., Jason N. Houle, and Daniel Simon. "Young, Black, and (Still) in the Red: Parental Wealth, Race, and Student Loan Debt." *Race and Social Problems* 8, no. 1 (2016): 64–76. https://doi.org/10.1007/s12552-016-9162-0.

AFL-CIO. "Take Action: Cancel Student Debt." May 17, 2022. https://act.aflcio.org/forms/cancelstudentdebt?source=051622-email&link_id=2&can_id=4b1d230bdd76d781cd31531d560bb240&email_referrer=email_1545570&email_subject=petition-cancel-student-debt.

Akers, Beth, and Matthew M. Chingos. "Student Loan Safety Nets: Estimating the Costs and Benefits of Income-Based Repayment." Brookings Institution, April 14, 2014. https://www.brookings.edu/research/student-loan-safety -nets-estimating-the-costs-and-benefits-of-income-based-repayment/.

American Council on Education Government and Public Affairs. "The College Cost Reduction and Access Act of 2007." https://www.acenet.edu/Documents /Summary-of-the-College-Cost-Reduction-and-Access-Act-of-2007.pdf.

Anderson, Nick. "Tighter Federal Lending Standards Yield Turmoil for Historically Black Colleges." *Washington Post*, June 22, 2013. https://www .washingtonpost.com/local/education/tighter-federal-lending-standards -yield-turmoil-for-historically-black-colleges/2013/06/22/6ade4acc-d9a5 -11e2-a9f2-42ee3912ae0e_story.html.

Anthony, Marshall, Jr., Casey Nguyen, and Nick Hillman. "Introducing the 2022 Pell Access and Completion Series." Institute for College Access and Success, June 29, 2022. https://ticas.org/affordability-2/student-aid/grant-aid-stu dent-aid/introducing-the-2022-pell-access-and-completion-series/#

Arenson, Karen W. "College Savings Plans Are a Growing Draw." *New York Times*, August 12, 2002. https://www.nytimes.com/2002/08/12/business/college -savings-plans-are-a-growing-draw.html.

Aronson, Raney, Jackie Bennion, Missy Frederick, John Maggio, and Arun Rath. "Educating Sergeant Pantzke." *Frontline*, episode 16, June 28, 2011. https:// www.pbs.org/wgbh/pages/frontline/educating-sergeant-pantzke/etc/tran script.html.

Asch, David A., Justin Grischkan, and Sean Nicholson. "Lower the Cost of Producing Doctors, Not Just the Price of Going to Medical School." *STAT*, July 21, 2020. https://www.statnews.com/2020/07/21/lower-cost-producing -doctors-not-just-price-medical-school/.

Asher, Lauren. "The Institute for College Access & Success Letter to Vice President Joe Biden." National Archives, 2010. https://obamawhitehouse .archives.gov/sites/default/files/microsites/100226-capping-student-loan -payments.pdf.

Associated Press. "College Loan Scandal 'like Peeling an Onion.'" *NBC News*, April 10, 2007. https://www.nbcnews.com/id/wbna18040824.

———. "House Votes 900 Million in School Aid." *Chicago Tribune*, August 9, 1958.

———. "Local Students Pass Up Bankruptcy." *La Crosse (WI) Tribune*, February 12, 1976.

"Atherton, Legion Leader, Blasts Those Retarding War Effort." *Washington Post*, August 7, 1943.

Babcock, Charles. "Loan Abuses by Some Trade Schools Leave Taxpayers with Big Bill." *Washington Post*, October 29, 1997.

———. "Rising Tuitions Fill Loan Firm Coffers." *Washington Post*, October 27, 1997.

Badger, Emily. "The Dramatic Racial Bias of Subprime Lending during the Housing Boom." *Bloomberg*, August 16, 2013. https://www.bloomberg.com /news/articles/2013-08-16/the-dramatic-racial-bias-of-subprime-lending -during-the-housing-boom.

Barger, Harold. *College on Credit: A History of United Student Aid Funds (1960–1980)*. Indianapolis, IN: Hackett Publishing, 1981.

Barnes, Adam. "Former Education Secretary Calls for Cancellation of Debt for All Student Loan Holders." *The Hill*, March 23, 2022. https://thehill.com/changing-america/enrichment/education/599453-former-education-secretary-calls-for-complete-student/.

Bates, Karen Grigsby, and Shereen Marisol Meraji. "The Student Strike That Changed Higher Ed Forever." *Code Switch*, March 21, 2019. https://www.npr.org/sections/codeswitch/2019/03/21/704930088/the-student-strike-that-changed-higher-ed-forever.

Baum, Sandy, Kristin Blagg, and Rachel Fishman. "Reshaping Parent PLUS Loans, Recommendations for Reforming the Parent PLUS Program." Center on Education and Data Policy, April 2019. https://www.urban.org/sites/default/files/publication/100106/2019_04_30_reshaping_parent_plus_loans_finalizedv2.pdf.

Beamer, Laura, and Marshall Steinbaum. "Opinion: Student Loans Were Never Going to Be Repaid." *New York Times*, July 13, 2023. https://www.nytimes.com/interactive/2023/07/13/opinion/politics/student-loan-payments-resume.html.

Bell, Terrel H. *The Thirteenth Man: A Reagan Cabinet Memoir*. New York: Free Press, 1988.

Bennett, Christopher T. "Labor Market Returns to MBAs from Less-Selective Universities: Evidence from a Field Experiment during COVID-19." *Journal of Policy Analysis and Management* 42, no. 2 (2022): https://doi.org/10.1002/pam.22448.

Berg, B., S. Lee, B. Randolph, M. Ryu, and D. Shapiro. "Current Term Enrollment Estimates, Spring 2023." National Student Clearinghouse Research Center, Spring 2023. https://nscresearchcenter.org/wp-content/uploads/CTEE_Report_Spring_2023.pdf.

Berkeley Office of the Registrar. "Fee Schedule Archive." https://registrar.berkeley.edu/tuition-fees-residency/tuition-fees/fee-schedule-archive/.

Berman, Jillian. "All the Ways Student Debt Exacerbates Racial Inequality—'It's Like Landing in Quick Sand.'" *MarketWatch*, July 27, 2019. https://www.marketwatch.com/story/all-the-ways-student-debt-is-exacerbating-racial-inequality-its-like-landing-in-quick-sand-one-black-student-says-2019-07-18.

———. "America's Educational System Is an 'Aristocracy Posing as a Meritocracy.'" *MarketWatch*, June 18, 2019. https://www.marketwatch.com/story/americas-educational-system-is-an-aristocracy-posing-as-a-meritocracy-2019-05-15.

———. "America's $1.5 Trillion Student-Loan Industry Is a 'Failed Social Experiment.'" *MarketWatch*, October 18, 2018. https://www.marketwatch.com/story/americas-15-trillion-student-debt-is-a-failed-social-experiment-2018-10-16.

———. "Biden Vows to Cancel Student Debt for Millions More This Fall—But He Faces an Uphill Battle Getting Relief before the Election." *MarketWatch*, April 8, 2024. https://www.marketwatch.com/story/biden-vows-to-cancel

-student-debt-for-millions-more-this-fall-but-he-faces-an-uphill-battle
-getting-relief-before-the-election-d5f70664

———. "The Black-White Wealth Gap Is Fueled by Student Debt." *MarketWatch*, May 6, 2018. https://www.marketwatch.com/story/how-student-debt-is -fueling-the-racial-wealth-gap-2018-05-03.

———. "Borrowers Are Still Having Their Paychecks Seized over Defaulted Student Loans, Even Though the CARES Act Was Supposed to Stop Wage Garnishment, Lawsuit Says." *MarketWatch*, August 9, 2020. https://www .marketwatch.com/story/borrowers-are-still-having-their-paychecks-seized -over-defaulted-student-loans-even-though-the-cares-act-was-supposed-to -stop-wage-garnishment-lawsuit-says-11596727697.

———. "Companies Have a New Weapon in the Hunt for Talent: Free College Degrees. Why It's Important to Read the Fine Print." *MarketWatch*, October 15, 2021. https://www.marketwatch.com/story/amazon-walmart -and-others-offer-free-college-degrees-to-lure-talent-but-read-the-fine-print -first-11634320257.

———. "Corinthian Colleges Files for Bankruptcy Protection; Students Scramble for Restitution." *MarketWatch*, May 4, 2015. https://www.marketwatch.com /story/corinthian-colleges-files-for-bankruptcy protection-students-scram ble-for-restitution-2015-05-04.

———. "Debt Cancellation Got All the Attention, but This Biden Proposal Could Impact Student-Loan Borrowers More, Critics and Advocates Say." *MarketWatch*, September 29, 2022. https://www.marketwatch.com/story /debt-cancellation-got-all-the-attention-but-this-biden-proposal-could-im pact-student-loan-borrowers-more-critics-and-advocates-say-11664464061.

———. "The Educational Technology Stock That Went from $98 to $1: Inside the 2U Debacle." *MarketWatch*, November 21, 2023. https://www.marketwatch .com/story/the-educational-technology-stock-that-went-from-98-to-1-inside -the-2u-debacle-d1cee3a4

———. "Elizabeth Warren Accuses College Watchdog of Not Biting." *MarketWatch*, June 10, 2016. https://www.marketwatch.com/story/elizabeth -warren-accuses-college-watchdog-of-not-biting-2016-06-10.

———. "Elizabeth Warren Calls for New Leadership to Oversee Student Loans— and Calls Betsy DeVos Era a 'Disaster.'" *MarketWatch*, January 28, 2021. https://www.marketwatch.com/story/elizabeth-warren-calls-for-new -leadership-to-oversee-student-loans-and-calls-betsy-devos-era-a-disas ter-11611776622.

———. "The Fate of Student-Loan Forgiveness May Rest with the Courts." *MarketWatch*, September 25, 2022. https://www.marketwatch.com/story /the-fate-of-student-debt-relief-may-rest-with-the-courts-11661467247.

———. "Feds Sue Student Loan Giant Navient." *MarketWatch*, January 19, 2017. https://www.marketwatch.com/story/feds-sue-student-loan-giant-navient -2017-01-18.

———. "A High-School Diploma Is Pretty Much Useless These Days." *HuffPost*, May 28, 2014. https://www.huffpost.com/entry/value-college-degree_n _5399573.

———. "Hillary Says Bernie Will Play Robin to Her Batman in Crusade to Fix Student-Loan Mess." *MarketWatch*, July 31, 2016. https://www.marketwatch .com/story/hillary-clinton-bernie-sanders-and-i-will-work-together-to -make-college-more-affordable-2016-07-29.

———. "'I Can't Imagine the Day When I'm Not Paying.' Black Women Are Being Crushed by the Student Debt Crisis—And Demanding Action." *MarketWatch*, November 3, 2021. https://www.marketwatch.com/story/i-cant-imagine-the -day-when-im-not-paying-black-women-are-being-crushed-by-the-student -debt-crisis-and-demanding-action-11635948623.

———. "'It's Not Just about Tuition, It's about How I'm Going to Eat': Over 50% of Community Colleges Are Not Affordable for Low-Income Students." *MarketWatch*, May 17, 2021. https://www.marketwatch.com/story/more -than-half-of-community-colleges-are-not-affordable-for-low-income-stu dents-11620913585.

———. "ITT Is the Second Major For-Profit College to Declare Bankruptcy since Last Year." *MarketWatch*, September 18, 2016. https://www.marketwatch.com /story/itt-is-second-major-for-profit-college-to-declare-bankruptcy-since -last-year-2016-09-16.

———. "The Little-Known Student Loan Middlemen Who Are Threatening Debt Forgiveness." *MarketWatch*, November 19, 2022. https://www.marketwatch .com/story/the-little-known-student-loan-middlemen-who-are-threatening -debt-forgiveness-11668786732.

———. "Man Who Oversaw Mortgage Crisis Settlement to Guide Corinthian Debt Relief." *MarketWatch*, June 25, 2015. https://www.marketwatch.com/story /man-who-oversaw-mortgage-crisis-settlement-to-guide-corinthian-debt -relief-2015-06-26.

———. "The 'Morally Suspect' Way the Government Collects Student Loans during Tax Season." *MarketWatch*, March 21, 2018. https://www.marketwatch .com/story/the-morally-suspect-way-the-government-collects-student -loans-2018-03-15.

———. "More Than 800,000 Student-Loan Borrowers to Start Seeing Their Debt Canceled, Biden Administration Says." *MarketWatch*, August 15, 2023. https://www.marketwatch.com/story/more-than-800-000-student-loan -borrowers-to-start-seeing-their-debt-canceled-biden-administration-says -c3acb9ec#:~:text.

———. "More Than Half of Community Colleges Are Too Expensive for Low-Income Students." *MarketWatch*, June 4, 2019. https://www.marketwatch .com/story/more-than-half-of-community-colleges-are-too-expensive-for -low-income-students-2019-06-03.

———. "Nearly 200 For-Profit Colleges Get Over 90% of Their Funding from the Government." *MarketWatch*, December 23, 2016. https://www.market watch.com/story/nearly-200-for-profit-colleges-get-over-90-of-their-fund ing-from-the-government-2016-12-22.

———. "New Student-Loan Forgiveness Guidelines Explained: A Step-by-Step Guide to Taking Advantage of the PSLF Waiver." *MarketWatch*, October 8, 2021. https://www.marketwatch.com/story/how-to-take-advantage-of-the-biden

-administrations-changes-to-public-service-loan-forgiveness-and-make-a
-successful-claim-11633703342.

———. "90% of Borrowers Who Claim They Were Scammed by Their Schools
Were Denied Relief." *MarketWatch*, March 22, 2021. https://www.market
watch.com/story/90-of-borrowers-who-claim-they-were-scammed-by-their
-schools-were-denied-relief-11616417936.

———. "Obama Administration Prepares to Hand Student Debt Challenge to
Trump." *MarketWatch*, November 18, 2016. https://www.marketwatch.com
/story/obama-administration-prepares-to-hand-student-debt-challenge-to
-trump-2016-11-18.

———. "One Company Will Now Handle Close to Half of All Student Loan
Payments." *Market Watch*, March 6, 2018. https://www.marketwatch.com
/story/one-company-will-now-handle-close-to-half-of-all-student-loan
-payments-2018-02-09#:~:text=Every%20month%2C%20approximately%20
40%20million,of%20these%20firms%20%E2%80%94%20Nelnet%20Inc

———. "Online Courses Could Help Make College Affordable, but This $1 Billion
Industry Is Standing in the Way." *MarketWatch*, September 25, 2019. https://
www.marketwatch.com/story/for-profit-middlemen-may-be-driving-up-the
-cost-of-online-higher-education-2019-09-19.

———. "Public Servants to Have $24 Billion in Student Debt Canceled." *Market-
Watch*, November 18, 2022. https://www.marketwatch.com/story
/public-servants-to-have-24-billion-in-student-debt-canceled-11668801753.

———. "Scammed Student-Loan Borrowers Accuse Betsy DeVos of Illegally
Stalling on Debt-Cancellation Claims." *MarketWatch*, June 26, 2019. https://
www.marketwatch.com/story/scammed-student-loan-borrowers-accuse
-betsy-devos-of-illegally-stalling-on-debt-cancellation-claims-2019-06-25.

———. "Should the Biden Administration Cancel Student Debt? Read This before
You Decide." *MarketWatch*, November 18, 2020. https://www.marketwatch
.com/story/should-the-biden-administration-cancel-student-debt-this-guide
-might-help-you-decide-11605715377.

———. "States to DeVos: We'll Keep Cracking down on Student-Loan Companies." *MarketWatch*, March 3, 2018. https://www.marketwatch.com
/story/states-to-devos-well-keep-cracking-down-on-student-loan-compa
nies-2018-03-02.

———. "Student Loan Borrowers Share Tales of Woe with Regulators."
MarketWatch, October 27, 2016. https://www.marketwatch.com/story
/student-loan-borrowers-share-tales-of-woe-with-regulators-2016-10-27.

———. "Students Duped by For-Profit Colleges Might Get Some Relief."
MarketWatch, June 8, 2015. https://www.marketwatch.com/story
/students-duped-by-for-profit-colleges-might-get-some-relief-2015-06-08.

———. "These Colleges Use a Loophole to Make Billions Off the GI Bill."
MarketWatch, November 12, 2017. https://www.marketwatch.com/story/
these-colleges-use-a-loophole-to-make-billions-off-the-gi-bill-2017-11-09.

———. "They Lost Their Tax Refund over Defaulted Student Debt. Now, They're
Getting It Back, but the Yearslong Delay Took a Toll." *MarketWatch*, December 7, 2023. https://www.marketwatch.com/story/they-lost-their-tax-refund

-over-defaulted-student-debt-now-theyre-getting-it-back-but-the-years
long-delay-took-a-toll-eebc57d3

———. "They Thought a Degree Would Change Their Life. Instead, It Left Them Trapped in School and in Debt for Years." *MarketWatch*, April 15, 2024. https://www.marketwatch.com/story/they-thought-a-degree-would-change -their-life-instead-it-left-them-trapped-in-school-and-in-debt-for-years -4ef541d5.

———. "This Government Loan Forgiveness Program Has Rejected 99% of Borrowers So Far." *MarketWatch*, September 23, 2018. https://www.market watch.com/story/this-government-loan-forgiveness-program-has-rejected -99-of-borrowers-so-far-2018-09-20.

———. "12 Years after Starting College, White Men Have Paid Off 44% of Their Student Loans While Black Women Owe 13% More." *MarketWatch*, August 11, 2019. https://www.marketwatch.com/story/12-years-after-starting-college -white-men-have-paid-off-44-of-their-student-loans-and-black-women -owe-13-more-2019-06-06.

———. "2 Million Americans Have Been Repaying Their Student-Loans for 20 Years." *MarketWatch*, March 12, 2021. https://www.marketwatch.com /story/2-million-americans-have-been-repaying-their-federal-student -loans-for-20-years-11615566233.

———. "Why This Author Is Skeptical of the Student Loan Crisis." *MarketWatch*, August 8, 2016. https://www.marketwatch.com/story/why-this-author-is -skeptical-of-the-student-loan-crisis-2016-08-08.

———. "Would It Work in America? A Student Loan System That Protects People from Bad Luck." *MarketWatch*, November 27, 2015. https://www.marketwatch .com/story/would-it-work-in-america-a-student-loan-system-that-protects -people-from-bad-luck-2015-11-25?mod=article_inline.

———. "Why Teachers and Social Workers May Not Get the Student Debt Forgiveness They're Counting On." *MarketWatch*, November 30, 2016. https://www.marketwatch.com/story/why-teachers-and-social-workers -worry-they-wont-get-the-student-debt-forgiveness-theyre-counting -on-2016-11-23.

Bidwell, Allie. "ED Launches Student Aid Enforcement Unit, Asks for $13.6 Million in Funding." National Association of Student Financial Aid Administrators. February 9, 2016. https://www.nasfaa.org/news-item/7523 /ED_Launches_Student_Aid_Enforcement_Unit_Asks_for_13_6_Million_in _Funding.

Bigott, Joseph C. "Hammond, IN." In *Encyclopedia of Chicago*. Chicago: Chicago Historical Society, 2005. http://www.encyclopedia.chicagohistory.org/pages /562.html#:~:text=When%20the%20city%20incorporated%20in,role%20 in%20the%20Pullman%20Strike.

"A Bill for Minority Education." *Sacramento Observer*, May 29, 1969.

Black, Sandra, Lesley Turner, and Jeffrey Denning. "PLUS or Minus? The Effect of Graduate School Loans on Access, Attainment, and Prices." Working Paper No. 31291, National Bureau of Economic Research, Cambridge, MA, May 2023. https://doi.org/10.3386/w31291.

Blagg, Kristin. "The Rise of Master's Degrees." Urban Institute, December 2018. https://www.urban.org/sites/default/files/publication/99501/the_rise_of _masters_degrees_1.pdf.

Board of Governors of the Federal Reserve System. "Dealing with Unexpected Expenses." Economic Well-Being of US Households (SHED), August 22, 2022. https://www.federalreserve.gov/publications/2022-economic-well-being-of -us-households-in-2021-dealing-with-unexpected-expenses.htm.

Brink, Meghan. "For-Profits Seek to Intervene in Federal Borrower-Defense Settlement." *Inside Higher Ed*, July 14, 2022. https://www.insidehighered.com /news/2022/07/15/profits-seek-intervene-defrauded-borrower-settlement#

Brinkley, Alan. "Reagan's Revenge as Invented by Howard Jarvis." *New York Times*, June 19, 1994. https://www.nytimes.com/1994/06/19/magazine/rea gan-s-revenge-as-invented-by-howard-jarvis.html.

Broder, David S. "Bennett Replaces Watt . . ." *Philadelphia Inquirer*, February 24, 1985.

Brooks, David. "Has Biden Changed? He Tells Us." *New York Times*, May 20, 2021. https://www.nytimes.com/2021/05/20/opinion/joe-biden-david-brooks -interview.html.

Brooks, John R., and Adam J. Levitin. "Redesigning Education Finance: How Student Loans Outgrew the 'Debt' Paradigm." *Georgetown Law Journal* 109, no. 1 (2020): 5–80. https://www.law.georgetown.edu/georgetown-law-journal /wp-content/uploads/sites/26/2020/11/Brooks_Levitin_Redesigning -Education-Finance-How-Student-Loans-Outgrew-the-Debt-Paradigm.pdf.

Brooks, Kendra. "Calling on the Federal Government to Enact a Plan by the End of President Biden's First 100 Days in Office to Cancel All Student Loan Debt and Begin the Transition to Education as a Public Good." Philadelphia City Council, 2021. https://phila.legistar.com/LegislationDetail .aspx?ID=4809193&GUID=FEF6ECC9-37C6-4E67-AEB4-0B592F6CAEA2&Options =ID%7CText%7C&Search=210163.

Brown, Sherrod, and Elizabeth Warren. "Senators' Letter to OPM Providers," January 23, 2020. https://www.warren.senate.gov/imo/media/doc/Letters %20to%20multiple%20orgs.%20re%20OPM%20Business%20practices.pdf.

Burd, Stephen. "Crisis Point: How Enrollment Management and the Merit-Aid Arms Race Are Derailing Public Higher Education." New America, February 13, 2020. https://www.newamerica.org/education-policy/reports/crisis -point-how-enrollment-management-and-merit-aid-arms-race-are-destroy ing-public-higher-education/.

———. "Undermining Pell: How Colleges Compete for Wealthy Students and Leave the Low-Income Behind." New America, 2013. https://static.newamer ica.org/attachments/2320-undermining-pell-2/Merit_Aid%20Final.b3b89c 275d2249eeb19cb53d3fc049b6.pdf.

———. "Undermining Pell: Volume IV." New America, 2018. https:// www.newamerica.org/education-policy/reports/undermining-pell-iv /introduction.

Burd, Stephen, Rachel Fishman, Laura Keane, and Julie Habbart. "Decoding the Cost of College." New America, 2018. https://www.newamerica.org /education-policy/policy-papers/decoding-cost-college/

Burd, Stephen, and Douglas Lederman. "Clinton Proposes 25% Increase in Spending on Pell Grants." *Chronicle of Higher Education*, February 7, 1997.

"Business-Guaranteed Student Loans Spread in Massachusetts; Other States Eye Them." *Wall Street Journal*, February 6, 1958.

Bykowicz, Julie, and Douglas Belkin. "Why Biden's Plan for Free Community College Likely Will Be Cut from Budget Package." *Wall Street Journal*, October 20, 2021.

Cahalan, Margaret W., Marisha Addison, Nicole Brunt, Pooja R. Patel, Terry Vaughan III, Alysia Genao, and Laura W. Perna. "Indicators of Higher Education Equity in the United States, 2022 Historical Trend Report." Pell Institute, 2022. http://pellinstitute.org/downloads/publications-Indicators _of_Higher_Education_Equity_in_the_US_2022_Historical_Trend_Report .pdf.

California Budget Project. "Proposition 13: Its Impact on California and Implications." April 1997. https://calbudgetcenter.org/app/up loads/2018/09/Issue-Brief_Proposition-13-Its-Impact-on-California-and -Implications_04.1997.pdf.

"Care Urged on GI's in Picking Schools." *New York Times*, April 12, 1948.

Carey, Kevin. "The Creeping Capitalist Takeover of Higher Education." *HuffPost*, April 1, 2019. https://www.huffpost.com/highline/article/capitalist -takeover-college/.

———. "A Quiet Revolution in Helping Lift the Burden of Student Debt." *New York Times*, January 24, 2015. https://www.nytimes.com/2015/01/25/upshot /a-quiet-revolution-in-helping-lift-the-burden-of-student-debt.html.

Carnevale, Anthony P., Ban Cheah, and Andrew R. Hanson. "The Economic Value of College Majors." Georgetown University Center on Education and the Workforce, 2015. https://cew.georgetown.edu/wp-content/uploads/Exec -Summary-web-B.pdf.

Carnevale, Anthony P., Tamara Jayasundera, and Artem Gulish. "Good Jobs Are Back, College Graduates Are First in Line." Georgetown University Center on Education and the Workforce, 2015. https://cew.georgetown.edu /cew-reports/goodjobsareback/.

Carnevale, Anthony, and Jeff Strohl. "Separate & Unequal, How Higher Education Reinforces the Intergenerational Reproduction of White Racial Privilege." Georgetown University Center on Education and the Workforce, 2013. https://cew.georgetown.edu/wp-content/uploads/SeparateUnequal .FR_.pdf.

Carr, James H., Katrin B. Anacker, and Ines Hernandez. "The State of Housing in Black America." National Association of Real Estate Brokers, 2013. https:// www.chapa.org/sites/default/files/State%20of%20Black%20Housing%20 in%20American%20NAREB_final_080413.pdf.

Cendana, Gregory. "United States Students Association Letter to Vice President Joe Biden." National Archives, February 22, 2010. https://obamawhitehouse .archives.gov/sites/default/files/microsites/100226-capping-student-loan -payments.pdf.

Chambers, M. M. "Appropriations of State Tax Funds for Operating Expenses of Higher Education 1964–1965." Office of Institutional Research and National

Association of State Universities and Land-Grant Colleges, September 1, 1964. https://education.illinoisstate.edu/downloads/grapevine/historical/Appropriations1964-65.pdf.

Chandler, John. "Enrollment in Community Colleges Drops." *Los Angeles Times*, December 23, 1993.

Chandler, Michael Alison. "DC among First in Nation to Require Child-Care Workers to Get College Degrees." *Washington Post*, March 31, 2017. https://www.washingtonpost.com/local/social-issues/district-among-the-first-in-nation-to-require-child-care-workers-to-get-college-degrees/2017/03/30/d7d59e18-0fe9-11e7-9d5a-a83e627dc120_story.html.

Chavez, Lydia. *The Color Bind: California's Battle To End Affirmative Action.* Berkeley: University of California Press, 1998.

Chingos, Matthew M. "Why Student Loan Rhetoric Doesn't Match the Facts." Brookings Institution, 2014. https://www.brookings.edu/research/why-student-loan-rhetoric-doesnt-match-the-facts/.

Chisholm, Shirley. "Black Caucus Reports: Money Needed for Higher Education." *Sun Reporter (CA)*, March 2, 1978.

Clark, Andrew. "How I Did It: Andrew Clark, Bridgepoint Education." *Inc. Magazine*, September 1, 2008. https://www.inc.com/magazine/20080901/how-i-did-it-andrew-clark-bridgepoint-education.html.

Clinton, William J. "Address to the Nation on the Middle Class Bill of Rights." 1994. American Presidency Project. https://www.presidency.ucsb.edu/documents/address-the-nation-the-middle-class-bill-rights.

CNN Wire Staff. "CNN Fact Check: Obama's Student Aid Boast on the Mark." *CNN*, October 17, 2012. https://www.cnn.com/2012/10/17/politics/fact-check-student-aid/index.html.

"College Saving Plan Can Avoid Tax Bite." *Boston Globe*, August 7, 1967.

Collins, Randall. *The Credential Society: A Historical Sociology of Stratification and Education.* New York: Columbia University Press, 2019.

Colmery, Harry W. "Testimony Concerning the GI Bill of Rights Presented by Harry W. Colmery." Kansas Historical Society, Topeka, 1944. https://www.kansasmemory.org/item/207980.

Community College of Philadelphia. "Community College of Philadelphia Now Accepting Applications for Octavius Catto Scholarship, Providing Free Tuition to Eligible Students." October 8, 2020. https://www.ccp.edu/about-us/news/press-release/community-college-philadelphia-now-accepting-applications-octavius-catto-scholarship-providing-free.

Congressional Budget Office. "Federal Student Loan Programs—May 2022 Baseline." 2022. https://www.cbo.gov/system/files/2022-05/51310-2022-05-studentloan.pdf.

Consumer Financial Protection Bureau. "Private Student Loans: Report to the Senate Committee on Banking, Housing, and Urban Affairs, the Senate Committee on Health, Education, Labor, and Pensions, the House of Representatives Committee on Financial Services, and the House of Representatives Committee on Education and the Workforce." 2012. https://files.consumerfinance.gov/f/201207_cfpb_Reports_Private-Student-Loans.pdf.

———. "CFPB Sues For-Profit Corinthian Colleges for Predatory Lending Scheme." September 16, 2014. https://www.consumerfinance.gov/about-us/newsroom/cfpb-sues-for-profit-corinthian-colleges-for-predatory-lending-scheme/.

———. "CFPB Sues Nation's Largest Student Loan Company Navient for Failing Borrowers at Every Stage of Repayment." January 18, 2017. https://www.consumerfinance.gov/about-us/newsroom/cfpb-sues-nations-largest-student-loan-company-navient-failing-borrowers-every-stage-repayment/.

Cook, Bryan J., and Jacqueline E. King. "2007 Status Report on the Pell Grant Program." American Council on Education, 2007. https://www.acenet.edu/Documents/2007-Status-Report-on-the-Pell-Grant-Program.pdf.

Cooper, Kenneth J. "Lawmakers Pursue Money Owed to US: Two Representatives Draft Bill to Ease Budget Pressure by Reclaiming $50 Billion Past Due." *Washington Post*, July 31, 1995.

Cornuelle, Richard C. *Reclaiming the American Dream: The Role of Private Individuals and Voluntary Associations.* New York: Routledge, 1993.

Crenshaw, Albert. "If It's for College Taxes Are Deferred: New State Plans Offer Better Returns on Long-Term Savings for Higher Education." *Washington Post*, August 7, 1998.

Curwood, Steve. "College Grant Participation Down, Study Says Federal Income Guidelines Cited." *Boston Globe*, January 11, 1987.

Davies, Lawrence E. "Reagan Promises to Rid Campuses of 'Anarchists.'" *New York Times*, January 8, 1969. https://www.nytimes.com/1969/01/08/archives/reagan-promises-to-rid-campuses-of-anarchists.html.

———. "Regents Battle Reagan's Vetoes." *New York Times*, July 13, 1968.

DC Office of the State Superintendent of Education. "DC Tuition Assistance Grant (DCTAG)." https://osse.dc.gov/dctag.

DeBaun, Bill. "New FSA Data Revise Verification Melt Estimate Downward & Other Tidbits." National College Attainment Network, February 18, 2021. https://www.ncan.org/news/551034/New-FSA-Data-Revise-Verification-Melt-Estimate-Downward—Other-Tidbits.htm.

Demos. "When Congress Went to College: Comparing Tuition Then and Now at Our Elected Officials' Alma Maters." 2018. https://www.demos.org/research/when-congress-went-college-comparing-tuition-then-and-now-our-elected-officials-alma.

Department of Justice, Office of Public Affairs. "Justice Department and Department of Education Announce a Fairer and More Accessible Bankruptcy Discharge Process for Student Loan Borrowers." November 17, 2022. https://www.justice.gov/opa/pr/justice-department-and-department-education-announce-fairer-and-more-accessible-bankruptcy.

"Digest of Education Statistics." National Center for Education Statistics, 2020. https://nces.ed.gov/programs/digest/d20/tables/dt20_306.20.asp.

Dillon, Sam. "Whistle-Blower on Student Aid Is Vindicated." *New York Times*, May 7, 2007. https://www.nytimes.com/2007/05/07/washington/07loans.html.

"Diversity in Higher Education Series Part I." Center for Social Solutions University of Michigan, June 25, 2021. https://sites.lsa.umich.edu/leadership

-institute/2021/06/25/the-history-of-diversity-in-higher-education
-ali-series-part-i/.

Douglas-Gabriel, Danielle. "The Obama Administration's Plan to Lower the
Student Debt Payments of Millions More Americans." *Washington Post*, July 10,
2015. https://www.washingtonpost.com/news/get-there/wp/2015/07/10
/the-obama-administrations-plan-to-lower-the-student-debt-payments-of
-millions-more-americans/.

Douglas-Gabriel, Danielle, and John D. Harden. "To Protect Taxpayer Dollars,
the Education Dept. Is Disproportionately Auditing Black and Latino College
Students." *Washington Post*, February 7, 2021. https://www.washingtonpost
.com/education/2021/02/07/fafsa-verification-black-latino-college-aid/.

Douglass, John A., and Zachary Bleemer. "Approaching a Tipping Point? A
History and Prospectus of Funding for the University of California." 2018.
https://escholarship.org/uc/item/4gn6b778#author.

Drawbaugh, Kevin. "US Rep Miller Defends Student Loan Bill." *Reuters*, July 28,
2009. https://www.reuters.com/article/us-studentloans-miller-interview/u
-s-rep-miller-defends-student-loan-bill-idUSTRE56S0BU20090729.

"Drexel University Tuition & Financial Aid." *US News & World Report*, 2022.
https://www.usnews.com/best-colleges/drexel-university-3256.

Dunleavey, M. P. "Paying for College without the Home Equity Option." *New
York Times*, April 19, 2008. https://www.nytimes.com/2008/04/19/busi
ness/19money.html.

Eaton, Charlie. *Bankers in the Ivory Tower*. Chicago: University of Chicago Press,
2022.

Eaton, Charlie, Sheisha Kulkarni, Robert Birgeneau, Henry Brady, and Michael
Hout. "Affording the Dream: Student Debt and Need-Based Grant Aid
for Public University Students." Center for Studies in Higher Education,
University of California, Berkeley, 2017.

Economic Policy Institute. "State of Working America Data Library, Wages by
Education." 2022. https://www.epi.org/data/#?subject=wage-education.

Egan, Lauren. "The White House Promised a Memo on Biden's Authority to
Cancel Student Debt. Where Is It?" *NBC News*, May 29, 2021. https://www
.nbcnews.com/politics/white-house/white-house-promised-memo-biden
-s-authority-cancel-student-debt-n1268681.

Eide, Eric, Michael Hilmer, and Mark Showalter. "Is It Where You Go or What
You Study? The Relative Influence of College Selectivity and College Major on
Earnings." *Contemporary Economic Policy* 34, no. 1 (2015). https://onlinelibrary
.wiley.com/doi/epdf/10.1111/coep.12115.

Eisenhower, Dwight D. "Our Future Security, Speech." American Presidency
Project. https://www.presidency.ucsb.edu/documents/radio-and-televi
sion-address-the-american-people-our-future-security.

Elizabeth Warren Press Office. "Schumer, Warren: The Next President Can and
Should Cancel Up to $50,000 in Student Loan Debt Immediately; Democrats
Outline Plan for Immediate Action in 2021." 2020. https://www.warren
.senate.gov/newsroom/press-releases/schumer-warren-the-next-president
-can-and-should-cancel-up-to-50000-in-student-loan-debt-immediately
-democrats-outline-plan-for-immediate-action-in-2021.

Ellis, Kristina. "How to Pay for College Without Student Loans." Ramsey Solutions, February 3, 2022. https://www.ramseysolutions.com/saving /pay-for-college-without-student-loans.

Ellis, W. L. "General Accounting Office Report of Survey—Veterans' Education and Training Program." 1951. https://babel.hathitrust.org/cgi/pt?id=umn.3 1951d03549214g&view=1up&seq=3&skin=2021&q1=were organized for the specific purpose.

Evans, Rowland, and Robert Novak. "LBJ Out to Ax Loan Sharks." *Boston Globe*, January 4, 1965.

———. "Student Loans Are Big Business." *Los Angeles Times*, January 4, 1965.

Fain, Paul. "Education Department Slaps Serious Sanctions on ITT." *Inside Higher Ed*, August 25, 2016. https://www.insidehighered.com/quick takes/2016/08/25/breaking-education-department-slaps-serious -sanctions-itt.

Federal Student Aid. "Announcing the Next Generation of Federal Student Loan Servicing." May 19, 2022. https://blog.ed.gov/2022/05/announcing -the-next-generation-of-federal-student-loan-servicing/.

———. "Federal Student Aid Posts New Quarterly Reports to FSA Data Center." December 20, 2023. https://fsapartners.ed.gov/knowledge-center/library /electronic-announcements/2023-12-20/federal-student-aid-posts-new-quar terly-reports-fsa-data-center#:~:text=(GENERAL%2D23%2D119),Reports%20 to%20FSA%20Data%20Center&text=Today%2C%20Federal%20Student%20 Aid%20

Fishman, Rachel. "The Wealth Gap PLUS Debt: How Federal Loans Exacerbate Inequality for Black Families." New America, 2018. https://www.newamerica .org/education-policy/reports/wealth-gap-plus-debt/.

Fiske, Edward B. "Cuts in College Aid Placing Students in a Vise." *New York Times*, March 15, 1982.

———. "Minority Enrollment in Colleges Is Declining." *New York Times*, October 27, 1985.

———. "Quotation of the Day." *New York Times*, February 22, 1981.

———. "Student Debt Reshaping Colleges and Careers." *New York Times*, August 3, 1986. https://www.nytimes.com/1986/08/03/education/student-debt-re shaping-colleges-and-careers.html.

Folkenflik, David. "A Boon or a Shuffle of Benefits? Tax Break Plan Could Change College Choices." *Baltimore Sun*, January 8, 1995.

Folsom, Marion B. "Folsom's Memorandum on School Aid." *New York Times*, December 31, 1957. https://timesmachine.nytimes.com/timesma chine/1957/12/31/90882779.html?pageNumber=4.

Friedman, Milton. "The Role of Government in Education." In *Economics and the Public Interest*, edited by Robert Solo. New Brunswick, NJ: Rutgers University Press, 1955. https://la.utexas.edu/users/hcleaver/330T/350kPEEFriedman RoleOfGovttable.pdf.

Frotman, Seth. "Annual Report of the CFPB Student Loan Ombudsman, Trans itioning from Default to an Income-Driven Repayment Plan." 2016. https:// files.consumerfinance.gov/f/documents/102016_cfpb_Transmittal_DFA _1035_Student_Loan_Ombudsman_Report.pdf.

Frydl, Kathleen. *The GI Bill.* New York: Cambridge University Press, 2009.

Fulford, Scott, Samyak Jain, Greta Li, Elizabeth Saunders, and Eric Wilson. "Making Ends Meet in 2022: Insights from the CFPB Making Ends Meet Survey." 2022. https://files.consumerfinance.gov/f/documents/cfpb_making-ends-meet-in-2022_report_2022-12.pdf.

Fulton County Center for Regional Growth. "Fulton County, Then and Now." 2021. https://www.fccrg.org/then-now/.

"Funeral Service for Claiborne Pell." *C-SPAN*, January 5, 2009. https://www.c-span.org/video/?283114-1/funeral-service-senator-claiborne-pell.

Furman, Bess. "Conferences Back 900 Million Fund to Aid in Education." *New York Times*, August 22, 1958.

———. "President Backs House School Bill." *New York Times*, August 6, 1958.

———. "Senate Approves Science Aid Plan." *New York Times*, August 14, 1958.

Gallagher, Charlie, and Silvio Rendon. "CFI in Focus: Understanding Older Student Loan Borrowers." Federal Reserve Bank of Philadelphia, 2021. https://www.philadelphiafed.org/consumer-finance/education-finance/understanding-older-student-loan-borrowers.

Gallagher, Kristen. "Beauty School Employees Charged with Loan Fraud." *Orlando Sentinel*, October 21, 1988. https://www.orlandosentinel.com/news/os-xpm-1988-10-21-0070440162-story.html.

Gladieux, Lawrence E., and Thomas R. Wolanin. *Congress and the Colleges: The National Politics of Higher Education.* New York: Lexington Books, 1976.

Glantz, Aaron. "Legislation to Close a Loophole in GI Bill Fails." *Desert Sun (CA)*, July 24, 2014.

Goldrick-Rab, Sara, Christine Baker-Smith, Vanessa Coca, Elizabeth Looker, and Tiffani Williams. "College and University Basic Needs Insecurity: A National #RealCollege Survey Report." Hope Center at Temple University, April 2019. https://www.insidehighered.com/sites/default/files/media/HOPE_realcollege_National_report_EMBARGOED%20UNTIL%20APRIL%2030%203%20AM%20EST%20(1).pdf.

Goldstein, Steve. "Goldman Sachs Has Run the Numbers on Student-Loan Forgiveness. This Is Its Assessment." *MarketWatch*, August 25, 2022. https://www.marketwatch.com/story/goldman-sachs-has-run-the-numbers-on-student-loan-relief-heres-their-assessment-11661417918.

Gose, Ben. "Bush Administration Decides to Fight Lawsuit Brought by Lenders against the Education Dept." *Chronicle of Higher Education*, April 20, 2001.

"Gov. Reagan Proposes Cut Back In U. Of California Appropriation." *New York Times*, 1967.

Granville, Peter. "Parent PLUS Borrowers: The Hidden Casualties of the Student Debt Crisis." Century Foundation, 2022. https://tcf.org/content/report/parent-plus-borrowers-the-hidden-casualties-of-the-student-debt-crisis/?agreed=1.

Gray, Carl. "Report on Education and Training under the Servicemen's Readjustment Act, as Amended from the Administrator of Veterans' Affairs." 1950. https://babel.hathitrust.org/cgi/pt?id=ucl.c055437940&view=1up&seq=91&skin=2021&q1=carl gray.

Green, Erica L. "Lawsuit Charges For-Profit University Preyed on Black and Female Students." *New York Times*, April 8, 2022. https://www.nytimes.com/2022/04/08/us/politics/walden-university-lawsuit.html.

Green, Kenneth. "Statement Prepared for Public Hearings on College Costs Held by the Subcommittee on Postsecondary Education." Education Resources Information Center, 1987. https://files.eric.ed.gov/fulltext/ED286424.pdf.

Greenberg, Carl. "Reagan Hits Choice of Regents for UC Inquiry." *Los Angeles Times*, May 22, 1966.

Groeger, Cristina Viviana. *The Education Trap: Schools and the Remaking of Inequality in Boston.* Cambridge, MA: Harvard University Press, 2021.

Grunwald, Michael. "The US Government's Predatory-Lending Program." *Politico*, June 19, 2015. https://www.politico.com/agenda/story/2015/06/the-us-governments-predatory-lending-program-000094/.

Gunn, Sarah, Nicholas Haltom, and Urvi Neelakantan. Federal Reserve Bank of Richmond, 2021. "Should More Student Loan Borrowers Use Income-Driven Repayment Plans?" https://www.richmondfed.org/publications/research/economic_brief/2021/eb_21-20.

"Had Advance On UC Report, Reagan Says." *Los Angeles Times*, May 11, 1966.

Halperin, David. "Campus Progress Letter to Vice President Joe Biden." White House, 2010. https://obamawhitehouse.archives.gov/sites/default/files/microsites/100226-capping-student-loan-payments.pdf.

Hamilton, Laura T., Heather Daniels, Christian Michael Smith, and Charlie Eaton. "The Private Side of Public Universities: Third-Party Providers and Platform Capitalism." Center for Studies in Higher Education at the University of California, Berkeley, 2022. https://escholarship.org/uc/item/7p0114s8.

Hamilton, Laura, and Kelly Nielsen. *Broke: The Racial Consequences of Underfunding Public Universities.* Chicago: University of Chicago Press, 2021.

Hanono, Gerald Benjamin. "California Dreamin', Examining the Legacy of the Great Tax Revolt in Chula Vista, California." Undergraduate honors thesis, Stanford University, 2012. https://web.stanford.edu/~mrosenfe/Hanono_Thesis_California_Dreamin.pdf.

Harris, Adam. *The State Must Provide: Why America's Colleges Have Always Been Unequal—and How to Set Them Right.* New York: Ecco, 2021. https://doi.org/0062976486.

"Harry Walter Colmery on the Oberlin College B caseball Team." Kansas Historical Society. https://www.kansasmemory.org/item/310151.

Hechinger, Fred M. "The Reagan Effect: The Department That Would Not Die." *New York Times*, November 14, 1982. https://www.nytimes.com/1982/11/14/education/the-reagan-effect-the-department-that-would-not-die.html.

———. "Reagan vs. Kerr—Contest at Berkeley." *New York Times*, January 15, 1967. https://www.nytimes.com/1967/01/15/archives/education-reagan-vs-kerr-contest-at-berkeley.html.

Hegji, Alexandra. "The 90/10 Rule under HEA Title IV: Background and Issues." Congressional Research Service, 2021. https://files.eric.ed.gov/fulltext/ED614219.pdf.

Henry, Tamara. "Pell Grants Face Further Cutbacks." *USA Today*, February 5, 1983.

Hillman, Nicholas, and Taylor Weichman. "Education Deserts: The Continued Significance of 'Place' in the Twenty-First Century." American Council on Education, 2016. https://www.acenet.edu/Documents/Education-Deserts -The-Continued-Significance-of-Place-in-the-Twenty-First-Century.pdf.

Herrine, Luke. "The Future of the Education Department's Power to Cancel Student Loan Debt." *The Regulatory Review: A Publication of the Penn Program on Regulation*, January 6, 2017. https://www.theregreview.org/2017/01/06 /herrine-future-educations-power-to-cancel-debt/.

Hill, Phil. "OPM Market Landscape And Dynamics: Summer 2021 Updates." *On EdTech Newsletter*, September 1, 2021. https://philhillaa.com/onedtech /opm-market-landscape-and-dynamics-summer-2021-updates/.

"History of 529 Plans." College Savings Plan Network. https://www.collegesav ings.org/history-of-529-plans/.

Hobbs, Tawnell D., and Andrea Fuller. "How Baylor Steered Lower-Income Parents to Debt They Couldn't Afford." *Wall Street Journal*, October 13, 2021. https://www.wsj.com/articles/baylor-university-college-debt-parent -plus-loans-11634138239

Honan, William H. "Claiborne Pell, Patrician Senator Behind College Grant Program, Dies at 90." *New York Times*, January 1, 2009. https://www.nytimes .com/2009/01/02/us/politics/02pell.html.

"How the New SAVE Plan Will Transform Loan Repayment and Protect Borro wers." Department of Education, 2023. https://www2.ed.gov/policy/high ered/reg/hearulemaking/2021/idrfactsheetfinal.pdf.

Huber, Jane. "Student Loan Bankruptcies Soaring." *Lancaster (PA) New Era*, October 6, 1976.

Huelsman, Mark. "Attainment within 6 Years among Student Borrowers." 2020. https://x.com/MarkHuelsman/status/1329822197406453762?s=20.

Hunter, Marjorie. "Study Finds Large Overpayments in Aid for Needy College Students." *New York Times*, November 20, 1981.

Ifill, Gwen. "The 1992 Campaign: Clinton's Standard Campaign Speech: A Call for Responsibility." *New York Times*, April 26, 1992. https://www.nytimes .com/1992/04/26/us/the-1992-campaign-clinton-s-standard-campaign -speech-a-call-for-responsibility.html.

Institute for College Access & Success. "How to Secure and Strengthen Pell Grants to Increase College Access and Success." June 2020. https://ticas.org /wp-content/uploads/2020/06/How-to-Secure-and-Strengthen-Pell-Grants -to-Increase-College-Access-and-Success.pdf.

Jackson, Victoria, Brittani Williams, and Jalil Mustaffa Bishop. "Parent PLUS Loans Are a Double-Edged Sword for Black Borrowers." Education Trust, 2023. https://edtrust.org/resource/parent-plus-loans-are-a-double-edged -sword-for-black-borrowers/.

Jaquette, Ozan. "In Pursuit of Revenue and Prestige: The Adoption and Produc tion of Master's Degrees by US Colleges and Universities." PhD diss., Univ ersity of Michigan, 2011. https://scholar.google.com/citations?view_op=view

citation&hl=en&user=rtr0-EAAAAJ&cstart=20&pagesize=80&citation
_for_view=rtr0_-EAAAAJ:hqOjcs7Dif8C.

Johnson, Lyndon B. "Remarks at Southwest Texas State College upon Signing the Higher Education Act of 1965." 1965. American Presidency Project. https://www.presidency.ucsb.edu/documents/remarks-southwest-texas-state-college-upon-signing-the-higher-education-act-1965.

———. "Remarks upon Signing the Higher Education Facilities Act." Public Papers of the Presidents of the United States, 1963.

———. "Special Message to the Congress: 'Toward Full Educational Opportunity.'" 1965. American Presidency Project. https://www.presidency.ucsb.edu/documents/special-message-the-congress-toward-full-educational-opportunity.

"Johnson Offers 100-Million Bill on Student Loans." *New York Herald Tribune*, September 15, 1959.

Jones, Tiffany, Jaime Ramirez-Mendoza, and Victoria Jackson. "A Promise Worth Keeping." Education Trust, October 21, 2020. https://edtrust.org/resource/a-promise-worth-keeping/.

Katznelson, Ian. *When Affirmative Action was White: An Untold History of Racial Inequality in Twentieth-Century America.* New York: W. W. Norton & Co., 2005.

Kelchen, Robert. "An Empirical Examination of the Bennett Hypothesis in Law School Prices." *SSRN Electronic Journal* (2017). https://doi.org/10.2139/ssrn.3067252.

Kelly, Dennis. "Gingrich Spells Out 'Revolution' to College Heads." *USA Today*, February 2, 1995.

King, Wayne. "School Still Feels Bakke Aftermath." *New York Times*, December 6, 1981. https://www.nytimes.com/1981/12/06/us/school-still-feels-bakke-aftermath.html.

Kirkham, Chris, and Alan Zarembo. "Recruiting Vets for Cash: GI Bill Money Helps Prop Up Distressed For-Profit Colleges." *Los Angeles Times*, August 18, 2015.

Klaus, Mary. "Remembering: Kenneth Reeher Was a 'Visionary' in Pennsylvania Higher Education." *Patriot News (PA)*, June 4, 2011. https://www.pennlive.com/midstate/2011/06/remembering_kenneth_reeher_was.html.

Klein, Ezra. "Alice Rivlin, Queen of Washington's Budget Wonks." *Ezra Klein Show*, May 17, 2016. https://podbay.fm/p/the-ezra-klein-show/e/1463482800.

———. "How Wall Street Recruits So Many Insecure Ivy League Grads." *Vox*, May 15, 2014. https://www.vox.com/2014/5/15/5720596/how-wall-street-recruits-so-many-insecure-ivy-league-grads.

Kokalis, Jerry, Jr. "Proprietary Schools: The Origin and Growth of National, Institutional Accrediting Bodies." PhD diss., University of Pittsburgh, 1982. https://www.proquest.com/openview/fc7090b6b481f7769aaa37dafee28caa/1?pq-origsite=gscholar&cbl=18750&diss=y.

Korman, Seymour. "Brown And Reagan Clash Over S.N.C.C." *Chicago Tribune*, October 22, 1966.

———. "Reagan Loses Tuition Fight with Regents, However He Gains Special Funds." *Chicago Tribune*, February 17, 1967.

———. "Tuition Imposed at U. of Cal." *Chicago Tribune*, February 21, 1970.

Korn, Melissa, and Andrea Fuller. "'Financially Hobbled for Life': The Elite Master's Degrees That Don't Pay Off." *Wall Street Journal*, July 8, 2021. https://www.wsj.com/articles/financially-hobbled-for-life-the-elite-masters-degrees-that-dont-pay-off-11625752773.

Korn, Melissa, Andrea Fuller, and Jennifer S. Forsyth. "Colleges Spend Like There's No Tomorrow: 'These Places Are Just Devouring Money.'" *Wall Street Journal*, August 10, 2023. https://www.wsj.com/articles/state-university-tuition-increase-spending-41a58100

Knott, Katherine. "Congressional Democrats Want Legal Review of OPMs." *Inside Higher Ed*, December 5, 2022. https://www.insidehighered.com/news/2022/12/06/democrats-want-more-oversight-online-program-providers.

Krivacsy, Kevin, and Thomas Usher. "Requirements of the Job: Tracking Changes to the Education Component." Indiana Business Research Center, Kelley School of Business, Indiana University, 2016. https://www.incontext.indiana.edu/2016/nov-dec/article1.asp.

Krop, Cathy, Stephen Carroll, and Carlos Rivera. "Trends in the California Higher Education Sector and Its Environment." RAND, 1997. https://www.ucop.edu/acadinit/mastplan/ProjectL.pdf.

Krugman, Paul. "The Two Big Questions about Student Debt Relief." *New York Times*, August 4, 2022. https://www.nytimes.com/2022/08/25/opinion/student-debt-relief-biden.html.

Larson, Ann. "Chapter Eleven, A Movement Is Born." *Leverage* (blog), November 16, 2020. https://annlarson.substack.com/p/chapter-11.

———. "Chapter Fifteen, An Historic Meeting in Washington." *Leverage* (blog), November 16, 2020. https://annlarson.substack.com/p/chapter-15.

———. "Chapter Five, The Rolling Jubilee." *Leverage* (blog), November 16, 2020. https://annlarson.substack.com/p/chapter-five.

———. "Chapter Fourteen, Student Debtors on Strike." *Leverage* (blog), November 16, 2020. https://annlarson.substack.com/p/chapter-14.

———. "Chapter Nine, A Meeting with Corinthian College Protestors." *Leverage* (blog), November 16, 2020. https://annlarson.substack.com/p/chapter-9.

———. "Chapter One, Occupy Wall Street." *Leverage* (blog), November 16, 2020. https://annlarson.substack.com/p/chapter-one.

———. "Chapter Thirteen, Recruiting Debt Strikers." *Leverage* (blog), November 16, 2020. https://annlarson.substack.com/p/chapter-thirteen.

Lee, Vivien, and Adam Looney. "Headwinds for Graduate Student Borrowers: Rising Balances and Slowing Repayment Rates." Brookings Institution, 2018. https://www.brookings.edu/research/headwinds-for-graduate-student-borrowers-rising-balances-and-slowing-repayment-rates/.

Leland, John. "Cheers and Boos after Ruling." *New York Times*, December 8, 2005. https://www.nytimes.com/2005/12/08/us/cheers-and-boos-after-ruling.html.

Levine, Phillip, and Dubravka Ritter. "The Racial Wealth Gap, Financial Aid, and College Access." Brookings Institution, September 27, 2022. https://www

.brookings.edu/blog/up-front/2022/09/27/the-racial-wealth-gap-financial
-aid-and-college-access/.

Loonin, Deanne. "No Way Out: Student Loans, Financial Distress, and the Need
for Policy Reform." National Consumer Law Center, 2006. https://www
.studentloanborrowerassistance.org/wp-content/uploads/2013/05/noway
out.pdf.

Loonin, Deanne, and Persis Yu. "Pounding Student Loan Borrowers: The Heavy
Costs of the government's Partnership with Debt Collection Agencies."
National Consumer Law Center, September 2014. https://www.nclc.org/wp
-content/uploads/2022/11/report-sl-debt-collectors.pdf.

Lumina Foundation. "Today's Student." Lumina Foundation. https://www.lumina
foundation.org/campaign/todays-student/.

Ma, Jennifer, and Matea Pender. "Trends in College Pricing." College Board,
2023.

———. "Trends in College Pricing and Student Aid 2022." College Board, 2022.
https://research.collegeboard.org/trends/student-aid.

Maloney, Carolyn. "Debt Collection Bill Could Reduce Deficit." *New York Times*,
March 2, 1996.

Marcus, Jon. "Graduate Programs Have Become a Cash Cow for Struggling
Colleges: What Does That Mean for Students?" *Hechinger Report*, September 18,
2017. https://www.pbs.org/newshour/education/graduate-programs-become
-cash-cow-struggling-colleges-mean-students.

Marginson, Simon. *The Dream Is Over: The Crisis of Clark Kerr's California Idea of
Higher Education.* Oakland: University of California Press, 2016.

Master Plan Survey Team. "A Master Plan for Higher Education in California,
1960–1975." Liaison Committee of the State Board of Education and Regents of
the University of California, 1960. https://babel.hathitrust.org/cgi/pt?id=mdp
.39015033885750&view=1up&seq=7&skin=2021.

McCullers, Madeline, and Irina Stefanescu. "Introducing Section 529 Plans
into the US Financial Accounts and Enhanced Financial Accounts." Federal
Reserve Board of Governors, December 18, 2015. https://www.federalreserve
.gov/econresdata/notes/feds-notes/2015/introducing-section-529-plans
-into-the-us-financial-accounts-and-enhanced-financial-accounts-20151218
.html.

McPherson, Michael S., and Morton Owen Shapiro. "New Higher Education Act
Worth Little to College Students." *Sun Sentinel (FL)*, August 2, 1992.

Meislin, Richard J. "Tax Relief Plan for College Costs Enacted by Albany." *New
York Times*, April 6, 1978. https://www.nytimes.com/1978/04/16/archives/2
-taxrelief-plans-for-college-costs-enacted-by-albany-believed-to.html.

Meyer, Katharine. "The Causes and Consequences of Graduate School Debt."
Brown Center on Education Policy, Brookings Institution, October 4, 2022.
https://www.brookings.edu/blog/brown-center-chalkboard/2022/10/04
/the-causes-and-consequences-of-graduate-school-debt/.

Miller, Ben. "Graduate School Debt: Ideas for Reducing the $37 Billion in Annual
Student Loans That No One Is Talking About." Center for American Progress,
2020. https://www.americanprogress.org/article/graduate-school-debt/

Miller, Holly. *From the Ground Up, an Early History of Lumina Foundation for Education*. Indianapolis, IN: Lumina Foundation for Education, 2007. https://www.luminafoundation.org/files/resources/from-the-ground-up.pdf.

Miller, G. Wayne. *An Uncommon Man: The Life & Times of Senator Claiborne Pell*. Hanover, NH: University Press of New England, 2011.

Mitchell, Josh. "Is the US Student Loan Program Facing a $500 Billion Hole? One Banker Thinks So." *Wall Street Journal*, April 29, 2021. https://www.wsj.com/articles/is-the-u-s-student-loan-program-in-a-deep-hole-one-banker-thinks-so-11619707091.

Mitchell, Ted. "Letter from Ted Mitchell on Bundled Services." Regulations.gov, 2023. https://www.regulations.gov/comment/ED-2023-OPE-0030-0228

Modestino, Alicia Sasser, Daniel Shoag, and Joshua Ballance. "Upskilling: Do Employers Demand Greater Skill When Workers Are Plentiful?" *Review of Economics and Statistics* 102, no. 4 (2020). https://direct.mit.edu/rest/article-abstract/102/4/793/96774/Upskilling-Do-Employers-Demand-Greater-Skill-When?redirectedFrom=fulltext.

MOHELA. "Letter from MOHELA to Cori Bush." The Office of Rep. Cori Bush, October 28, 2022. https://bush.house.gov/imo/media/doc/letter_to_hon_cori_bush.pdf.

Monarrez, Tomas, and Jordan Matsudaira. "Trends in Federal Student Loans for Graduate School." US Department of Education, 2023. https://sites.ed.gov/ous/files/2023/08/OCE_GraduateDebtReport202308.pdf.

Morgan, Dan. "Change Means Fewer Students Will Be Eligible for Pell Grants." *Washington Post*, December 24, 2004.

Mui, Ylan Q., and Felicia Sonmez. "Obama, Romney Focus on Student Debt as Campaign Issue." *Washington Post*, April 23, 2012. https://www.washingtonpost.com/business/economy/obama-romney-focus-on-student-debt-as-campaign-issue/2012/04/23/gIQAnEz6cT_story.html.

Nagourney, Adam. "Dole to Advocate 15% Cut in Taxes, His Campaign Says." *New York Times*, August 5, 1996. https://www.nytimes.com/1996/08/05/us/dole-to-advocate-15-cut-in-taxes-his-campaign-says.html.

National Association of Realtors. "Student Loan Debt Holding Back Majority of Millennials from Homeownership." September 14, 2021. https://www.nar.realtor/newsroom/student-loan-debt-holding-back-majority-of-millennials-from-homeownership.

National Center for Education Statistics. "Average Undergraduate Tuition, Fees, Room and Board Rates Charged for Full-Time Students in Degree-Granting Postsecondary Institutions, by Level and Control of Institution: Selected Years, 1963–64 through 2020–21." 2022. https://nces.ed.gov/programs/digest/d21/tables/dt21_330.10.asp.

———. "College Enrollment Rates." 2023. https://nces.ed.gov/programs/coe/indicator/cpb/college-enrollment-rate.

———. "Fast Facts: Undergraduate Graduation Rates." 2022. https://nces.ed.gov/fastfacts/display.asp?id=40.

———. "Graduate Degree Fields." 2022. https://nces.ed.gov/programs/coe/indicator/ctb/graduate-degree-fields?tid=74.

———. "Status and Trends in the Education of Racial and Ethnic Groups, Indicator 22: Financial Aid." 2019. https://nces.ed.gov/programs/raceindica tors/indicator_rec.asp.

"Nationwide Loan Fund for College Students Gets $2 Million Grant." *Wall Street Journal*, May 7, 1962.

Navient. "Legal Action Facts." 2024. https://news.navient.com/legal-action -facts.

———. "Navient Announces Successful Resolution of Legal Matters with State Attorneys General." January 13, 2022. https://news.navient.com/news -releases/news-release-details/navient-announces-successful-resolution -legal-matters-state.

New York Legal Assistance Group. "Ana Salazar, Marilyn Mercado, Ana Bernardez, Jeannette Poole, Edna Villatoro, Lisa Bryant and Cherryline Stevens, on Behalf of Themselves and All Others Similarly Situated vs. Arne Duncan." 2014. https://nylag.org/wp-content/uploads/2019/08/NYLAG -sues-Secretary-of-Education-for-Failing-to-Notify-Former-Wilfred-Stu dents-Amended-Complaint.pdf.

New York Times News Service. "Bankruptcy Being Used to Lapse Student Loans." *Freeport (IL) Journal-Standard*, November 22, 1976.

———. "Reagan Cuts State Budget By $503 Million." *Louisville (KY) Courier-Journal*, July 4, 1971.

Ngo, Madeleine. "After Dropping Free Community College Plan, Democrats Explore Options." *New York Times*, October 22, 2021. https://www.nytimes. com/2021/10/22/us/politics/free-community-college-democrats.html.

Nichols, Chris. "Proposition 13: The Birth of California's Taxpayer Revolt." Capitol Public Radio, October 25, 2018. https://www.kpbs.org/news /midday-edition/2018/10/25/birth-californias-taxpayer-revolt.

Ochoa, Eduardo M. "Dear Colleague Letter on Program Integrity Regulations." US Department of Education, 2011. https://fsapartners.ed.gov/sites/default /files/attachments/dpcletters/GEN1105.pdf.

Office of Postsecondary Education, US Department of Education. "A Rule by the Education Department." *Federal Register*, 2016. https://www.federalregister .gov/documents/2016/11/01/2016-25448/student-assistance-general-provi sions-federal-perkins-loan-program-federal-family-education-loan.

Office of the Attorney General Maura Healey. "AG Healey Submits Application to US Department of Education to Cancel Thousands of Loans for Former Corinthian Students." Office of the Attorney General of Massachusetts, November 30, 2015. https://www.mass.gov/news/ag-healey-submits-applica tion-to-us-department-of-education-to-cancel-thousands-of-loans-for -former-corinthian-students.

Office of Inspector General, US Department of Education. "The Department's Decision to Terminate Private Collection Agency Contracts." 2022. https:// www2.ed.gov/about/offices/list/oig/misc/terminate-pca-contracts.pdf.

———. "FAFSA Data by Demographic Characteristics." 2024. https://studentaid .gov/data-center/student/application-volume/fafsa-school-state#fafsa-data -by-demographic-characteristics.

———. "US Department of Education Launches Review of Prohibition on Incentive Compensation for College Recruiters." 2023. https://www.ed.gov /news/press-releases/us-department-education-launches-review-prohibi tion-incentive-compensation-college-recruiters.

O'Neill, James M. "With Less Aid, College Dreams Slip Away." *Philadelphia Inquirer*, June 9, 2002.

Pastor, Manuel. "After Tax Cuts Derailed the 'California Dream,' Is the State Getting Back on Track?" *The Conversation*, November 1, 2017. https://thecon versation.com/after-tax-cuts-derailed-the-california-dream-is-the-state -getting-back-on-track-77919.

Penn, Nathaniel. "Hello, Cruel World." *New York Times Magazine*, March 23, 2012. https://www.nytimes.com/2012/03/25/magazine/what-the-fate-of-one -class-of-2011-says-about-the-job-market.html.

Pennsylvania Attorney General's Press Office. "Attorney General Josh Shapiro Announces $1.85 Billion Landmark Settlement with Student Loan Servicer Navient." 2022. https://www.attorneygeneral.gov/taking-action/attorney -general-josh-shapiro-announces-1-85-billion-landmark-settlement-with -student-loan-servicer-navient/#:~:text=HARRISBURG%E2%80%93Attor ney%20General%20Josh%20Shapiro,abuses%20in%20originating%20 predatory%20student.

Perry, Andre M., and Randi Weingarten. "Gov. Tom Corbett Has Slashed Funding for Pennsylvania's Neediest Students. Fixing Schools Means Voting Him Out." *Washington Post*, October 29, 2014. https://www.washingtonpost.com/post everything/wp/2014/10/29/gov-tom-corbett-has-slashed-funding-for-penn sylvanias-neediest-students-fixing-schools-means-voting-him-out/.

Petersen, Anne Helen. "The Master's Trap. What Makes a Graduate Program Predatory?" *Culture Study*, July 21, 2021. https://annehelen.substack.com /p/the-masters-trap.

Petraeus, Hollister K. "For-Profit Colleges, Vulnerable GI's." *New York Times*, September 22, 2011. https://www.nytimes.com/2011/09/22/opinion/for -profit-colleges-vulnerable-gis.html.

Pine, Art. "Carter Aid Plan Seeks to Head Off a Tuition Credit." *Washington Post*, February 8, 1978.

———. "Senate Votes to Expand Student Loan Programs." *Los Angeles Times*, February 22, 1992. https://www.latimes.com/archives/la-xpm-1992-02-22 -mn-1942-story.html.

———. "Tuition Tax Credit Gets Boost in the House." *Washington Post*, April 4, 1978.

Pinto, Sergio, and Marshall Steinbaum. "The Long-Run Impact of the Great Recession on Student Debt." *Labour Economics* 85 (2023). https://marshall steinbaum.org/assets/pinto_steinbaum_full_article_accepted_9-2023.pdf.

Pomfret, John D. "Bankers Promote Student Aid Loan." *New York Times*, June 11, 1966.

Potempa, Philip. "Indiana Locations a Real World Reminder of Jean Shepherd's 'A Christmas Story.'" *Chicago Tribune*, December 3, 2020. https://www.chicago tribune.com/suburbs/post-tribune/ct-ptb-ent-christmas-story-st-1211 -20201203-b5oxjkrmlbhzbnrrgg3xmpwp5a-story.html.

Project on Predatory Student Lending. "Tina Carr and Yvette Colon v. Elisabeth DeVos, in Her Official Capacity as Secretary of the US Department of Education." Project on Predatory Student Lending, 2019. https://nylag.org/wp-content/uploads/2019/08/NYLAG-Sues-Department-of-Education-for-4-Year-Delay-in-Deciding-Loan-Cancellation-Applications-Complaint.pdf.

Public Policy Institute of California Higher Education Center. "Investing in Public Higher Education." 2019. https://www.ppic.org/wp-content/uploads/higher-education-in-california-investing-in-public-higher-education-october-2019.pdf.

Quinn, Jayne Briant. "Student Loans: Paying The Price of Education." *Washington Post*, February 17, 1991.

Rankin, Deborah. "Your Money; Reagan Cuts in Student Aid." *New York Times*, October 24, 1981. https://www.nytimes.com/1981/10/24/business/your-money-reagan-cuts-in-student-aid.html.

"Reagan Ax Falls: State Agency Budgets Cut 10% UC, State Colleges Included; Tuition Left Up to Educators." *Los Angeles Times*, January 13, 1967.

Reardon, Patrick. "Dukakis' College Tuition Loan Plan Has Some Merit, Experts Say." *Chicago Tribune*, October 9, 1988. https://www.chicagotribune.com/news/ct-xpm-1988-09-09-8801290070-story.html.

Riley, Richard W. "January 19, 2001 Letter from Richard Riley to College Presidents." 2001.

Rivera, Lauren. *Pedigree: How Elite Students Get Elite Jobs.* Princeton, NJ: Princeton University Press, 2015.

Rivlin, Alice M. *The Role of the Federal Government in Financing Higher Education.* Washington, DC: Brookings Institution, 1961.

Roache, Marlo. "College Plans Get Some Low Grades." *Sarasota (FL) Herald Tribune*, October 21, 1996.

Roosevelt, Franklin D. "Message to Congress on the Education of War Veterans." 1943. Franklin D. Roosevelt Presidential Library and Museum. http://docs.fdrlibrary.marist.edu/odgiced.html.

Rothwell, Jonathan. "Using Earnings Data to Rank Colleges: A Value-Added Approach Updated with College Scorecard Data." Brookings Institution, 2015. https://www.brookings.edu/research/using-earnings-data-to-rank-colleges-a-value-added-approach-updated-with-college-scorecard-data/.

Sampson, Vincent. "Dear Colleague Letter: The Ensuring Continued Access to Student Loans Act of 2008." Department of Education, 2008. https://fsapartners.ed.gov/knowledge-center/library/dear-colleague-letters/2008-06-19/gen-08-08-ensuring-continued-access-student-loans-act-2008.

Sanger, David E. "Bush's Budget Will Seek Modest Rise in Pell Grants." *New York Times*, January 15, 2005. https://www.nytimes.com/2005/01/15/politics/bushs-budget-will-seek-modest-rise-in-pell-grants.html.

Sattelmeyer, Sarah, and Tia Caldwell. "In Default and Left Behind." New America, November 30, 2022. https://www.newamerica.org/education-policy/reports/in-default-and-left-behind/.

Scott-Clayton, Judith, and Jing Li. "Black-White Disparity in Student Loan Debt More than Triples after Graduation." Brookings Institution, 2016. https://

www.brookings.edu/research/black-white-disparity-in-student-loan-debt
-more-than-triples-after-graduation/.

Senator Dick Durbin Press Office. "Durbin Meets with Department of Education
Special Master to Encourage Fair Debt Relief Process for Former For-Profit
Students." July 9, 2015. https://www.durbin.senate.gov/newsroom/press
-releases/durbin-meets-with-department-of-education-special-master-to
-encourage-fair-debt-relief-process-for-former-for-profit-students.

Shane, Leo, III. "Feds Close 90/10 Loophole Involving Veterans Education
Benefits." *Military Times*, October 27, 2022. https://www.militarytimes.com
/education-transition/2022/10/27/feds-close-9010-loophole-involving
-veterans-education-benefits/.

Shebanow, Alexander. *Fail State.* Gravitas Ventures, 2017. https://failstatemovie.com.

Shireman, Robert. "Learn Now, Pay Later: A History of Income-Contingent
Student Loans in the United States." *Annals of the American Academy of Political
and Social Science*, April, 184–201 (2017).

Shiro, Ariel Gelrud, and Richard V. Reeves. "The For-Profit College System Is
Broken and the Biden Administration Needs to Fix It." Brookings Institution,
2021. https://www.brookings.edu/blog/how-we-rise/2021/01/12/the-for
-profit-college-system-is-broken-and-the-biden-administration-needs-to
-fix-it/#:~:text=There%20is%20an%20immense%20amount,of%20all%20
student%2Dloan%20defaults.

Sigelman, Matt, Joseph Fuller, and Alex Martin. "Skills-Based Hiring: The Long
Road from Pronouncements to Practice." Burning Glass Institute, 2024.
https://static1.squarespace.com/static/6197797102be715f55c0e0a1/t/65cc355c
4935cb001349a4cd/1707881822922/Skills-Based+Hiring+02122024+vF.pdf.

Slack, Megan. "Income Based Repayment: Everything You Need to Know." White
House: President Barack Obama, June 7, 2012. https://obamawhitehouse
.archives.gov/blog/2012/06/07/income-based-repayment-everything
-you-need-know.

Smith, Christian Michael, Amber D. Villalobos, Laura Hamilton, and Charlie
Eaton. "Promising or Predatory? Online Education in Non-Profit and For-
Profit Universities." Centre for Global Higher Education, 2023. https://re
searchcghe.org/publications/working-paper/promising-or-predatory
-online-education-in-non-profit-and-for-profit-universities/.

Snyder, Thomas D. "120 Years of American Education: A Statistical Portrait."
National Center for Education Statistics, 1993. https://nces.ed.gov/pubs93
/93442.pdf.

Special to the New York Times. "George Zook Dies; Education Leader." *New York
Times*, August 19, 1951. https://www.nytimes.com/1951/08/19/archives
/george-zook-dies-education-leader-former-us-commissioner-headed.html.

Special to the New York Times. "Bell Assails Criticism of Plans to Cut Student
Aid as Unjust." *New York Times*, May 4, 1982. https://www.nytimes.com
/1982/05/04/us/bell-assails-criticism-of-plans-to-cut-student-aid-as
-unjust.html#:~:text=Education%20Secretary%20T.H.%20Bell%20
charged,proposed%20cutbacks%20in%20student%20aid.&text=Bell%20
said%20at%20a%20news,to%20trim%20the%20education%20budget.

Staff of the National Performance Review. "Department of Education: Accompanying Report of the National Performance Review." 1993. https://files.eric.ed.gov/fulltext/ED379992.pdf.

State Higher Education Finance. "State Profile: California." 2021. https://shef.sheeo.org/state-profile/california/.

Steinbaum, Marshall. "The Student Debt Crisis Is a Crisis of Non-Repayment." Jain Family Institute, 2020. https://www.phenomenalworld.org/analysis/crisis-of-non-repayment/.

Stratford, Michael. "Warren Promises to Cancel Student Loan Debt Using Executive Powers." *Politico*, January 14, 2020. https://www.politico.com/news/2020/01/14/elizabeth-warren-cancel-student-debt-executive-powers-098623.

General Accountability Office. "Student Loans: Education Has Increased Federal Cost Estimates of Direct Loans by Billions Due to Programmatic and Other Changes." 2022. https://www.gao.gov/products/gao-22-105365.

Taylor, Benjamin. "Reagan Sends Congress Plan to Limit Student Aid Programs." *Boston Globe*, March 18, 1983.

"Tiger Teague to Give Congress Plenty Color." *Austin American-Statesman*, September 10, 1946.

Trombley, William. "Changing University—A Look at the Reagan Era." *Los Angeles Times*, January 7, 1973.

———. "Education Budget Fight Looming for Governor." *Los Angeles Times*, October 13, 1969.

———. "Spending Dip Called Threat to Education." *Los Angeles Times*, February 13, 1992.

———. "UC Regent Group Backs Rise in Fees." *Los Angeles Times*, January 10, 1968.

"Tuition & Costs." Temple University Undergraduate Admissions. 2022. https://admissions.temple.edu/costs-aid-scholarships/tuition-costs.

Turner, Lesley J. "The Economic Incidence of Federal Student Grant Aid." Unpublished manuscript, 2017. https://lesleyjturner.com/Turner_FedAidIncidence_Jan2017.pdf.

United Press International. "Governor Renews Tuition Plan Campaign." *San Francisco Examiner*, July 26, 1967.

Urban Institute. "Sandy Baum Author Bio." https://www.urban.org/author/sandy-baum.

US Bureau of Labor Statistics. "Union Membership Rate Fell by 0.2 Percentage Point to 10.1 Percent in 2022." 2023. https://www.bls.gov/opub/ted/2023/union-membership-rate-fell-by-0-2-percentage-point-to-10-1-percent-in-2022.htm#:~:text.

US Census Bureau. "Historical Census of Housing Tables: Gross Rents." October 8, 2021. https://www.census.gov/data/tables/time-series/dec/coh-grossrents.html.

———. "QuickFacts Hammond City, Indiana." https://www.census.gov/quickfacts/fact/table/hammondcityindiana/PST045219.

US Commission on Civil Rights. "Equal Protection of the Laws in Higher Education," 1960. https://www.crmvet.org/docs/ccr_rights_us_6000.pdf.

US Department of Education. "Biden-Harris Administration Announces Additional $7.7 Billion in Student Debt Relief in Approved Student Debt Relief for 160,000 Borrowers." May 21, 2024. https://www.ed.gov/news/press -releases/biden-harris-administration-announces-additional-77-billion -approved-student-debt-relief-160000-borrowers.

———. "Biden-Harris Administration Approves Additional $5.8 Billion in Student Debt Relief for 78,000 Public Service Workers." March 21, 2024. https://www.ed.gov/news/press-releases/biden-harris-administration -approves-additional-58-billion-student-debt-relief-78000-public-service -workers#:~:text=Public%20Service%20Workers-,Biden%2DHarris%20 Administration%20Approves%20Additional%20%245.8%20Billion%20in%20 Student%20Debt,for%2078%2C000%20Public%20Service%20Workers &text=The%20Biden%2DHarris%20Administration%20announced,debt%20 relief%20for%2077%2C700%20borrowers.

———. "Debt Collection Practices." Office of Information and Regulatory Affairs, Office of Management and Budget, 2021.

———. "Delivering on President Trump's Promise, Secretary DeVos Suspends Federal Student Loan Payments, Waives Interest during National Emergency." March 20, 2020. https://content.govdelivery.com/accounts/USED/bulletins /2823e37.

———. "Department of Education Announces Actions to Fix Longstanding Failures in the Student Loan Programs." April 19, 2022. https://www.ed.gov /news/press-releases/department-education-announces-actions-fix-long standing-failures-student-loan-programs.

———. "Education Department Approves $5.8 Billion Group Discharge to Cancel All Remaining Loans for 560,000 Borrowers Who Attended Corinthian." June 1, 2022. https://www.ed.gov/news/press-releases/education-department -approves-58-billion-group-discharge-cancel-all-remaining-loans-560000-bor rowers-who-attended-corinthian-colleges.

———. "A Fresh Start for Federal Student Loan Borrowers in Default." April 6, 2022. https://studentaid.gov/announcements-events/default-fresh-start.

———. "Over 323,000 Federal Student Loan Borrowers to Receive $5.8 Billion in Automatic Total and Permanent Disability Discharges." August 19, 2021. https://www.ed.gov/news/press-releases/over-323000-federal-student-loan -borrowers-receive-58-billion-automatic-total-and-permanent-disability -discharges

US Department of Education, College Scorecard. "Albright College." https://col legescorecard.ed.gov/school/?210571-Albright_College.

———. "Eureka College." https://collegescorecard.ed.gov/school/?144971-Eureka -College.

———. "University of California-Merced." https://collegescorecard.ed.gov /school/?445188-University-of-California-Merced.

US Department of Justice. "Justice Department Reaches $60 Million Settlement with Sallie Mae to Resolve Allegations of Charging Military Servicemembers Excessive Rates on Student Loans." May 13, 2014. https://www.justice.gov /opa/pr/justice-department-reaches-60-million-settlement-sallie-mae -resolve-allegations-charging.

US Government Accountability Office. "Education Needs to Strengthen Its Approach to Monitoring Colleges' Arrangements with Online Program Managers." 2022. https://www.gao.gov/assets/gao-22-104463.pdf.

———. "Higher Education: A Small Percentage of Families Save in 529 Plans." 2012. https://www.gao.gov/products/gao-13-64.

US Senate Committee on Health, Education, Labor and Pensions. "For Profit Higher Education: The Failure to Safeguard the Federal Investment and Ensure Student Success." 2012. https://www.help.senate.gov/imo/media /for_profit_report/PartII/Corinthian.pdf.

Veterans Education Success. "GI Bill History." 2017. https://veteranseducation success.org/gi-bill-history.

"Veteran's Whirl." *Cleveland (OH) Call and Post*, March 11, 1950.

Vidal, David. "Students Default on College Loans." *Spokesman-Review (WA)*, August 1, 1976.

Vobejda, Barbara. "Educators Score Reagan's Spending Proposals; Lower College Enrollment, Especially among Minorities, Foreseen If Aid Is Cut." *Washington Post*, January 8, 1987.

Waldman, Annie. "How a For-Profit College Targeted the Homeless and Kids with Low Self-Esteem." ProPublica, March 18, 2016. https://www.propublica .org/article/how-a-for-profit-college-targeted-homeless-and-kids-with-low -self-esteem.

———. "Who's Regulating For-Profit Schools? Execs from For-Profit Colleges." ProPublica, February 26, 2016. https://www.propublica.org/article/whos -regulating-for-profit-schools-execs-from-for-profit-colleges.

Waldman, Steven. *The Bill: How Legislation Really Becomes Law: A Case Study of the National Service Bill*. New York: Penguin Books, 1996.

Ward, Marguerite. "6 Alternatives to an Expensive Undergrad Degree, and What Exactly to Do to Avoid Massive Student Debt." *Business Insider*, February 25, 2020. https://www.businessinsider.com/heres-exactly-what-to-do-to-avoid -massive-college-debt-2020-2.

Warren, Elizabeth. "My Plan to Cancel Student Loan Debt on Day One of My Presidency." 2020. https://elizabethwarren.com/plans/student -loan-debt-day-one#:~:text=So%20I%20will%20start%20to,profit%20 institutions%2C%20and%20eliminate%20predatory.

Weil, Julie Zauzmer. "DC Government Will Send $10,000 Checks to the City's Day-Care Workers." *Washington Post*, February 1, 2022. https://www.wash ingtonpost.com/dc-md-va/2022/02/01/childcare-workers-checks-dc -council/.

Weisman, Jonathan. "Obama Relents on Proposal to End '529' College Savings Plans." *New York Times*, January 27, 2015. https://www.nytimes .com/2015/01/28/us/politics/obama-will-drop-proposal-to-end-529-college -savings-plans.html.

White House. "The Biden-Harris Administration Launches the SAVE Plan, the Most Affordable Student Loan Repayment Plan Ever to Lower Monthly Payments for Millions of Borrowers." August 22, 2023. https://www.white house.gov/briefing-room/statements-releases/2023/08/22/fact-sheet-the -biden-harris-administration-launches-the-save-plan-the-most-affordable

-student-loan-repayment-plan-ever-to-lower-monthly-payments-for-mil
lions-of-borrowers/.

———. "The Clinton Presidency: Timeline of Major Actions." https://clinton
whitehouse5.archives.gov/WH/Accomplishments/eightyears-02.html.

———. "FACT SHEET: President Biden Announces New Actions to Provide Debt
Relief and Support for Student Loan Borrowers." 2023. https://www.white
house.gov/briefing-room/statements-releases/2023/06/30/fact-sheet
-president-biden-announces-new-actions-to-provide-debt-relief-and-sup
port-for-student-loan-borrowers/.

———. "FACT SHEET: President Biden Announces Student Loan Relief for
Borrowers Who Need It Most," August 24, 2022. https://www.whitehouse
.gov/briefing-room/statements-releases/2022/08/24/fact-sheet-president
-biden-announces-student-loan-relief-for-borrowers-who-need-it-most/.

———. "President Biden Announces Student Loan Relief for Borrowers Who
Need It Most." August 24, 2022. https://www.whitehouse.gov/briefing-room
/statements-releases/2022/08/24/fact-sheet-president-biden-announces
-student-loan-relief-for-borrowers-who-need-it-most/.

———. "Remarks by President Biden Announcing Student Loan Relief Plan."
August 24, 2022. https://www.whitehouse.gov/briefing-room/statements
-releases/2022/08/24/fact-sheet-president-biden-announces-student-loan
-relief-for-borrowers-who-need-it-most/.

———. "Remarks by President Biden Announcing Student Loan Debt Relief Plan."
August 25, 2022. https://www.whitehouse.gov/briefing-room/speeches
-remarks/2022/08/25/remarks-by-president-biden-announcing-student
-loan-debt-relief-plan/.

———. "Statement from President Joe Biden on Student Loan Debt Cancellation
for More than 800,000 Borrowers." 2023. https://www.whitehouse.gov
/briefing-room/statements-releases/2023/08/22/fact-sheet-the-biden
-harris-administration-launches-the-save-plan-the-most-affordable-stu
dent-loan-repayment-plan-ever-to-lower-monthly-payments-for-millions
-of-borrowers/.

White House Office of the Press Secretary. "Fact Sheet: A Simpler, Fairer Tax
Code That Responsibly Invests in Middle Class Families." White House:
President Barack Obama, January 17, 2015. https://obamawhitehouse
.archives.gov/the-press-office/2015/01/17/
fact-sheet-simpler-fairer-tax-code-responsibly-invests-middle-class-fami.

White House Task Force on the Middle Class. "Annual Report of the White
House Task Force on the Middle Class." 2010. https://obamawhitehouse
.archives.gov/sites/default/files/microsites/100226-annual-report-middle
-class.pdf.

Whitman, David. "The GOP Reversal on For-Profit Colleges in the George W.
Bush Era." Century Foundation, 2018. https://tcf.org/content/report
/gop-reversal-profit-colleges-george-w-bush-era/.

———. *The Profits of Failure: For-Profit Colleges and the Closing of the Conservative
Mind.* N.p.: Cypress House, 2021.

Winerip, Michael. "Billions for School Are Lost in Fraud, Waste and Abuse." *New York Times*, February 2, 1994. https://www.nytimes.com/1994/02/02/us/billions-for-school-are-lost-in-fraud-waste-and-abuse.html.

———. "House Panel Is Facing Vote on School Aid." *New York Times*, June 19, 1994.

———. "Overhauling School Grants: Much Debate but Little Gain." *New York Times*, February 4, 1994.

Winter, Greg, and Diana Jean Schemo. "Bill Clears Way for Government to Cut Back College Loans." *New York Times*, November 21, 2004.

Wurtz, Donald R. "Guaranteed Student Loan Program's Internal Controls and Structure Need Improvement." Government Accountability Office, 1993. https://www.gao.gov/assets/afmd-93-20.pdf.

"Young Men Declared Dodging Military Duty." *Christian Science Monitor*, December 7, 1943.

Zeman, Ray. "Reagan Favors Tuition Fee but No Budget Cuts." *Los Angeles Times*, January 11, 1967.

———. "Reagan Drops Tuition Plans, Raises Budgets $38 Million." *Los Angeles Times*, March 1, 1967.

Zillow. "San Francisco Home Values." https://www.zillow.com/san-francisco-ca/home-values/.

Zimmerman, Fred L. "Student Loan Program Troubled Increasingly by Lagging Repayment." *Wall Street Journal*, February 4, 1965.

Zumper. "San Francisco, CA Rent Prices." July 27, 2022. https://www.zumper.com/rent-research/san-francisco-ca.

Index